# The New Guinea Diaries
## 1871-1883

# The New Guinea Diaries
## 1871-1883

## by N.N. Miklouho-Maclay

Translation from the Russian edition
and Commentary Essays
by B. Wongar

© Text and photographs B. Wongar

The New Guinea Diaries 1871 – 1883
Wongar, B.
First published 2007 by Dingo Books,
an imprint of The Wongar Foundation
PO Box 147
Carnegie, Victoria, Australia 3163

Miklouho-Maclay, 1846-1888.
The New Guinea diaries.

Bibliography.
Includes index.

1. Miklouho-Maclay, 1846-1888.
2. Ethnologists - Russia - Biography.
3. Explorers - Russia - Biography.
4. Scientists - Russia - Biography.
5. Ethnology - Papua New Guinea.
6. Papua New Guinea - Discovery and exploration - Russian.
7. Papua New Guinea - Description and travel.
I. Wongar, B. II. Title.

305.80092

ISBN Paperback 978-0-9775078-1-8
ISBN Hardback 978-0-9775078-2-5

Illustrations by N. N. Miklouho-Maclay

Designed and packaged by Lynda Patullo, Green Poles Design
Editorial assistance by Susan Utber, Red Camel Publishing
Printed in China

# Contents

ATTRIBUTIONS

Publication of this title was assisted by the Australia Council,
the Federal Government's art funding and advisory body.

# Translator's Note

I began translating the *New Guinea Diaries* in 1973 and soon found out that Miklouho-Maclay was politically unacceptable in Australia because of his correct understanding of indigenous people and their culture. He wrote at a time when the work of Charles Darwin was being misused to 'justify' colonial expansionism. The British had declared Australia *terra nullius*, an empty land, and the natives who were there were presumed to be sub-human. Subsequently Miklouho-Maclay became deleted from Australian and British history.

This is the first time that Miklouho-Maclay's diaries have been translated and published in Australia. Two earlier translations appeared some decades ago: one by C.L. Sentinella, *Miklouho-Maclay: New Guinea Diaries 1871–1883*, published in New Guinea in 1975; another by the Russian historian, D. Tumarkin, *Miklouho-Maclay: Travels to New Guinea*, Moscow 1982. Two biographical books about Miklouho-Maclay's life and work were published in Australia: F.S. Greenop, *Who Travels Alone*, Sydney 1944; and E.M. Webster, *The Moon Man*, Melbourne University Press/University of California Press, 1984.

I have followed the version of the *New Guinea Diaries*, originally edited by Miklouho-Maclay on advice from the Russian author, Leo Tolstoy. The book sold millions of copies in Eastern Europe.

The dates of the diaries are by the Julian calendar. Maclay uses both Imperial and metric measurements.

Australia was Miklouho-Maclay's adopted country and Sydney the home town of his family — no politician or historian can take that away from him. It is my hope that my version of his book may do justice to his great work and to his descendents (grandchildren Kenneth, Robertson and Paul Maclay) in Australia, as well as justice to the Australian Aborigines, the Papuans and Kanaka people.

I am grateful to Prue Grieve for her help in the initial stages of the translation, and to academics Patrick Morgan, Patricia Excell, Thomas Shapcott and Tom Thompson, for their professional advice. Thanks also, to Lynda Patullo for her wonderful design and production expertise, and Susan Utber for her editorial eye.

My special thanks to Lynda Bilcich who put considerable time and effort into the research and editing of this book.

*B. Wongar*
*Dingoes Den 2003*

# Commentary

## The Early Years

One of the first scientists, if not the first, who endeavoured to save life on earth was undoubtedly N.N. Miklouho-Maclay. He did not invent the words 'ecology' and 'humanity' but he was a devoted believer in both and gave his life for them. Had his work been published and acted upon at the time, he could have towered over Darwin, but Miklouho-Maclay fell into oblivion before the western world came to know about him.

Miklouho-Maclay lived over a century ago at a time when any struggle on behalf of indigenous people and their environment was unheard of — his determination to help them has been unmatched since. After two millennia of European civilisation with its system of statehood that has outlived itself and is moving towards destruction, Miklouho-Maclay gives us an opportunity to look back from where that system began — for better or worse, more likely the latter.

I was eighteen years old when I came across the *New Guinea Diaries*, the first serious book I had ever attempted to read. I began one cold wintry night, sitting by a kerosene lamp. It took me all night just to go over a dozen pages, but by the time I had finished the book I had changed from a peasant boy into Miklouho-Maclay's disciple. The book had become available to readers only a few years earlier when in 1949 the manuscript of his diary was acquired by the Saltikov-Shchredrin Library in Moscow from a private citizen, into whose possession it had come by sheer accident. Prior to that time it was thought that the entire work of the scientist had been destroyed after his death, as he had requested in his will.

1

Nikolai Nikolayevich Miklouho-Maclay was born on the 17 July 1846 in the village of Rozhdestvenskoye in the Novgorod Province. His paternal ancestor came from Scotland, brought to Russia to help build Saint Petersburg and given the title of a nobleman. At the time of Miklouho-Maclay's birth his father worked as engineer-in-charge of construction of the Moscow-Saint Petersburg railway line. His father died when Miklouho-Maclay was eleven years of age. During his schooling in Saint Petersburg, the young Miklouho-Maclay showed a strong, independent mind which soon brought him into conflict with the educational authorities for taking part in student demonstrations. Miklouho-Maclay was eventually barred from entering any Russian university but, undeterred he went abroad to Germany and enrolled in the Faculty of Philosophy at the University of Heidelberg. There he studied medicine, chemistry and other scientific disciplines. Later he entered Jena University in Germany, the leading university in Europe at that time, where he studied comparative anatomy and zoology under the famous Ernst Haeckel.

His education abroad caused considerable financial strain on his mother in Russia, who also had to care for his three brothers and a sister. The family, considered nobility, had very limited means of support. In her letters his mother asked him to be as frugal as possible; however, the young Miklouho-Maclay's spending was already minimised — his worn out clothes were covered with patches and there were barely any soles left on his footwear.

Humble as he might have looked, Miklouho-Maclay's student records were brilliant, attracting the attention of Haeckel who made him his assistant. During the summer of 1866 Haeckel included the young Miklouho-Maclay in a field expedition to the Canary Islands. They spent four months on fieldwork, mostly on the small island Lanzerote where Miklouho-Maclay took an interest in sponges and studied the brains of *Selachia* (a species of fish). There he discovered a new species of sponge with polymorphic changing form and behaviour which he named

*Guancha blanca* in tribute to the Guanchas, the original inhabitants of the Canary Islands who had been exterminated by European invaders. Even though the sponges represented a primitive life form, Miklouho-Maclay associated their fate with that of humans.

To further his research Miklouho-Maclay travelled alone from the Canary Islands to Morocco, then journeyed on foot through North Africa. He returned to Europe where, after the publication of his findings, he unveiled his much larger project — to research into the comparative anatomy of the brain. The first two parts of the project would be on fish followed by work on the brains of mammals and the final part on the brains of humans. He wanted to prove that the changes among species were conditioned by the external environment; the influence of humidity, temperature, light, population density, food, and so on, a pattern that also produced differences among various races within the human species.

After graduating from Jena University, Miklouho-Maclay went to the Red Sea area to do further research on sponges. He travelled disguised as an Arab to avoid possible hostility from Muslims in the area. However, he soon found himself in serious trouble when, travelling on an Arab *dhow*, he was recognised as a European — the sole unbeliever on board. Although about to be thrown into the sea, Mikloulo Maclay remained unafraid. He seized the main Arab agitator, locked him in the vessel's hold and so quelled the hostility.

During his visit to the Red Sea region, Miklouho-Maclay's interests broadened from studying primitive life forms into observing humans of various race and culture. While in Jeddah he saw masses of Muslim pilgrims on their way to Mecca — people from distant areas of Africa and Asia, speaking different languages and wearing different clothes. He soon became as interested in those people and their culture as in the sponges he was studying.

On his return to Russia, aged only twenty-three years, Miklouho-Maclay already had a sound scientific reputation in the European academic establishment. Soon afterwards he submitted to the Russian Geographical Society a plan for an expedition to the Far East, in order to undertake a study of the relationship between marine organisms and the local environment in an area extending from the Sea of Okhotsk in the far north, to the Equator. On that trip he also intended to carry out anthropological research, being interested in both the humans and the environment around them. Research into the behaviour of sponges and the marine environment was not exactly a priority on the list of European scientific community concerns in the wake of the Industrial Revolution and colonial expansionism — social Darwinism was also on the increase. Miklouho-Maclay sensed that with the rapid increase of industrialisation, accompanied by human population increases, the resulting strain on the natural environment would cause pollution and eventually the extinction of various species, including humans. He had already found that sponges, with their delicate life system, reacted strongly to any minute environmental change. Miklouho-Maclay placed himself between the environment and progress.

A leading Russian scientist at that time, Karl von Baer, suggested to Miklouho-Maclay that he might like to visit the unexplored island of New Guinea. Little was known, if anything at all, about New Guinea and the people living there. It was thought, however, that the inhabitants of the island, because of their isolation, had utterly preserved their primitive way of life and culture; intact from outside influence, they were most likely cannibals. The Russian Geographical Society agreed to sponsor Miklouho-Maclay's expedition but provided him with the paltry sum of 1200 roubles — an amount barely enough to purchase equipment for the expedition. Fortunately for Miklouho-Maclay, the President of the Russian Geographical Society, the Grand Duke Constantine (the Czar's brother) was also the administrative head of the Russian Navy, and he organised for Miklouho-Maclay to travel to the Far East on the steam corvette *Vitiaz*. The corvette, commandeered by Captain Pavel Nikolayevich Nazimov, was to join a squadron of the Russian Fleet in the Far East.

The *Vitiaz* left the Russian Baltic port of Kronstadt on 27 October 1870 for a ten-month voyage around South America, calling at various ports and stopping at Easter Island for some weeks to recover from the strenuous journey. While the seamen recuperated Miklouho-Maclay used the time to acquaint himself with the island, an experience that gave him the opportunity to foresee the fate of earth in centuries to come. Limited in resources and isolated in the Pacific, Easter Island suffered ecological devastation even before Europeans had colonised the island. Because of increased population and diminishing local resources on which life depended, the original indigenous population eventually perished. The Europeans who later colonised the island further escalated the ecological disaster by introducing grazing and plantation activities; outsider slaves were also brought in for the benefit of the colonial masters. The impact of all these encounters on the fate of Easter Island was dramatic — so much so that Miklouho-Maclay abandoned sponges altogether to devote the rest of his life to the study of humans and their environment.

Troubled by frequent illness during the sea journey, Miklouho-Maclay looked in sad physical condition. Captain Nazimov strongly advised him to abandon his idea of going to New Guinea and proceed with him to the Russian Far East where care could be taken of his ailing health. The advice was declined and when the *Vitiaz* called at Samoa, Miklouho-Maclay hired two servants for this expedition: a Polynesian man, Boy, and a Swedish whaler, Olsson. He had hoped to make the Swede his assistant but this idea never materialised; for years to come Olsson often caused him more trouble than help. This was frequently to be Miklouho-Maclay's fate when dealing with Europeans.

# The First Journey to New Guinea

## 19 September

Morning. At about 10 a.m. the mountain ridges of New Guinea, partly covered in cloud, appeared at last. The corvette *Vitiaz* headed towards them moving parallel with the north-east coast of New Britain. The land in sight was Cape King William on the north-coast of New Guinea. A high mountain range rising to over 10,000 feet runs parallel to the coast, marked on geographical charts with the name of Finisterre.

In the straits between Rooke Island and New Guinea a number of flatter islands covered in extensive vegetation could be seen. Assisted by a favourable current, the ship moved smoothly forward.

At 2.00 p.m. the *Vitiaz* came so close to the coast that even the smallest details on shore were distinguishable. In the distance lay the mountains, cloud masses totally obscuring the main peaks. On the lower slopes the forest had a dark and eerie appearance, greatly differing in colour from the coastal belt of pale green jungle. This belt extended from the sea to the mountains, rising consistently in ridges and terraces.

Numerous ravines and gorges covered in a heavy cloak of jungle were carved into this panorama, connecting the area of tall forest with the coastal belt. The strip of jungle along the coast was irregular and in some places extended deeply inland to where the mountains lay, giving the impression of jungle-clad coastal plains. In two places near the beach smoke was seen, betraying the presence of man.

At 6.00 p.m. a small jungle-covered island appeared close to the mainland and through the palms, roofs of rough huts could be seen. A few minutes later figures of people on the beach became distinguishable. A stream flowed across the island, seeming to meander across an area of grassland.

Unable to find suitable anchorage the *Vitiaz* cut steam and remained in the open sea. The evening was clear with bright stars and although the mountain peaks were still wreathed in clouds, it looked as if the island had subsided slightly as the cloud mass crept down towards the coastal areas. Lightning flashed constantly in the clouds hanging over the mountains, but the accompanying thunder could not be heard from such a distance.

## 20 September

During the night a strong current had swept us about twenty miles to the north. I rose early and went on deck, hoping to see the mountain peaks free of cloud before sunrise. Indeed, the peaks could be seen quite clearly. They were by no means many in number; rather the range had the appearance of a high, compact wall, almost uniform in height. With the first sunrays the tops and bases of the peaks were still visible, while the intervening areas remained veiled in mist.

As we moved the scene changed. The terraces gradually disappeared as the long mountain ridges dissolved into undulating hills towards the coast. The vegetation was richer here.

Around 10.30 p.m. heading in the direction of Astrolabe Bay we saw Cape Rigny and Cape Duperrey, both looking very low, the latter protruding into the sea. The clouds fled towards the mountain peaks, probably swept up by wild currents, rapidly changing their shape before becoming static on reaching the summit. Columns of smoke rose here and there in the foothills.

At noon we were in the middle of Astrolabe Bay[1] and Captain P.N. Nazimov asked me at which point I wished to disembark. I indicated a cliff lying to our right thinking that a landing among the mangroves might prove treacherous. We observed the coast for some time hoping to sight more native huts, but saw only sporadic columns of smoke. The *Vitiaz* moved closer inshore and second-in-command P.P. Novosilsky excitedly announced that he had seen natives running on the beach. Indeed, on the sandy shore a number of dark figures could be seen rushing about, stopping occasionally to look at us.

At this point a small cove extended inland, appearing to shelter a small bay. We moved towards the cove, then the *Vitiaz* dropped anchor approximately 150 yards from the shore at about 27 fathoms depth. Huge trees grew on the edge of the cove's protective coral reef, their heavy foliage pulling the branches close to the surface of the water. Behind these a sandy beach could be seen and as we watched, a group of natives came into view, apparently shy and apprehensive. They were engaged in some consultation and after a long discussion one moved forward carrying a coconut. This he left on the beach, indicating through mime that the fruit was meant for us, then quickly disappeared into the thick jungle.

I asked the captain for the use of a dinghy but on being told that I would be accompanied by a number of armed men, I insisted on rowing ashore with just Olsson and Boy.[2] We got into the dinghy and set off to meet my future friends. I carried many and various gifts with me — beads, strips of red cotton cloth, mirrors and such. Following the coastline, we approached the place where natives were first seen. After half an hour's rowing we were near the shore, where I sighted several native pirogues on the sand. I wanted to land there but the rough sea prevented this.

A native appeared from the jungle armed with a spear. He raised this over his head and gestured for me to move away from the beach. I stood up and showed him a few pieces of red cloth, whereupon a dozen armed natives appeared from the jungle, apparently too cautious to come closer. I was not eager to wade through the sea to them so I dropped the cloth into the water, hoping that the waves would carry my gift to the shore. The natives began to wave excitedly, signalling me to move away; our presence was obviously disturbing them so I ordered my men to row seaward. However, as soon as we began to move away, the natives jumped into the sea to collect the red cloth that had attracted much attention. On shore they peered at the bits of cloth curiously, chattering amongst themselves. Realising that my first attempt at making a friendly contact had failed, I returned to the ship.

Back on the *Vitiaz* I was told that more natives had been sighted on another part of the beach. I made haste to this place but found no one. In a small cove behind low branches close to the water, several empty pirogues could be seen. I sighted a strip of sandy beach in a small inlet not far away and headed towards it. A track led from the inlet into the jungle and as soon as I landed I set off along this. So eager was I to make contact with the natives that I forgot to give my men appropriate orders for beaching the dinghy. After a short walk through the jungle I could see the roofs of huts. Further on the footpath widened into a clearing surrounded by rows of huts with roofs that reached down to the ground.

The village appeared tidy and rather pleasant. The central area of the clearing was of beaten earth, while the entire settlement was surrounded by tropical oak trees (varied in the colour of their leaves) and tall shady palms. The palm fronds on the roofs, aged and weather-beaten white, contrasted sharply with the dark background of heavy greenery. Vivid red Siamese Rose (hibiscus) and the variegated red, green and yellow of *Croton* and *Coleus* completed the wild scenery. The surrounding flora consisted chiefly of tall pandanus, banana palms, bread fruit trees, areca and coconut palms that also sheltered the clearing from the wind.

Although the village was totally deserted, evidence of recent habitation could be seen everywhere, giving the appearance of having been abandoned only a few moments ago; smouldering embers in fires on the ground still flared occasionally. Nearby lay coconuts already punctured for drinking, a few steps away a hastily abandoned paddle.

The doorways of some huts were closed with a shelter

fashioned from tree-bark, but two were wide open as though the inhabitants had left in a great hurry. The huts had but one opening that also served to admit the only light into the dwelling. As I peered inside the semi-darkness, objects were barely visible: a resting platform built of bamboo; a few stones leaning against a clay vessel with a section of the top knocked out. Here gleamed the flickering flames of a fire. Hanging from the walls were bundles of feathers and strings of variously shaped shells, and from the roof hung skulls darkened by smoke.

The setting sun cast its soft rays on the palm fronds and from the jungle drifted the songs of many unknown birds. It was remote, pleasant, but at the same time strange and unknown — more like a dream than reality.

I approached another hut but heard some disturbance. When I turned I saw a few paces from me a man who seemed to have emerged from the ground; he faced me for an instant, then fled into the jungle. I dashed after him waving a red cloth I had in my hand. The man turned and, realising that I was alone and unarmed and pleading for him to wait, halted while I approached slowly proffering the gift. The Papuan took the cloth, examined it with curiosity and admiration, and finally wound it around his head. This native was of average height and dark chocolate in colour. His short, dark, dull hair was curly like an African's. His nose was flat, his eyes deep-set, his full mouth partly covered by a wild moustache and beard. His entire clothing consisted of a grey rag hardly wider than eight centimetres, which encircled his waist as a belt, then passed between his legs and tied at the back into the belt. Bands of knotted dried grass on both his upper arms appeared to be meant as decorations. Thrust into the right arm band was a betel leaf, and in the other a primitive knife fashioned from polished bone. The solidly built man was well muscled. He was my first native acquaintance and from his facial expression I judged him to be sympathetic. Without knowing why, I had the feeling that he would obey me so I took him by the hand and, without meeting any resistance, led him back to the village.

In the clearing I found my men, Olsson and Boy, worrying about my absence and about to search for me. Olsson gave my Papuan friend several tobacco leaves which he took silently, but not knowing what to do with them, hung them next to the betel leaf on his right arm bracelet.

As we stood in the clearing, natives began to appear from behind the surrounding bushes still too apprehensive to approach, tensed to flee at a single movement. Extremely nervous of us, they kept some distance away. I endeavoured to encourage them to come closer but was unsuccessful so was obliged to go to them and, taking each by the hand, pulled them individually to the centre of the clearing.

After having assembled the natives, I sat upon a rock and distributed the gifts — beads, nails, fish-hooks and coloured cloth. No one refused the gifts, though they clearly did not comprehend the use of the nails and hooks. Around me stood eight Papuans of varying height and physiognomy; even their skin tones differed slightly.

In striking contrast to my first native acquaintance was one taller than the average Papuan, skinny, with a long hooked nose. His forehead was narrow and appeared flat above the temples. His beard and moustache were shaved, wiry reddish-brown hair stood out on top of his head like a bush, and long coils of hair fell over his neck and shoulders as commonly seen on the natives of New Ireland. Stuck in his hair were two bamboo combs, the rear one decorated in the style of a fan consisting of black and white cassowary and cockatoo feathers. Tortoiseshell rings hung from his ears and his nostrils were pierced with a pencil-sized bamboo stick. Around his neck hung necklaces of the teeth of dogs and other animals as well as a small bag, while a larger bag suspended from his left shoulder held his personal possessions. All the natives wore woven armbands from which hung bones, leaves, flowers and so on.

Some of the men had a stone axe slung upon one shoulder while others carried bows as tall as themselves and arrows a full metre long Not only did the colour of their hair vary — some dark, others like red clay — but their style of dressing varied also. Some had their hair combed in the form of a fur hat, some had it cut short, and others had hair falling to the shoulder. Regardless of the style, the hair curled like that of a Negro and even the hair of their beards grew in spiralling curly tufts. The skin pigmentation varied with the age group, the younger natives being of a paler complexion than the older ones.

Satisfied with my first contacts and findings, I returned to the *Vitiaz* at sunset. The natives accompanied me to the beach, carrying gifts for me of coconuts, bananas and two squealing piglets whose legs were firmly bound together. The Papuans placed their offerings in the dinghy. Eager to continue my contact and introduce my new friends to the officers, I urged the assembled natives to follow us in their pirogues. After some consultation, five of them occupied two pirogues while the others remained ashore and obviously tried to discourage the adventurers from exposing themselves to danger. I tied one pirogue to my dinghy and rowed towards the *Vitiaz*.

We had covered approximately half the distance when my courageous companions began to change their minds and expressed a desire not to continue. They endeavoured to cast off their pirogue while the other group had already headed towards shore. One of the Papuans even attempted to cut the rope with an axe so impatient was he to free the pirogue. I persuaded them to go further but once we reached the *Vitiaz* we experienced great difficulty in getting the visitors on board. Olsson and Boy had to almost carry them up the ladder against their wishes. My help was sorely needed otherwise the Papuans would have collapsed with fright, obviously fearing that they were about to be executed. In the meantime night had fallen and on the mess deck, candles were lit. The natives became calmer, even cheerful when the officers presented them with gifts. Tea was served to them which they immediately drank.

Despite this warm welcome, the Papuans were very happy to

leave and descended with great speed into their pirogue, then paddled as quickly as possible back to the beach. I was told on the corvette that the natives had appeared again where we had first seen them. They brought with them a gift of two dogs, slaughtered the animals on the spot and left them for us.

## 21 September

After breakfast I returned to the village I had visited the previous day. My first local friend Tui, accompanied by other Papuans, came forward to greet me.

That day a celebration was to be held on board ship to mark the birthday of His Highness, the Grand Duke Constantine. I decided to remain in the village during the festivities, hoping my presence would cushion the impact upon the natives when the celebratory salvoes started firing from the ship. As there was some time to wait before the gun salute began, I decided to employ my time in searching for the future site for my hut. As I was unfamiliar with the customs and habits of my new neighbours, I felt it unwise to settle in the village; particularly, not knowing their language, I could not ask for their permission to do so.

My decision to live apart from them was influenced not only by a hesitance in imposing my presence upon them, but also to stay in the village would involve being disturbed by excessive noises of life — crying children, barking dogs and so on.

After following a foot-track through the jungle for about ten minutes, I reached a small cape where a stream was discharging into the sea. The area was covered with large trees and appeared quite comfortable as it was isolated, close to water, and located on a track between two villages.

After choosing this location for my camp, I hurried back to the village. As I arrived, the gun salute started. At first it seemed that the booming of the guns surprised rather than frightened the Papuans, but with each new salvo they started to run about, bending down with their hands over their ears, trembling in fear.

This noisy celebration placed me in an uncomfortable position because, although I tried to preserve a calm and serious demeanour, I could not help laughing. However, it turned out that this had a reassuring effect on the natives; laughter spread like an epidemic as they followed my example. The Papuans were soon looking at each other and smiling.

Happy that the incident had passed without serious results, I returned to the *Vitiaz*. Captain Nazimov wished to accompany me ashore to help with the choice of a camp site, and the first officer and ship's doctor came with us. Although I had already chosen a site for the hut, it was useful to look at other possible places too. We inspected three locations, one of which was particularly favoured by my companions. Here a large creek entered the sea and because of this, I disliked the site as it was obvious that the place was often visited by Papuans using their pirogues kept at the mouth of the creek; also, not far away an area of land was partly cultivated, suggesting the existence of native gardens. I felt my presence there would be an intrusion into their life, so told the captain I wished to build on the site of my original choice. At mid-afternoon a gang of seamen came ashore to help clear the jungle for my camping site. Carpenters began the hut by erecting two poles in the shade of a gigantic tree (*Canarium commune*).

## 22, 23, 24 and 25 September

On each of these days I concentrated upon the erection of the hut, leaving the *Vitiaz* daily at 6.00 a.m. accompanied by the carpenters and staying ashore until nightfall.

My hut, 7 feet by 14 feet, was divided by waxed sail cloth into two rooms, one for myself and the other for my two men. We had brought planks from Tahiti with us but these proved insufficient, so we were obliged to construct only the lower portion of the walls with them. The upper sections of the walls and the door we fashioned from waxed cloth, the roof of palm leaves skilfully woven into mats by Boy. The floor, wall-frames and planking of

Tahitian timber were all manufactured in the corvette's workshop. The poles and beams had to be cut locally but, thanks to the generosity of the captain, many seamen were assigned to this task and it progressed at some speed.

The Papuans kept away from the building site, perhaps remembering their fear on the 21 September or perhaps in awe of so many men, so only occasionally did we see a native or two. The ship's officers began to survey the bay, naming several promontories after themselves and many geographical sites after high ranking Russian authorities. The small nearby island called Bili Bili by the natives was temporarily renamed Vitiaz.

On 25 September, Boy began the roofing, the last day before the *Vitiaz* was to sail. Presently the Papuan, Tui, who was quite sympathetic to me, came to the site. Expressing himself through mime he explained that when the ship left (indicating the *Vitiaz* and then the horizon) leaving us behind (he pointed to me, Olsson, Boy and the ground), natives from the local villages would come (gesturing towards the jungle then naming the villages), they would demolish the hut (he approached the poles and made as if he were cutting them) and then spear us (here he made spear throwing motions, came to me, pushed me with his finger, and imitated a man dying from a spear thrust). The same demonstration was performed on Boy and Olsson.

Although I understood my Papuan friend quite well, I pretended ignorance. In a new attempt to make me more aware of the danger, Tui emphasised the names of the villages — Bongu, Gorendu and Gumbu — at the same time demonstrating how the poles would be cut and the hut demolished. I pretended not to understand and presented him with a nail as a gift.

That evening on the corvette, I told the ship's crew about Tui and his mime. The officer in charge of armoury, Lieutenant Chirikov, offered help, suggesting the placement of landmines around the hut. I found his offer a practical one as some protection would be valuable in the event of the natives acting in accordance with Tui's fears.

## 26 September

Yesterday I went to bed at 11.00 p.m. and rose at 2.00 a.m. All morning I was extremely busy attending to my European correspondence and sorting out my belongings. My baggage had to be organised into two parts — one part to remain with me in New Guinea and the other to go with the *Vitiaz* to Japan. As I had come to New Guinea intending not only to visit but also to take up residence, possibly for many years, it was clear to me that I must not rely on European food for my diet. However, being aware that the Papuan gardens were quite productive and that I could obtain even a pig from time to time, I was sure that I would never starve.

After many months spent at sea, tinned food had become so distasteful to me that I had totally neglected to purchase further supplies at the last port. I had brought so little with me that Captain Nazimov was surprised and kindly offered a supply of his food. I accepted his offer gratefully, feeling that it was necessary to have a reserve in case of illness. The captain also gave me the smallest dinghy from the *Vitiaz* which in an emergency could be rowed by only one man — a boon indeed! Having a boat at my disposal would enable me to visit a number of villages along the coast; also, in case I should fail to build a friendly relationship with the local natives, I could make a move into a more hospitable area.

When the last of my tasks on board the *Vitiaz* were completed, I began to transfer supplies from ship to shore and my small hut soon became overcrowded with baggage. Some of the crates had to be placed underneath the hut in the hope they would be safer from weather and looting than left outside.

Since early morning Lieutenant Chirikov had been engaged in laying mines around the hut. He placed them in a half circle, a protective shield against a possible attack from the jungle. Approximately thirty seamen were under his direction, stripping bare an area of 70 metres square around the hut. Behind the hut lay the sea, so consequently protection was unnecessary from this direction. Captain Nazimov was also present, offering helpful advice. I showed the captain and officers the place in the bush immediately behind the hut where, in case of serious illness or attack by natives, I would bury my diaries and notes. I had brought with me to New Guinea several metal cylinders in which my papers could safely lie buried underground for a number of years. The spot chosen was beneath a big tree close to the hut and, to mark the spot, bark had been stripped from the appropriate side of the tree and an arrow carved on it pointing in the direction of the particular spot on the ground.

At about 3.00 p.m. Port Constantine (the name given to the cove where my hut was located) made an impressive picture of life and action. A small steamboat transported firewood from shore to ship surrounded by several other small boats busily engaged in some activity, one of them still transferring my goods ashore. Intense activity continued around the hut; carpenters were busy with the final construction work, while a gang of seamen not only dug holes for the mines but also took care to tidy the area around the hut — even clearing a foot track to the creek and to the shore.

I was not able to supervise the work at the hut — there was still packing to be done on board the *Vitiaz* and this required my presence. Now, totally exhausted from constant activity and little sleep during the past days and nights, I was nervous and tense. I could hardly stand up and my actions and thoughts were mechanical and dreamlike. At 1.00 a.m. I had finished packing the last of the baggage and went ashore to write several letters.

### 27 September

About 2.00 a.m. I brought the last load of baggage to the hut. Boy slept heavily after his labours on the roof. The hut was so filled with goods that I could scarcely find space to stretch out for sleep. Although extremely exhausted, I found sleep difficult — the ants and mosquitoes gave me no peace. Nevertheless, it was most relaxing simply to lie with my eyes closed. Later I returned to the ship to finish my letters, due to lack of space and quiet to accomplish this in my hut. After expressing my thanks to the captain and crew of the *Vitiaz* for their generous assistance, I bade farewell to all, descended into the dinghy and moved ashore. I had ordered Olsson to lower the flag from the mast erected near my hut, in salute as soon as the *Vitiaz* weighed anchor. Observing, however, that the flag had not moved, I hastened to investigate and was astonished to find that my servant, so courageous of speech, had shaking hands and tear-filled eyes. Angrily I snatched the rope and told him that if he was so afraid, it was not too late to be transferred to the ship which had not yet departed. In fact, the *Vitiaz* was already under way from Port Constantine and I made the farewell salute myself.

Suddenly I was aware that the natives might use the opportunity, as *Vitiaz* sailed out of sight, to attack. From this moment on it seemed that everything, the whole project and even our lives, would depend wholly on my efforts and ingenuity.

As soon as the *Vitiaz* had steamed from sight, a group of natives appeared on the cape. They were engaged in some kind of ritual, running in a circle and dancing. Abruptly all stopped and looked towards my camp, their attention most likely attracted by the large Russian flag flapping on the mast beside my hut. They grouped together, talked between themselves, turned towards the camp, shouted several words, and then disappeared.

The baggage and all my gear were still heaped untidily about. In the event of an attack I would find myself in a totally unprepared situation. Clearly I must immediately unpack and sort the goods in the hut and tents. Suffering from total exhaustion due to lack of sleep, I felt physically incapable of the task. I felt faint, unsteady on my feet, lacking energy enough to even move my hands. My Papuan friend Tui arrived at this juncture, presumably to ascertain that I had stayed when the ship sailed. He did not treat me as courteously as before, sceptically inspecting the details of the hut and wanting to go inside, but I prevented this with a gesture and the word "taboo".

It would be difficult to be sure what had the most impression upon him, word or gesture, but he abandoned his efforts to enter the hut. Using mime once more, Tui enquired about the movements of the corvette and I explained that it would return. The presence of my visitor delayed my unpacking, so, in order to divert him, I asked if he could bring me coconuts (I already knew approximately twenty Papuan words) and presented him with a piece of red cloth.

Tui left immediately, but within an hour returned accompanied by two boys and a middle-aged man. The newcomers did not speak at all, remaining serious and formal throughout the visit; even the youngest, about seven years old, observed me with some suspicion. Tui suddenly decided to sleep and stretched himself upon the ground, following all my movements while pretending slumber. Acting as though all was normal, I proceeded with my unpacking. Eventually Tui rose and looked around. Puzzled about the mines, he inspected them cautiously while keeping an appropriate distance, curious to know more about their installation but fearful of getting too close. Leaving at last, he made a strange sign with his hand and said a few unintelligible words (since my arrival I had carried a notebook for noting down new Papuan words).

At approximately 4.00 p.m. a sharp whistle was heard and a group of natives armed with spears and arrows appeared from the bush. I hurried towards them and with gestures, invited them to come closer. They split up into two groups — some left their arrows against trees as they came forward carrying coconuts and pieces of sugar cane, while about six others stayed behind with their weapons. These were the inhabitants of the village beyond the nearby cape whom I had seen dancing during the ship's departure. It was this village (named Gumbu) where I had tried to disembark when I first arrived.

I gave my visitors a variety of small items in return for their gifts and when I had explained that I needed sleep, they finally left.

## 28 September

There was bright, beautiful moonlight last night. I divided the night into three sections, rostering a guard for each, personally taking the first and most difficult share from 9.00 p.m. to 12.00 p.m. When Olsson replaced me at midnight I found sleep impossible in my exhausted condition. Thus the night, though majestic in its moonlit beauty, was a long and boring one for me.

The day passed in the same way as the one before and I was kept busy unpacking and arranging the hut. Having so much baggage and too little space, I was faced with many problems. Nonetheless I managed to stack it all, after some items were hung from the ceiling and the rest stowed away in the tiny attic which Olsson helped me build in the roof. One part of my room (being only 7 foot by 7 foot) was occupied by a table and the other part by two large hampers to serve as my bed. A passageway three feet wide between these sections was occupied by a folding chair — so necessary for my relaxation.

Today we saw Papuans on the shore engaged in fishing, using large oblong baskets.

I rested all day and made no trips. I expected to sleep well that night.

## 29 September

Last night I slept as one dead. The weather was pleasant and the Papuans were not seen the entire day. I found out that my men had taken turns to be on guard all night, so I told them to sleep in future and not to worry. This they refused to do however, still being afraid of the Papuans.

Our hands and faces were swollen from the bites of mosquitoes, ants and other insects. It seemed strange but it appeared that I attracted fewer insects than Olsson and Boy. Each morning they complained bitterly to me of sleep disturbed by these insect pests.

## 30 September

During the day I sighted a number of Papuans; it now appeared that their life, disturbed by the *Vitiaz*, was returning to its normal routine. I needed to be cautious however, as existing scientific data on their racial traits stresses a tendency toward cunning and untrustworthiness. Until I collect new data, I must rely on previous information and remain cautious.

I watched the evening spectacle of a splendid sunset upon the mountain peaks, each evening a different and impressive picture. After the *Vitiaz* departed, an air of total peace settled in. It was hard to imagine human sounds of talking, shouting and quarrelling. The silence was broken from time to time only by the sea sounds, the wind and occasional bird-songs. This change of environment made a happy impact upon me; I was content. The temperature was quite constant, the surrounding vegetation varied and luxuriant and the entire scenery picturesque, helping me to forget the past, ignore the future and enjoy each new experience as it came along. My only thought was to collect information and research into the life surrounding me. What more could one hope for indeed? Behind me lay the sea and a coral reef, in front a tropical jungle, both of which abounded in only partly-known flora and fauna. In the far distance the silhouette of the mountains was seen, with peaks partially enveloped in cloud. Thinking about all this, I rested on a fallen log well satisfied with my destiny, although I knew I was only on the first rung of a great ladder yet to be scaled.

Tui arrived again. I received an hour's tuition in the Papuan language and my vocabulary was increased by several new words. After writing these words in my notebook with as much phonetic accuracy as possible, I presented Tui with a cigarette box and Olsson gave him an old hat. Tui was so pleased with his gifts that he left quickly, either in fear of having them taken away again, or in haste to show them to the other villagers. Less than an hour later, a column of some twenty-five natives appeared from the bush. Two men heading the column carried a pig slung on a bamboo pole. Following them came two more bearing pots on their heads while others carried coconuts. Among them were Tui and other natives known to me.

The Papuans laid their goods on the ground in front of me, then each made a presentation of his personal gift. Some of them gathered about me while others, including Tui, formed a separate group. Tui was explaining to them all he had learnt about my equipment and me. The natives observed the gear with great curiosity, quickly moving from one object to another. They spoke little and behaved in a reserved manner, staying clear of the hut doorway either out of fear or politeness. The natives knew my name already and used it always when addressing me. A group formed around Boy as he played a harmonica, a musical instrument popular on the island of Samoa, and which Boy could play with some proficiency. The music made a considerable impression, holding the natives' entire interest to the exclusion of all else. I made gifts of several harmonicas to the Papuans; they immediately began to experiment with the instruments. The visit ended about an hour later and on leaving, the Papuans shook hands using the left hand. In many of the natives, symptoms of elephantiasis were quite noticeable.

At 10.00 p.m. a storm broke unexpectedly, rain fell in torrents and the sky was riven by lightning. I was encouraged to find my roof watertight.

## 1 October

I woke before daybreak and decided to visit one of the neighbouring villages; the time having come to make more moves towards familiarising myself with the Papuans.

Before leaving, I needed to solve a problem — should I carry a firearm? I followed my inclinations and proceeded unarmed, not knowing how I would be greeted on arrival at the village. I was quite aware that the use of arms would be disastrous to the success of my research and could place my life in jeopardy; if, in the defence of my person, I used a gun to kill a number of natives, this would be the beginning of problems, not the end of them. Protection would be only temporary, out of fear — but protection for how long? The desire for revenge among the numerous natives would override fear of a gun so I needed to make an entirely different approach to these people, and this conviction sent me forth unarmed.

It would be absurd to predict how a man will behave in circumstances not before experienced; therefore it was hard to foresee how I would act if I knew a gun was at my waist when hostility grew and tension rose. Would I remain calm and restrain my impulses? The only aspect that I could be sure of was that if I fired one shot, that bullet would kill the natives' confidence in me and ruin all my chances of success. Thinking about this, I was strongly convinced that patience and peace should be the basis of my approaches, thus I left the gun behind and carried only my notebook and pencil.

I had in mind to visit Gorendu, the village closest to my hut. However, once in the jungle I took the wrong track. Although I realised my mistake, I decided not to retrace my steps feeling sure the track would lead to one village or another. Preoccupied with thoughts of my Papuan neighbours whom I hardly knew and imagining the details of the approaching meeting, I was almost lost in meditation when suddenly, I realised I was about to enter a village — which one I knew not.

The noises of village life were heard and I stopped to familiarise myself with my surroundings. While I stood struggling with my thoughts, a lad of about fifteen years emerged from the bush a few steps from me. For a moment we silently exchanged looks and as I wasn't able to talk with him and fearing a movement or gesture would frighten him away, the inactivity remained. The boy glanced towards the direction of the village from where came the cries of a woman. Then the sound faded into a chill silence.

I walked out into the clearing where a group of armed Papuans stood absorbed in discussion. Behind them waited a larger group of silent, armed warriors — no woman or child could be seen. At sight of me, several natives readied themselves to dispatch their spears, but at the same time a series of calls were heard, apparently causing these natives to lower their arms. Tired by my walk and surprised at this welcome, I moved forward searching for a familiar face among the warriors.

In the centre of the clearing stood a small platform and here I stopped. A few Papuans moved closer to me. Suddenly two arrows flashed in rapid succession close by me — it was hard to ascertain whether on purpose or accidentally. The Papuans who had approached me said something loudly, obviously addressing the bowmen who had loosed the arrows. Then they addressed me, indicating the tree tops and leading me to believe the arrows were aimed at birds. No birds could be seen, and the arrows were surely launched to test my reaction. As the first arrow passed me by, the eyes of many natives were fixed upon me, trying to read the impressions in my face. However, except for fatigue and curiosity, I registered no emotion.

I looked around at the glum faces of the natives, suspecting a sense of anger in their silence — why indeed had I come to trouble these people? With the exception of a few elders, the warriors held their arms at the ready while more natives arrived and the numbers steadily increased. Perhaps the news of my presence had reached a neighbouring village? A small group of men completely surrounded me and three of them spoke loudly with hostile glances in my direction. Then, in order to give support to their words, they brandished their spears. One was so impassioned in his gestures that during his discourse, unintelligible to me, his spear nearly struck my nose. The gesture was so rapid that I scarcely saw the spear, so it was not I who avoided contact, but the bearer's skill in manipulating his weapon with such mastery that it enabled him to halt the spear only centimetres in front of my face. I took several steps to one side and caught the voices of some of the other natives, apparently protesting at this attempted assault. At this moment I was glad not to have brought my gun, for if I were armed, would I permit my challenger to repeat his experiment with the spear?

I found myself in an awkward situation; I could not communicate with the natives and nothing remained but to leave. I felt tired and sleepy so, considering the distance to my hut, I decided to sleep where I was. I had no alternative but to rest; without further delay, I chose a place beneath a tree, dragged a mat into the shade and stretched out on it. It was pleasant to close my eyes against the sunlight and, to increase my comfort further, I loosened my shoe-laces, unbuttoned my shirt, unfastened my belt and cushioned my head.

The natives grouped in a half circle but at a respectful distance, wondering what new surprise I might have in store. I was aware that behind me, inspecting my shoes, was my would-be assailant of some minutes before.[3] The earlier incident flashed through my mind and I realised it was likely only the forerunner to further events about to begin. If no other choice be offered but death, then there can be no difference if it should overtake one running, sitting, lying still or asleep. I know not why, but I found myself thinking that I would die less happy if I knew that three or four natives had paid for my life. Thus, once more I was glad that I had not brought my gun.

Through my drowsiness I was aware of bird noises; the screech of some lorikeet darting about startled me awake several times, but the *koko* (*Chlamydodera*) sounded a sweet lullaby to calm me again. A chorus of insects was heard from all around; rather than being an annoyance, only served to increase my drowsiness.

I awoke fresh and rested, calculating the time to be 3.00 p.m. from the position of the sun — I had slept for at least two hours. On opening my eyes I sighted several Papuans sitting hardly a yard from me busily chewing betel. The men were unarmed and appeared not as hostile as before. I regretted not being able to converse and decided to tidy myself and return to camp. The procedure of dressing myself was a phenomenon of enormous interest to my audience. Finally I rose, bowed to all about me and took the path leading towards my camp.

All night heavy rain fell and dawn brought more rain and a gloomy aspect. The ants were really troublesome, often gaining access to my hair and beard, stinging painfully. Boy was so badly bitten by them and had scratched his skin so much, that both his legs were swollen and one arm quite badly affected. After bathing the suffering areas, I treated those that looked most severe, using some of my chemicals instead of medicaments.

At sundown Tui visited me armed with a spear and asked to borrow the axe — he needed it to cut something and promised to return it without delay. I quickly fulfilled his wish, eager to test his trustworthiness. Although neither of us spoke the other's language, we nonetheless communicated.

Early morning at low tide, I walked in the shallows along the beach but found nothing to arrest my attention. The Papuans brought me several bamboo poles about 20 feet in length to build a verandah. Tui also brought bamboo, but did not mention the borrowed axe.

I had earlier noticed that pictures in books caused anxiety in the natives. After showing them magazine illustrations, I saw my visitors become restless and eager to leave. They begged me to take the magazine into the hut and leave it there; their anxiety eased only when I complied with their wishes.

I was mistaken to doubt Tui's honesty; it was not yet 6.00 p.m. when he entered the camp carrying the axe. Satisfied with his character and bearing, I presented my friend with a mirror, which he took straight back to the village to exhibit. This gift inspired other natives to come calling bringing coconuts and sugar-cane, and my return gifts included empty boxes and nails. I must clarify here that I did not regard these exchanges of gifts as a business matter but only as a means of building friendship, for such a gift is given spontaneously, without thought of benefit. On several occasions I put my Papuan friends to a test by accepting their gifts of coconuts and sugarcane, but offering nothing in return. The natives made no sign of expecting anything, and left without having asked for the return of their own offerings. It became noticeable that my hut, and I as its owner, was making some impact on the villagers. Whenever they visited me the natives exhibited restlessness and looked about curiously, expecting momentarily some miraculous happening.

There were few with the fortitude to look me straight in the eye; they usually turned or glanced away when I looked at them. Some of them looked upon me and my equipment with a strange attitude (I could not precisely describe the expression on their faces but I had the feeling it was a type of jealousy). On several occasions I was visited by natives who exhibited some anger and hostility. Their faces were dark, their upper lips raised a little, and at each moment I expected these to widen even further into a snarl.

Traces of the *Vitiaz's* visit still remained in parts of the island. Felled trees lay across jungle paths, in places almost rendering them impassable, impressing the natives who would take years to cut so many with only the stone axe as a tool.

Throughout the night, flute and drum sounds could be heard from Gorendu. The flutes were made by drilling several holes in a small coconut. The drums were fashioned from a section of log two or three metres long and half a metre in diameter, and when beaten projected a sound heard for several miles. My neighbours in Gorendu seemed to be celebrating some occasion. Some of the inhabitants who visited me that day had their faces and backs painted with red ochre and most wore the comb hair-ornament decorated with feathers.

By his son, Tui sent me some pork, breadfruit, bananas and taro; all well-cooked and wrapped in large leaves of *Arthocarpus incisa*.

## 2 October

On this day the Gorendu villagers came again and brought with them some of the inhabitants of Bili Bili Island, the latter traditionally dressed in shell ornaments hung with dog and boar teeth. Their faces and bodies were splendidly painted with figures and designs; even their hairdressing was of particular note, combed upward and coloured. Although there were no obvious physical differences between the Gorendu villagers and the nearby island peoples, the Bili Bili natives were quite distinguishable by their folk-lore.

My friends from Bongu played the role of hosts and conducted the visitors about the camp, discussing my goods and equipment. The Gorendu and Bili Bili guests were most impressed, staring wide-eyed and occasionally putting two fingers into their open mouths (the native gesture of astonishment).

With the fall of evening I was moved to stroll along a bush track, feeling it necessary to ascertain whether or not I could move about the jungle at night, for example the return journey from a nearby village. In the jungle, however, the darkness was so intense I was soon forced to abandon my experiment. Though the journey was so short, I returned to camp with several scratches, a wound on my forehead and a twisted knee; so concluded that jungle walks at night were not practicable.

(The ink bottle is almost empty and I am not sure if I have more in reserve.)

## 3 October

Early this morning I walked upon the reef at low tide in the hope of catching fish. Wading knee-deep I unexpectedly came upon some interesting sponges of rare varieties (*Calcispongia*). After half an hour of collecting these, I assured myself of an occupation for the rest of the day. However, returning from the reef I did not rush to the microscope and postponed the study of the sponges. I decided, instead, to go to the village east of Cape Observation and introduce myself to the natives.

I made my way without knowledge of the right track, trusting my judgment to choose what path seemed appropriate. The early part of my journey led through dense forest and as I walked, I admired the abundant tropical flora — so much of which was unknown to the scientific world. The track terminated at the shore and from there, by following the beach, it was not difficult to locate the village I sought.

I met no one in transit by whom I could send advance word of my intending visit. From the beach I followed fresh footprints inland and heard, after only a few steps, sounds of habitation.

A little further on, roofs of huts could be seen. I passed one and gained a clearing in the village centre. It was a busy place, throbbing with life and movement. Two men, absorbed in their work, were mending the roof of a hut; a group of boys and girls wove palm fronds for this purpose and passed the completed mats aloft to the men on the roof; women were occupied attending to children of different ages; two large pigs, with litters of piglets, were just finishing a meal. Although the sun was high, the clearing was steeped in shade and stayed cool and fresh. The villagers chattered incessantly among themselves and the whole scene, rich in its originality, was of great interest to me. Suddenly someone cried out — all conversation immediately stopped and chaos descended upon the village.

Shrieking in unison, the women and girls abandoned their work, caught up the babies and roughly wakened small children who screamed loudly. Children, bewildered by their mothers' fear, yelled as they were dragged away into the jungle. The girls and older children followed, in company of barking dogs and squealing pigs.

Alarmed by the hubbub, villagers rushed from everywhere and encircled me. Surprised by my welcome, I nonetheless remained calm and controlled, though wondering why my presence had caused such a storm. I wished I could have reassured these people in some way, but not knowing the right words to do so, feared gestures might cause further confusion.

The men encircling me had ominous expressions and were talking together in words quite unintelligible. Tired by my long journey, I walked towards a small platform, stepped upon it and made myself comfortable. I gestured to the natives to come and sit close by me, and some seemed to realise I had no hostile intentions. The tone of their discussion became friendlier and a few laid down their arms; others, still filled with reserve and doubt, clung to their weapons.

The natives grouped about me were of considerable interest. Their uneasiness at my presence kept them tense; many had fear in their eyes, and my departure would obviously be a relief to them. I took my notebook and made sketches of the huts with their tall platforms similar to that upon which I sat. I began to make notes about the inhabitants, observing each native from head to heel as I wrote. My behaviour disconcerted them; they obviously resented being so closely scrutinised and some left the circle muttering in protest.

I felt very thirsty and wished to have a coconut, but was offered none of those lying scattered about. Not one villager approached or attempted a conversation, and a feeling of hostility prevailed. Finally, I realised that to prolong my visit would damage my relationship with the natives and stood up. The only reaction to this and to my departure was silence, and I followed the track to the beach again.

Considering the visit as I made my way home, I concluded that my task to build up confidence among the natives would be a difficult one, which must be approached in future with more patience and caution.

On reaching my camp at sunset, I found my servants very worried at my long absence. I was told that during the day two villagers had brought a small parcel for each of us. I ordered the parcels be opened; they revealed cooked bananas, bread fruit and some meat resembling pork. The meat did not appeal to me, but

Boy and Olsson ate of it with gusto. After the meal was finished, I suggested to my servants that in all possibility they had eaten human flesh. The men were bemused and tried to convince me that it was pork — I however, doubted this.

## 4 October

The previous evening, a small insect flew into my eye and though I successfully removed the trespasser, the eye remained painful all night; the eye-lid grew swollen, thus preventing my microscope examination of the sponges. Early in the morning, on the turn of the tide, I visited the reef and became so absorbed in the fascinating prospects for research that I was unaware of the rising waters, so my return journey necessitated wading, in parts, more than waist-deep.

The verandah roof was finished this day and other small jobs done to make our camp tidier and more comfortable — I cleared the camp area of fallen leaves and branches. Day by day the camp gained a homelier air.

During the evening the sound of laboured breathing drew me to the hut to find Boy, wrapped in blankets and almost too weak to speak. He had a high fever.

## 6 October

At approximately 4.00 p.m. a sail appeared around Cape Observation followed by a large pirogue specially equipped with an improvised canopy. Under this could be seen a group of natives where one of them handled sail and tiller. The boat approached our cape with the pilot calling and gesturing to us. I was unaware that my neighbours had a pirogue of such size. Its course bore it towards Gorendu and it was followed by an even larger vessel. This carried more natives who were protected from the sun and wind by an extensive cabin-like construction. Each pirogue had two masts, which slanted obliquely to fore and aft.

I guessed my neighbours would be anxious to introduce their guests to the creature none had seen before — a white man — and so prepared the camp for such a visit. Indeed, only half an hour had elapsed before Papuans began to appear from two directions, from both Gorendu and Gumbu. I understood that the visitors were from Bili Bili Island and had been brought to the camp to see the unusual objects in the white man's hut.

The Bili Bili islanders observed with wonder and curiosity the pots and cooking utensils, my deck-chair and the small table in front of the hut. My boots and striped socks really astonished them. Often their mouths were open saying "aaa" and "eee", their tongues clicking in surprise and disbelief and, in the final stages of amazement, putting fingers in their mouths. Nails fascinated them and I gave them eight of these, some beads and red cloth. Olsson objected to this, as he pointed out that the natives had brought nothing for us.

Part of each islander's hair was coloured red, as were their foreheads and noses and some shoulders. Some natives had necklaces hanging to their waists, fashioned from two pig tusks. The natives of Gorendu called this ornament, apparently a valued piece of decoration, *bul-ra*. I offered a knife in exchange for a *bul-ra* but was rejected, despite obvious keenness to have the knife. The natives seemed pleased with the small gifts I had given them and left in high spirits. I was surprised, however, to see them returning some half an hour later; they carried quantities of coconuts and bananas, after apparently stowing their presents in the pirogues.

The ceremony of presenting gifts had a strict form of protocol; for example, a man personally carried his gift to the recipient. So each islander gave me a gift, a smaller one to Olsson and an even smaller one to Boy. The visitors stayed by my hut for some time and on leaving, mimed an invitation to me to visit their island. They indicated my dinghy and the direction of their island, mimed assurance they would not kill and eat me, and that coconuts and bananas were plentiful. As each man left he gripped my upper arm by way of farewell. Two natives, to whom I had inadvertently given more gifts than the others, slung an arm around my neck, pulled my head onto their chests and repeated "O Maklai, O Maklai!" They moved a short distance only, stopped, turned and saluted with upraised bent arm and clenched fist.

## 10 October

This date marked my first attack of fever. No matter how fiercely I resisted this, I was forced to lie abed all day — truly a hellish day.

## 12 October

Olsson's turn for fever had come. When I rose I found myself weak and my legs nearly useless. Boy also complained of feeling unwell, so the hut was quite like a hospital ward.

I learned from Tui the names of the villages which could be seen from the reef. I was surprised to hear so many names. Everything, even the smallest reef, creek or part of the beach had its native title. The cape where my hut is located, though previously uninhabited, is named Garagassi. Cape Observation, lying opposite, is called Gabina, and so on. The village I had visited the day *Vitiaz* arrived in Port Constantine bore the name previously mentioned, Gorendu. Behind this village lies Bongu; further on Male; still further on Bogatim. Again, further along the beach almost level with Bili Bili Island, lies Gorima village; east of Garagassi is Gumbu village where I had unsuccessfully tried to land on my arrival, behind it Barangu and then further on Rai.

While collecting this information from Tui, I was puzzled because although I admired his natural intelligence, I detected a lack of enthusiasm. On hearing the names of the villages I wrote them into a sketch I had made of the bay and its surrounds, as I marked the location of each. Tui understood all of this and I twice checked the pronunciation of the village names. Tui not only corrected my pronunciation but my geographical sketching as well. But the act of my writing and drawing was of no interest to him whatsoever. It would even appear that he had not noticed it, though I had expected him to show great curiosity regarding the skill of writing.

## 13 October

The fever caught me again and so all of us lay ill. It was horrible and with the onset of the monsoon, worse could be expected.

## 14 October

After I had given a dose of quinine to my patients, I cooked rice for breakfast, gave a bowlful to each and left immediately to walk in the jungle, mainly to escape the moaning of the sick men. The surrounding bush abounded with birdlife. Once I had become more familiar with the natives, I planned to hunt birds for the pot as tinned food was becoming so abhorrent to me. On my return to camp I found Olsson still in bed with a high fever, but Boy was on his feet and cooking beans for the evening meal.

Tui, accompanied by three friends from Gumbu, came to visit. The tobacco I had given him earlier (an American brand) was becoming more and more favoured. The natives usually mixed it with some of their own leaf and when smoking, the men would pass the cigarette from one to another, each taking a puff and swallowing the smoke slowly.

I watched with interest a Papuan at work splitting slivers from a section of parasitic vine. First he peeled the bark, and then smoothed the inner wood with the edge of a shell. As the edge became blunt, the man cracked the shell across, forming a new blade.

When a number of these strips were prepared, they were woven into a bracelet such as the natives wear on elbow and knee. The Papuans used their primitive implements with such skill that, watching, I became convinced that no other tool could possibly be more convenient.

## 15 October

In consequence of my previous day's conversation with Tui, I concluded that the hills flanking Astrolabe Bay were quite densely inhabited. He mentioned numerous names, all prefixed with *mana* meaning "mount". Boy had spent three days in bed and was still very pale.

## 16 October

A heavy storm blew last night with such downpour that my roof began to leak and the interior of the hut was awash. I did my best to protect books and papers, and spent the rest of the night in a damp state.

During the day, visits were made by about forty natives from various villages. I was becoming more and more bored by such visits, though the situation would be improved by being able to converse. My progress in learning the language was slow.

## 17 October

Boy's condition was a little improved, but symptoms of a new sickness now appeared — swollen glands and difficulty of movement. Olsson also was ill, could scarcely speak, lying in bed all day with the appearance of a dying man, and moaning and crying out in the night. He emerged only secretly at sunset to cool himself against my orders without his hat in the fresh sea breeze. During the previous week I had done most of the necessary cooking. I was, therefore, tied to the hut by my two patients as the natives took no notice of the servants during my absence. If I were present however, the Papuans would rush to do my bidding. For some reason the Papuans disliked me staring at them and if given even a frown, would run away.

## 18 – 21 October

We began work on a vegetable garden by digging the ground. The surface soil was shallow and we soon struck a bed of coral, making cultivation hard labour. The limited layer of topsoil was crammed with a net-work of roots, so operations had to be performed as often with an axe as with a spade. We planted beans, Tahitian gourds and Indian corn. I was not sure if these would germinate as the seed was inferior, years old.

I spent a considerable amount of time in the bush admiring the vegetation and lamenting my inadequate knowledge of botany. A group of thirteen men from Jambombe (an island near Bili Bili) visited, no doubt having heard stories about me from other islanders. Of the presents I made them, they most fancied the nails.

For a time I observed Tui's son of about fifteen years, attempting to catch fish with arrows. His efforts were unrewarded as the arrow flashed into the water but a moment later, floated to the surface again. At intervals the lad collected the floating arrows before continuing his fishing. The fishing arrows used were slightly different from the conventional, having several branched heads. The arrow heads were made independently from hard wood and then fitted to the shaft.

I decided to increase my living space by enclosing the verandah, and in just one day the thought was made reality. I took Boy with me to cut suitable timber and, working from noon until late afternoon, we completed the extension. Thus I gained an extra 28 square foot of space. Stacking one packing case upon another I formed an adequate work table which, placed in the new extension, gained more light than in its previous position and was more convenient for greeting visiting natives. In addition, the view of the sea from there was splendid.

## 22 October

The following is a description of how I spent an average day. I usually rose earlier than my servants, at daybreak around 5.00 a.m. The first task was to walk around the hut to see if anything untoward had occurred during the night. Then I would go to the creek to wash, usually forgetting to take the soap. Generally I only realised this when I had reached the creek, so I seldom felt like returning for it. However, the sandy clay on the bank of the creek made an adequate substitute and solved my dilemma. Rubbed with this, the skin on my hands became red but quite clean; sometimes I even used it on my face, with eyes tightly closed. Unfortunately though, grains of sand were left in my beard.

Returning to camp around 5.45 a.m. I would find the day already started. Boy would have built the fire and put water on for tea. I waited on the verandah for tea to be served with rusks and baked bananas. At 7.00 a.m. I recorded the temperatures of the air and water of both creek and sea, the height of the tide, the barometric reading and the quantity of water evaporated in the atmometer. After making these thermal observations I went to the coral reef to collect sea creatures, or into the jungle looking for insects. Returning to the hut, I would sit at my microscope, preserve in alcohol any specimens collected and complete various other tasks until breakfast at 11.00 a.m. — usually curry and rice. After breakfast I rested in my hammock slung underneath the verandah and slept often until 1.00 p.m. At approximately 1.00 p.m. I repeated the meteorological readings made at 7.00 a.m. and then turned to some other activity — recording collected data, classifying details from my notebook and on rare occasions, reading.

My work was often interrupted by the arrival of Papuans. As they appeared I would hurry to them, eager to use any opportunity to increase my Papuan vocabulary. After 5.00 p.m. I would take a short walk in the jungle until Boy served dinner at 6.00 p.m. Dinner was usually a plate of Chilean beans and a piece of charki (smoked beef brought from Valparaiso) accompanied by one or two cups of tea. Rice in the morning, beans at night and several cups of tea made up the bulk of my daily diet. The tinned food, fish and meat which I had brought with me, I left for the servants as I had come to loathe the taste of it.

The period of time after dinner I usually employed with various domestic jobs — cleaning the weapons and attending to my clothing or relaxing on a tree stump watching the tide. Often, as I lay in my hammock, I listened to the sounds of crickets and songs of birds.

From 8.00 p.m. to 9.00 p.m. I recorded the meteorological data again and finally drank coconut milk before checking the readiness of the guns, and then stretching upon my hard bed for sleep. The bed was a simple arrangement of a blanket across two hampers, but I fell quickly asleep.

The constant visits of the natives and the illness of Olsson and Boy broke the continuity of such a monotonous routine but, to me, quite an active day.

## 23 October

Tui visited with two companions who were armed with spears and arrows, and carried axes upon their shoulders. I expressed a desire to examine my visitors' skill with arrows and they immediately complied. The arrows flew some 65 paces, drifting slightly off course in the wind. I doubted if they could kill a man at such a distance but at 20 or 30 paces, would have had a much more lethal effect. Perhaps Tui was correct when he exhibited his palm and intimated that an arrow could pierce it completely. Tui then described to me the manoeuvres of a tribal war. Holding an arrow over his left shoulder and his spear in his right hand, he ran about ten yards, dodging to left and right and emitting at intervals a battle cry. He made several strikes with the arrow and lunged with the spear as if attacking an enemy. From time to time he hid behind a tree or leaped aside as if avoiding arrows. Inspired by Tui's example the other natives joined him, playing the role of enemy, and the enacted battle was quite graphic and most interesting.

## 24 October

The appearance of fungi of various sizes surprised me as I had not seen any here before. They had sprung up virtually everywhere: on trees, soil, rocks and even on the rails of my verandah. They had not been evident the previous evening and had obviously grown up during the night. I could not explain the phenomenon and thinking about these fungi I realised their appearance was as mysterious to me as that of an epidemic illness. Both must run on the same pattern — a rapid increase in the growth of primitive cells.

I made a drawing of one fungus, grown in matter of a few hours out of the earth but remarkable in its size.

## 25 October

My evening rest in the hammock did not pass without accident — last night I had a fever and woke with a high temperature, bathed in perspiration. During the morning I felt so exhausted that I was unfit for work and could not even read, as a book of the smallest size was too heavy to hold. After lunch I attempted to draw but the light failed before my work was finished. Rain fell again and I was forced to move the baggage to a different location. Boy was still in bed with fever and although Olsson was up and about, he could scarcely move. I was almost settled by now, often walking to admire my surroundings, though perforce leaving these pleasures from time to time to solve domestic problems. One such crisis which claimed my immediate attention was a leaking roof, with great drops of water falling upon my head and endangering work and papers.

I worked all day in the jungle with Olsson and on our return attempted to repair the roof. Boy still suffered from swollen glands, frequently crying out in a fashion which I found irritating. After administering a small dose of morphine to him, I went for a short walk. The night was magnificent and although the sounds of the ailing man could still be heard, I scarcely noticed them.

## 27 October

Boy's cries disturbed me throughout the night, waking me several times. I fell asleep close to dawn and woke only when Olsson brought breakfast with the news that Tui had been waiting in the kitchen for some time.

After taking my tea, I went to the kitchen-tent to find not Tui but an unknown Papuan. I stared at him but could not recall having seen him before. I assumed the native had first arrived in company with Tui, but Olsson surprised me by asking, did I not recognise the man? I looked at the native again. He smiled at me, indicated a piece of glass and pointed at himself before I realised that he was indeed Tui, but that he had cut his moustache and shaved part of his beard. The absence of hair from his face had changed his physiognomy to such an extent as to make him unrecognisable. The man's face was close-shaven so skilfully that not one scratch marked his skin. Tui's discovery of using glass as a shaving implement, quite an accidental one but already common on many Polynesian islands, would increase the demand for broken bottles. This surmise was proved correct several minutes later, when I saw Tui accepting a handful of broken glass from Olsson. Tui's discovery was the result of a similarity between broken glass, stone implements and shells — the usual Papuan cutting tools. Tui demonstrated the ability of native peoples to adapt themselves to the use of new objects driven by traditional instincts.

Emerging on the verandah I was shocked to find the roof, the fruits of five hours' labour, leaking again. I had not expected further trouble as such care had been taken to weave the coconut fronds. On consideration I concluded that the fault could not lie in materials or workmanship but in the low pitch of the roof. Most Pacific Island huts have a steeply inclined roof to shed water and lessen the chance of leaking.

Feeling ill again, I decided to take quinine and was glad I had done so as the fever, which returned at 1.00 p.m., was lessened by the medicine. Olsson felt ill also, behaving in gait and speech like a seriously affected victim. Boy was in bed and the hut was a hospital again. I was at home only during the evening and night and spent the rest of the day in the jungle, or on the verandah, or otherwise out of doors.

Hardly any evening passed without some distant thunder and lightning and this night was no exception. The roof leaked and water fell upon my gear. All was damp.

## 28 October

Tui came again, his appearance so changed by his shaven face that I had difficulty in recognising him. Before this I had thought that his facial characteristics, so familiar to me, differed markedly from others but represented the typical native man. This impression was lost when his shaven face revealed his mouth. Generally the mouth is the most revealing feature of the face and Tui was a most outstanding example of this theory.

At about 2.00 p.m. the sail of a pirogue was seen again in the distance. At first I assumed I would have guests, but the visitors did not turn up.

Boy moaned pitifully. Horrible! A small dose of morphine soon calmed him however. At 8.00 p.m. the rain began and an hour later I had finished my meteorological records and was about to retire when moans were heard again — Olsson this time with an attack of the fever. I should not have made arrangements to be accommodated under the same roof as the others; this has taught me a lesson for the future.

## 29 October

I fell asleep in spite of Olsson's cries, but half an hour later was wakened by an indistinct humming noise, coming from I knew not where. Still half asleep, I walked onto the verandah from which point the noise sounded different and could be distinguished. It came from the direction of Gorendu where the natives were holding some kind of ceremony. The rain had ceased, the sky had become lighter and I decided to dress, venture to Gorendu and hear the ceremony properly. Olsson needed to be told, but was not happy to have me go. He tried to convince me that during my absence the Papuans would descend to kill him and Boy and, weakened as they were by illness, my servants would be unable to defend themselves. To reassure him, I leaned the double-barrelled rifle against his bed with the arrangement that, on hearing a single shot, I would return at speed from the village to Garagassi.

Although the rain had stopped, the sky remained overcast and the rising moon was hidden in cloud. Nonetheless, my feet found the footpath as I strode cautiously upon it. As I advanced toward Gorendu the singing could be heard more and more clearly. Presently, fatigued with walking, I sat upon a stump and enjoyed the distant sounds of the ceremony. The native song was quite simple, a single melody repeated with similar patterns of expression. The irregular waves of melody rose and fell constantly — at once loud and penetrating, then receding almost to nothing, only to rise again. In accompaniment to the singing a *barum* (native drum) was heard. The pattern of the native singing ran thus — a hushed beginning sounding like one attenuated note; then came a slight rise in pitch and the tempo increased; gradually the rhythm became faster and finally the singing took on a likeness to a wailing in unison.

Twice I nearly fell from my tree stump, having the sensation of experiencing an unpleasant dream. After the second awakening from my torpor, I felt too fatigued to continue to the village and returned instead to the camp. I cannot remember my journey home, but recall falling on my bed without undressing. Later through my sleep, I heard fragments of the native concert.

## 30 October

It rained during the morning, the first rain I had seen in daylight, so perhaps the beginning of the monsoon. After the rain I sat by the flag-pole and watched an unusual fishing scene. It was low tide and school after school of small fish (very likely pursued by sharks, so common in these waters) darted forward, even leaping at times upon the sand of the beach. From the jungle came Tui who watched the behaviour of the fish. A sudden wave of fish crowded towards the shore and Tui, wading quickly into the water, gained the rear of the bank of fish. The transparent water was hardly knee-deep and Tui expertly trapped a fish with his toes, first stepping upon it, then gripping it between his largest and next toe and lifting it up behind him. Swiftly stooping, he grasped the fish and put it in his bag. A stone picked from the sea-bed and hurled back into the water provided another catch to be picked up again between the toes. As he fished my friend moved gracefully and with vigour, showing skill and speed despite his probable 45 years. Becoming aware of me sitting on the reef, Tui came to Garagassi. I dropped a piece of paper and asked him to pick it up with his toes, eager to ascertain if his power and skill were sufficient to grip an object thus. It took him only a second to pick the paper up with his toe, pass to his hand held behind him, and then hand it to me. He did the same with a pebble, lifting it without hesitation.

Each day I saw new varieties of butterfly but had no opportunity to catch them. I was not successful in chasing them in the open space (bounded by jungle and sea) where pursuit was possible but limited. I did, however, finally catch one. My health seemed to be deteriorating; pains appeared in my back, my head felt heavy and I was unsteady on my legs. Boy had a restful night after I had, almost by force, opened an ulcer while Olsson held him as I operated.

A moaning wakened me at about 1.00 a.m. Olsson again racked with fever. His health was rapidly deteriorating, his eyes becoming sunken in his pinched face and his movements lethargic. However, it was Boy's health which concerned me more as, although his fever was over, his temperature was still high. His ulcer had been treated but his cough, an old trouble he told me, was much worse. Two weeks had passed during which he lay in bed taking almost no food as he held a superstition that his chances of recovery would be better if he ate little.

## 31 October

I received visitors from Bongu who brought with them guests from the hills — mountain dwellers distinguishable from the coastal natives by the untidiness of their hair and slightly paler skin tone.

## 1 November

Once more, the sails of two native pirogues appeared in the distance from the direction of Bogatim. They were approaching us and carried two groups of twenty men each, all bent on paying me a visit. I remained silent during most of their stay to discourage my guests, but observed them closely while they sat about my chair. No favourite native-style attitude of repose was apparent as frequent changes of position took place — kneeling, squatting, sitting on heels, lying prone with chin on hand, but still incessantly chattering or eating.

Olsson brought out his harmonica and on hearing the first sounds, the natives started up and backed away. Gradually some moved forward, but only with diffidence. The music, although an unusual buzzing to their ears (Olsson played a sea-shanty), was obviously approved as the audience whistled and swayed in appreciation. To disperse my guests I distributed red cloth which was instantly utilised as head gear. The young boys especially were fond of personal ornamentation and spent a considerable time making their toilet.

During arrival and leave taking, the Papuans rarely exchange any salute with their friends, this only occurring under special circumstances. Tui, who visited Garagassi more than anyone else, never greets me on arrival or departure with even the smallest gesture.

## 2 November

During the night I decided I should take the dinghy parallel to the beach to study the topography of the coastal hills. I rose before dawn, drank cold tea (not wishing to waste time waiting for breakfast) and set off in the dinghy towards Cape Gabina (Point Observation) following the coastline to Male village. From the jungle rose a number of hills about 300 feet high; parts of the lower slopes were bare of jungle growth and covered only by tall grass. At intervals rose columns of smoke suggesting the existence of villages.

The same morning I spent some time collecting animal specimens from the sea's surface and filled my jar with small *Medusae siphonophores* (sea anemone) and various species of crab. The day's trip convinced me of the richness of marine life thereabouts. Tired and hungry I returned to Garagassi for breakfast; afterwards I spent several hours at the microscope studying the captives of the morning.

After my day's labours and as evening approached, I relaxed in my hammock on the verandah. Although not late (6.45 p.m. approximately) it was already dusk and dark, stormy clouds poured down from the mountains. Busily observing the lightning splitting the skies, I suddenly felt the hammock shake; the first shock faded, then returned with an intensity which caused a trembling of the roof, walls and uprights of the hut. Olsson emerged from the kitchen full of agitated questions regarding the possible return and subsequent seriousness of the earthquake.

Two hours later as I read the aneroid barometer, the tremor was felt again — this time more intense and of longer duration. My readings completed and recorded in my meteorological diary, I retired, instructing Olsson to wake me in the event of further tremors. I feared I would sleep through an earthquake as I had done in Messina in 1869, although all other residents had been in a state of panic. I did wake during the night, however, with my bed and the floor beneath trembling violently. As the shaking diminished I heard Olsson's voice calling me, but the earthquake was already over.

The inevitable storm which broke during the night had blown itself out and the dawn sky was quite clear. A journey into the jungle to cut saplings was necessary and on my return I was greeted by Olsson reporting that the earth still trembled. "What do you mean by 'still'?" I asked. He was amazed that I had noticed nothing, assuring me that he had, on several occasions, felt further tremors. "It is not the earth which quakes but the hut itself," I explained. My servant was sceptical with my answer and repeated his concerns with much agitation; in a few hours time he was proved correct when I noticed two or three weak quakes.

The previous few days the barometer had been unusually high, even registering 464° as against a previous maximum of 410°.

Tui visited after lunch, shaven even more extensively than before. His hair attracted my notice and I studied it closely. He was almost hairless on arms, legs and body and the hair of his head seemed not to grow in tufts from his scalp.

### 4 November

It was not six weeks since my first meeting with the Papuans and in all that time they had never seen me armed. I had firearms of course, but kept them in the hut and not about my person even when venturing into the jungle, and certainly not when going into native villages.

The Papuans were puzzled by my lack of weapons; on many occasions they tried to determine whether I kept a spear, or bow and arrow in my hut, and several times offered me the use of their own weapons. These overtures I declined with polite smiles and explained that I had no need of arms; I planned to keep them unenlightened regarding my weapons for as long as possible.

### 5 November

Mosquitoes and ants were persistently troublesome all night and my rest was disturbed. At about 2.00 a.m. the earth trembled again for barely half a minute, but with the greatest intensity yet experienced. Whenever I felt the tremors beneath me, I grew curious and asked myself: "What will follow?" I stayed awake for a time in expectation of further shocks.

The readings of the aneroid barometer stayed consistently high and during the earthquake rose to 515°, though the reason for this evaded me. Rain fell during the morning but cleared as the day progressed. It had stormed fiercely during the night, such a storm as could not be imagined but must be experienced. The entire sky was shattered into fragments by lightning; the rain streamed, not in drops but jets of water.

After such a wild night the morning dawned fresh and clear, and the remainder of the day followed this pleasant pattern. With no effort I collected many insects sunning themselves after the downpour, and in the same fashion obtained long-tailed lizards.

### 7 November

The fever overtook Olsson once more, this time accompanied by vomiting and delirium. I completed a portrait of one of the visiting natives and could probably have successfully executed more, but such tasks were difficult with both my servants ill. My daily routine included cooking, medical duties and playing host to guests, not only uninvited but also inquisitive and bothersome; all this consumed my valuable time, which should have been spent exploring and recording my findings. I found these domestic occupations onerous and more exhausting than any other work I had ever undertaken.

## 8 November

A storm raged again and the interior of the hut was damp. I was forced to rise several times during the night to administer medicine to both servants, who moaned incessantly. Around midnight an earth tremor was felt and the ground trembled beneath me without pause. The surrounding hills, coral reef and hut, all fell victims to the subterranean disturbance as the storm continued unabated — such lightning, thunder, flooding rain and gale force wind as seemed to be unending.

## 9 November

A humid but clear morning dawned, 22°C. Warmly dressed I sat on the verandah taking my tea. Tui approached, obviously chilled without adequate clothing, but overcoming his difficulty by carrying a primitive but practical portable heater — a smouldering billet. He seated himself close by and I was interested to watch him shifting the brand from one side to the other of his body, distributing its warmth to his chest, his thighs, or whatever part of his body needed comfort. Presently a group of Bongu villagers arrived and with them a small man of particularly ferocious appearance. As there seemed to be some hesitation in his manner, I made an approach, and though he attempted to retreat, his companions prevented this. As he watched me, he began suddenly to laugh and to jig about — obviously such an extreme reaction was prompted by his first sight of a white man. The other Papuans explained to me that our laughing guest was from the distant highland village of Maragum, and that he had made the journey expressly to see me and my house.

As a result of the chill in the air, many natives could be seen carrying portable heating devices. Some carried, instead of a burning branch, a bundle of canes which slowly smouldered. As they assembled near me, the Papuans threw their various brands into a heap and made a fire.

Later a group of Gumbu villagers arrived with guests from Maragum-mana, hill people who were of great interest to me. Their physiognomy resembled that of their contemporaries from the coastal plain; however, the skin of the Maragum-mana residents was slightly lighter — a comparable pigment to that of the Samoan islanders — and some I noticed were paler of face than of body. The inhabitants of Maragum-mana were short and solidly built, with strong and well-muscled legs. I distributed gifts amongst the strangers and they left happily, in undisguised admiration of my hut, armchair and clothes.

The rainy weather became a trial to me as the limited space in my hut was even further encroached upon by the use of the living area as a depot for stores. During fine weather the overcrowded atmosphere was not as noticeable as much of the domestic activity could be carried on outdoors. Some rough furniture had been improvised from logs and stumps to provide convenient seating for my guests in a shady place in front of the hut but, with the onset of rain, of course, the use of this rustic setting became impractical.

*10 November*

The local natives were of a practical nature, placing importance on items of particular domestic use. The gifts most appreciated, for example, were knives, axes and bottles — these were more popular than beads, cloth or mirrors which, of course, were acceptable but seldom asked for.

The lack of confidence shown in me by my neighbours was often amusing. On one occasion they were curiously examining my knife and, for additional interest, I brought out two larger ones, approximately 18 inches long. I explained that they might have these knives in exchange for a small Papuan boy in their company, to be left in my care at Garagassi. The Papuans glanced one to another, then held some discussion amongst themselves. Then some words were spoken to the small boy, who ran straight away into the bush. There were ten or more natives, all armed and all concerned that I might claim the child, despite their having been constant visitors and surely familiar with me after twenty, or perhaps more, calls.

Often a small group of unarmed natives would visit, but I was aware that their actions were watched by an armed party, hidden and poised for rescue should such be needed. A point seemed to be made of demonstrating that each visiting party was unarmed. Another example of the Papuans' lack of confidence in me was the care taken to keep women out of my sight. So far I had seen them only at a distance, and then already in flight as from a wild beast.

## 11 November

My turn today for a bout of illness. I was overtaken by fever early in the morning and, as a result, did not work all day. With the help of quinine I got Olsson on his feet, but Boy remained ill. I had been dosing Boy regularly with quinine, trying to persuade him to eat, but he lived exclusively on bananas and sugarcane. I learned from Olsson that Boy also secretly drank large quantities of water, although I had strictly instructed him to drink only hot or cold tea.

My evenings were made unpleasant with constant repetitions of Olsson's life story. Some men suffer an extreme need to converse and cannot live without constant conversation; I have always been bored by this phenomenon.

The morning brought a piece of good luck — I achieved a satisfactory likeness of Tui.

## 12 November

The nights proved far noisier than the days, for from midday until 3.00 p.m. scarcely any sound could be heard except cicadas and the calls of birds. After sunset however, a veritable concert would commence: croaking frogs, chirruping crickets, calling night birds, and animal noises, the origins of which I have not yet discovered. On most nights the chorus was accompanied by rumbling thunder not heard during the day. The sound of waves crashing upon the reef was more distinct at night, the persistent whine of mosquitoes an annoying factor, and always in the background were the echoes of the Papuans' festivities —and yet I slept soundly. As a result of the previous day's fever I was in a state of exhaustion all day. The natives hereabouts applied but one verb for both 'writing' and 'drawing', and logically so as the tribe was not literate. As I made notes with book and pencil they said "*Maklai negrengva*" — if I made a portrait of one of their number, they said again "*negrengva*". On one occasion when a Papuan was explaining to others how useful a small nail to score decorative patterns on bamboo was, still the word *negrengva* was used.

The Papuans from Bongu again came to visit and I tried to ascertain how they obtained fire, but my inadequate grasp of the language prevented me from acquiring any details.

The Papuans persisted in asking me to join them in chewing betel; according to their custom the action had symbolic meaning — to offer betel to another meant an expression of friendship. Unfortunately, it was necessary for me to refuse, having burnt the tip of my tongue during an earlier attempt to chew the leaf.

## 15 November

During the high tide at about 4.00 p.m. Olsson and I beached the dinghy in preparation for repainting. The job was a hellish one for only two men, but we accomplished it within an hour and pulled the dinghy well above the high-water mark. An exhausting day.

## 16 November

Soon after morning tea I went back to work on the dinghy, which had to be turned over for cleaning, scraping and finally painting. The work was almost injurious and we considered it fortunate that the most severe effort lasted but an hour. In other circumstances the assistance of a number of men would have been enlisted, but there and almost alone, I was forced to meet the challenge and thus put my strength to the test. This physical encounter brought me closer to the thought processes of primitive man, forced daily to face such difficulties without the advantages of modern conveniences. In such an environment man must rely upon not only his intellect, but also his muscle.

## 17 November

Nothing new happened, a new day but the same routine. Early in the morning I was zoologist and scientist, then if the servants were unwell, a cook and physician, pharmacist, painter, tailor and even laundry attendant — a variety of professions to pursue in one day. Although systematically learning the Papuan language, my communication is achieved mostly by guessing the content of a conversation, so expressing myself was even more difficult.

It appeared that my presence was being accepted more by the natives as our relationship gradually developed. My tactic of patience and reserve was proving successful; I did not approach the Papuans, but they came often to me. Overtures of friendship were made by the natives, and efforts to please me as they became more relaxed in my presence. No longer were their visits of a few moments' duration before a hasty return to the group, but were becoming quite prolonged.

I found contact with Papuans more pleasant on my home ground than on theirs as during my visits to their village, they became tense and unsettled. The exception was Garagassi where the natives answered my queries with calm and patience, and even permitted me to examine and to sketch them. Apart from this, in Garagassi my anthropological measuring equipment, my instruments and drawing materials were all close at hand. In return for their co-operation, these natives had various gifts from me, reciprocated with presents of implements, ornaments and other small objects to be found in the donors' bags.

During visits made by the hill people, I took the opportunity to obtain anthropological data, and also samples of human hair for my collection.

Studying and comparing hair of various races is of great anthropological importance, thus I took every opportunity to enrich my collection with new samples. At first, obtaining these samples caused me some embarrassment; for instance, while clipping Tui's hair my scissors came too close to his scalp. The man immediately flinched, became poised for flight, and never again approached if I was seen to be equipped with scissors. Tui was one of the most familiar natives, and meeting such mistrust from him made me wonder what to expect from others still holding doubts and fears. As reassurance I offered to exchange tufts of my hair for Tui's. On acceptance of this plan I chose and clipped some of the native's hair, then did the same to myself. I packed the collected hair in a piece of paper, labelling each with the sex and age of the donor, and the part of the head from where the hair was taken. In imitation, Tui wrapped my hair in a large leaf picked from a tree.

Exchanging locks of hair in this fashion, I accumulated a sizable collection without too much effort. One day, however, I reached a point when the entire left side of my head was close-cropped, and it became necessary to begin clipping the locks for exchange from the right side.

Walking in the jungle, I became disoriented and suspected myself lost. In time, however, I crossed a foot-track and, following it, reached the shore. From here I regained my bearings, being not far from Male village — but rather than proceed there, I decided to visit Bongu as it lay on my route homeward. However, I failed to reach Bongu and as night fell, I was only as far as Gorendu. To the surprise of the Gorendu villagers I elected to stay overnight with them. On reaching the village clearing, I made for Tui's *buambramra* (a large native hut to accommodate the young males and guests from other villages), intending not to disturb the natives more than necessary. However, my arrival had already caused some stir and the fearful cries of women and children could be heard. Tui came forward and I explained to him my need for hospitality. We talked for some time and, although I did not understand every word, it seemed he would prefer to escort me to Garagassi, lighting our way with a flaming torch. In his efforts to persuade me, he referred often to the women and children. I made no sign that I had understood and laid myself upon a *barla* (a plank-bed platform made of bamboo). Closing my eyes, I repeated "*nyavar, nyavar*" (sleep, sleep). It was yet early evening, but tired as I was from my trek, I was soon asleep. When I woke, chilled from lack of covering, it was still deep night. The draught circulating through the *buambramra* (it had but two walls, the other sides being open) caused considerable discomfort.

I awoke hungry after a whole day without food and ventured from the hut. Around the central fire sat a group of natives, including Tui, whom I addressed, saying "*uyar*" (to eat). He immediately understood and brought a *tabir* (a flat wooden dish) filled with taro and cooked bananas. Although not salted, I ate several pieces of taro and sampled the bananas, the latter being a disappointment.

The rest and food refreshed me; filled with new strength I asked two young natives to escort me with flares to Garagassi as the night was intensely dark and travel would be impossible without some form of light. The Papuans understood my request and gladly complied in order to see me away. Torches were brought, made from dry-palm fronds bound in a special fashion. My escorts took up their spears and we proceeded.

By the light of the flickering torches the jungle showed even more beauty than by daylight. My companions, too, were interesting to observe, moving with ease and speed as they held their flaring lights high, deflecting intrusive branches with their spears. One man travelled ahead of me, the other behind, and when I turned to watch the rear-guard I thought how easy it would be for him to plunge his spear in my back. As usual I was unarmed, which the natives knew, but despite my doubts we reached Garagassi without mishap. My servants had been alarmed at my absence and had already given up hope of ever again seeing me alive.

## 22 November

Some time ago I had killed a pigeon of a rare species I had not seen before, and had hung the carcase on a tree to dry in preparation for stuffing at some later date. An hour later the dead bird disappeared from its position, although but a few steps from the house. From the verandah I sighted a dog making for the shelter of some bushes, but did not realise he was the thief of my bird that I had worked upon for nearly an hour.

This morning I killed another such pigeon but it fell into the sea, and as I chose not to get wet myself or to interrupt Olsson at work cooking the meal, I solved my dilemma by waiting for the rising tide to carry my trophy ashore. From a vantage point on the verandah I could follow the progress of the pigeon as it drifted towards the beach. Suddenly the bird was flicked upwards and then the body disappeared, leaving only a disturbance upon the surface of the water — the fin of a shark showed itself for a moment, then submerged.

Tui demonstrated his growing confidence by requesting at sundown, if he might stay overnight in my hut. I offered immediate hospitality, but the Papuan left with a promise to return later. I did not take this seriously and retired to bed, but in fact heard his voice calling later during the night. I went out to investigate and, yes — it was indeed Tui. By moonlight he appeared the archetype of all primitive warriors; his strongly built body was impressively silhouetted against the darkness of the jungle, one arm leaning upon a spear while the other arm held aloft a flare. The red glare of the torch was reflected on one side of his body, illuminating a colourful tapa-cloth mat falling across his shoulder. Tui asked me where he should lie; I indicated a space on the verandah and gave him some bedding upon which to stretch out. This pleased him well and he readied himself for sleep at about 10.00 p.m. When I rose to check the air temperature at about midnight in bright moonlight and looked at the verandah, Tui was missing. The mat and blanket were neatly rolled up, but the occupant seemed to have preferred, at the last, to sleep in his own hut.

## 23 November

I shot a bird — one of those often perched high and noisily in the trees about the hut. The natives called these birds *koko* in imitation of their call "*kokonui-kai*".

I made the discovery this day that ants had devoured my entire butterfly collection, with the exception of the tips of their wings. Olsson's fever had returned and I was employed again in chopping wood, cooking beans, and making tea. Some evenings I spent contriving ear-ornaments from empty food-tins, copying those the natives made from tortoiseshell. My first efforts I presented to Tui, and these proved so popular that many natives called to ask for a like gift. Tin earrings became the height of fashion and were in strong demand.

## 24 November

I killed a white *cacadua* (cockatoo) bird, which fell from the tree and into the sea. I stripped and sprang into the water to retrieve my prize, but the tide was receding and the bird rapidly carried with it. I swam in pursuit and was almost within reach when the fin of a shark made its appearance. I instantly decided to abandon my *cacadua* and made a hasty return to the beach.

Olsson had retired to his sick-bed suffering the severest bout of fever yet experienced, with eyelids, lips and tongue badly swollen. The domestic duties fell, again, to my lot.

## 25 November

In spite of a large does of quinine, Olsson was still in pain. His fever symptoms increased; his whole face, even his arms, was swollen. I was the domestic again, but also had to keep a close watch on my patient who often, in his delirium, would leap from his bed and attempt to cool himself in the sea. I found his constant crying and moaning upsetting. If it were not for the two servants, I would not have bothered with the preparation of meals, but have taken the chance of being offered yams or taro in one native village or another.

Many days had passed but my progress with the language was slow. It seemed that the most important words were still unknown to me, and I had not devised a satisfactory method of learning these. I still did not know the Papuan words for 'yes', 'no', 'bad', 'want', 'cold', 'father', 'mother' and so on. It seemed strange not to have acquired these words, but the opportunity seemed not to have arisen. I asked the natives on many occasions to tell me the words I needed, but could not make myself understood. Abstractions or objects to which I could not point an indicative finger, seemed doomed to remain a mystery, though at times I gained my goal by sheer accident. During that evening when Tui came to spend the night at my hut, I learned that the Papuan word for 'star' was *niri*. The word for 'sun' is *sing* though it was often referred to as *sing-niri*. The moon is called *kaaram-niri* (sun-star, moon-star).

## 27 November

Olsson was convinced that he would never rise again from his sick-bed; his eyelids were so swollen as to be nearly immovable, and his tongue, according to the poor man himself, had "grown far bigger than usual". My reaction was to discourage talk of death and defeatism as he would surely, the next day, be much improved. I persuaded him to take quinine — a dose of about one grain — and drink some tea.

I repeated this dose of quinine at intervals, four times, and despite Olsson's complaints at the unpleasant taste of the medicine, it appeared to be effective and the fever abated. During the night I was subjected to a bout of fever myself, suffering extreme chills and chattering teeth. The sleep I enjoyed was only in snatches and in the morning I could scarcely rise. Although unsteady on my feet, I made a journey into the bush to collect firewood, there being none to boil water for tea. During this search, I stumbled against a wasp's nest, and was attacked by the entire swarm. In my haste to regain the safety of the hut, I left behind not only the collected wood, but also the axe. The numerous wasp-stings were painful and took some hours to subside.

Late in the evening, Asel and Vuanvum, two lads from Gorendu, visited in regalia of red and white paint and flowers. The boys were in transit to Gumbu where ceremonials were to be held, as the date was of some particular significance. The younger Papuans were constantly travelling from one village to another.

As I was fatigued I slept soundly, paying little attention to the native festivities. I was wakened later by Olsson, asking if I had heard the sounds of celebration and should we not load the firearms in case of attack. I was about to reply when from the direction of Gorendu came a storm of sounds dominated by the cries of human voices. The note of the hubbub made us uneasy as it had an aggressive overtone, as of a war-cry. Olsson explained that over a period of ten minutes the cry had sounded repeatedly — at first so loud that he had thought it was a mass call to attack, and so had wakened me.

I rose and walked about the clearing behind the hut where the sounds of the *barum* could be heard from many villages. The full moon rose gracefully over the trees, and I felt the natives' ceremonies were likely to be in honour of this phenomenon, as such was their custom. I told Olsson not to fear an attack, but to return to his bed — whether he took my advice I know not as I fell asleep immediately.

## 30 *November*

The sun had been veiled with cloud and appeared only rarely. I found it pleasing to be able to leave the hut unattended, if necessary, for a whole day without fear of having anything disturbed or stolen. The exception to this was food, a prey to the many wandering dogs and impossible to protect from them. Never, during my entire stay, did I have anything taken from my hut without my consent. Such a circumstance has ceased to occur in the 'civilised' world, despite laws and the police.

## 3 *December*

I went to Gorendu in search of coconuts and, as usual, announced my arrival by whistling in order to give the women and children time to absent themselves. Gorendu had left the pleasantest impressions upon me, being clean, surrounded by greenery and having a peaceful atmosphere. Now, there were not so many men about to make a dramatic display when I arrived, as had previously occurred. The tranquillity was only disturbed by the occasional flight of a bird from tree to tree. Here and there on a tall *barla* (elevated platform) sat several natives, hardly speaking as they chewed upon coconut and peeled and ate hot yams, isolated from local dogs and pigs. Some natives were occupied in and around their huts, but most did nothing but lie in the sun, plucking hair from their arms.

On my arrival I settled myself immediately upon a *barla* and picked up a yam. A group of perhaps a dozen natives assembled about me, and one after another expressed his wish — one desired a long nail, another a piece of red cloth, there was one who required medicament for an afflicted leg, and another needed yet something different. I listened silently and when each had made his petition, I made mine for coconuts. Two boys immediately climbed a palm tree and despatched the fruit. I indicated by fingers in the air the number of nuts needed to be delivered to '*tal* Maklai' (house of Maclay) which was duly done. I distributed the presents, and then made successful portraits of several villagers.

A storm rose again during the evening with severe thunder and lightning, and such a wind as to several times extinguish my lamp. Often it was necessary to retire earlier than I would wish as the light was so consistently extinguished by the wind as to make work impossible. My hut had as many chinks as a basket and admitted the breeze from every direction — to seal all the gaps presented an impossible task.

The rain began at sunset and was unlikely to stop before 3.00 a.m. In October the rain was intolerable, but increased during November until in December, it seemed probable that it would pour every day. The roof leaked again, dripping water over my work table and bed, although the latter affected me little as I had a waterproof covering for my blankets.

I surely would be more comfortable without servants as I served them more than they me. Boy had been ill for two months and Olsson was susceptible to bouts of fever. However, even when feeling well he was fonder of lying down than of working — sleeping all day this day and when scheduled to cook the evening meal, being unwilling to risk a chill in the rain — so the work fell to me. Making tea in the wet season at Garagassi was an onerous task. Dry wood was stored in the tent separate from the house, but this needed to be chopped and the fire coaxed alight in the downpour.

This day, too, I found the samovar had not been filled and a trip to the creek in inky darkness had to be made. Moving by instinct, as the track was indistinguishable, I twice fell and had to wait for lightning flashes to illuminate the scene and set my feet upon the right way again (I could have carried the hurricane lamp but the wind would have extinguished it instantly).

By the time I regained the hut, I was soaked to the skin and grateful to be sheltered from the deluge. I changed my clothes hurriedly and as I settled to record the day's events, the tea I drank held special savour. The last sugar was used some weeks ago and this day the last of the rusks were thrown out, spoiled by weevils. We tried to save the precious rations by drying them out in the sun and on the fire, but this had no effect on the insects.

The absence of bread was compensated for by baked bananas or taro and I hardly considered it a hardship, but Olsson and Boy protested considerably, particularly at the absence of sugar. The remainder of our diet was as before — rice, curry, and beans — but, so much for our food. I frankly paid little attention to the manner in which my body was nourished, and gave my full enthusiasm to observing and recording scientific and natural history data. During my journey to the creek for water — stumbling, angry and unhappy — I slipped and grasped a thorny bush. A flash of lightning illuminated the far horizon for some seconds — the foaming sea, the driving rain, the wet leaves and the dripping forest. Although the scene was but momentary, I was enthralled, still gripping the thorns, such was the impression a dramatic scene in nature could make on me. All my troubles could be forgotten in my preoccupation with the grandeur and fascination of natural phenomena.

At 9.00 p.m. the candle was burnt low, my tea finished, and as the roof was still leaking, I made a speedy retreat to my bed.

## 5 December

After the rain I collected many insects and found a fine specimen of a very interesting fungus.

Boy had grown so weak he could hardly stand; the poor fellow fell while trying to negotiate the steps. Olsson was in bed moaning and instead of attempting to help with Boy, he pulled the bedclothes over his head. I found Boy sprawled upon the steps and dragged him back indoors. He was unconscious and thus did not recognise me. The rain started at about 4.00 o'clock, and dampness crept everywhere.

## 6 December

Boy's condition had deteriorated. It appeared he could not live for long and Olsson was concerned, obviously, that he might follow Boy to the grave.

Tui called and sitting on my verandah with a serious expression, told me Boy would soon die, and that 'Will' (the natives' name for Olsson) was seriously ill, and Maclay would be left alone. Then he raised his finger, indicated both east and west and said: "Many villagers from Bongu and Gumbu (showing all his fingers and toes to emphasize the numbers of natives) will come to kill Maklai." He demonstrated how the spears would enter my neck, chest and belly, and sadly sang "*O Maklai, O Maklai.*"

I made as if nothing untoward had been said (though I was convinced his suggestion was highly probable) and told him neither Boy, Will nor Maclay would die. Tui looked sceptically at me, and in an even sadder tone said "*O Maklai, O Maklai*". This conversation with him was doubly interesting, as firstly, his suppositions were quite possible, and secondly, my neighbours must have discussed the subject — otherwise why revert to the old topic of death by spear thrust. It was an uneasy situation requiring constant alertness; however the tension did not affect my sleep.

Eight Papuans from Gorendu and Male called in and as I was in a good humour, I gave them gifts despite the fact that they had come empty handed. Tui and Lali, another native, suddenly asked: "Will the corvette ever return?" Of course I could not answer as I did not know how to say "It will come, but I know not when" and in addition I had not learned to express in Papuan the concept of a big number. This was my opportunity to find out how the natives count. I took a few pieces of paper and tore them into strips, then into smaller pieces. After manufacturing a handful of such scraps, I explained to a Male villager that each one symbolised two days. The other natives grouped expectantly around us as the Papuan began to count on his fingers, but with little expertise; the other Papuans concluded he had little knowledge of counting, so grabbed the paper and handed it to another native.

The chosen man sat, called another to assist, and the counting began. The first man placed each piece of paper on his knee to be counted and pronounced each time the word *nare* (one). The second native repeated the word *nare* and at each pronouncement bent one of his fingers. When the fingers on both hands were folded the man dropped them to his knee, saying "two hands" and a third assistant bent one finger. Each time the tally reach ten, the third man bent another finger, and so on in a manner apparently satisfactory to the participants. I confused them, however, by displaying two fingers and saying "*bum, bum*" (day, day). The Papuans grouped together and a consultation began, the outcome of which was that the paper was wrapped inside a bread fruit leaf and carried off to the village for further study.

The Papuans' lack of confidence in me caused constant concern as, while the situation remained such, little progress could be made.

Boy was not likely to live very long. Olsson was so cowardly that the natives could even have burnt down the hut without resistance from him. However, I felt that once I had more mastery of the local language, I would be away from home far more than had been my custom, so I planned to bury some of my instruments and gear. I felt they would be safer underground than in the precarious care of Olsson.

## 8 December

During the evening two lighted pirogues passed around the cape, brilliant in the intense darkness. I fired a rocket, which must have impressed the voyagers greatly, as every torch upon the pirogues immediately dropped into the water, leaving only impenetrable darkness.

Lalai from Bili Bili came to call — a man of memorable features. His hooked nose could not be considered typical of the race, even his brother having the characteristic flatness of feature. The man's poorly developed calf muscles were, however, not unique and attributable to long periods of time spent sitting in a canoe travelling between islands.

A group of natives, including two boys, visited me from Bongu. The boys were probably eight years old and resembled the African Negro: broad nose, large mouth with full lips, and very curly hair. Their bellies were distended and appeared hard. Such African types were more commonly seen among the younger natives.

Boy's condition had deteriorated even further and Olsson tried to convince me that we should leave this place. I replied that firstly, I had not forced him to come to New Guinea, and secondly, had suggested that he should have left with the *Vitiaz*. Every night he trembled in expectation of the natives coming to kill us and had grown to hate Tui, suspecting him of being a spy.

As soon as I fell asleep I was wakened again to the sounds of humans outdoors. A bright light shone from the direction of the beach, presumably a number of pirogues arriving or perhaps already ashore. Olsson cried, "They are coming!" I moved to the verandah and into a blaze of light. Six or seven natives armed with spear and arrows called to me, but I did not move before ascertaining their purpose. Olsson stepped behind me and tried to force a rifle into my grasp, urging, "Don't let them come any closer." I knew one shot would be sufficient to repel the natives (though never having tried the effectiveness of firearms upon them) but decided to wait, and minutes later began to recognise a familiar voice.

On my call of "*gena*" (come here) the Papuans moved forward, stopped in the clearing in front of the verandah and each man handed me, with his right hand, a quantity of fish. Their left hands gripped their weapons and torches while they called repeatedly "*niki, niki*". I ordered the shamefaced Olsson to accept the fish from our benefactors.

The armed Papuans, beneath their flaring brands, made a deep impression upon me and I wished I were artist enough to record the scene. As the men returned to their pirogues, they repeatedly called in salute to me "*E, meme, e meme.*"

We enjoyed the fish.


## 13 December

Exhausted and anxious for rest, my impressions of the day past must be recorded as I sit in my armchair, although it is 11.30 p.m.

When I woke this morning, I decided to perform all preliminaries in preparation for the time when it became necessary to bury my papers — not only my diaries but also meteorological data, notes and unused sheets, in case of destruction by fire.

Tui was suspicious, looking about the hut and inspecting everything minutely. He later walked into Olsson's room calling "*O Boy, O Boy*" then approached me with a request for permission to take Boy to Gumbu. He was so persistent that I finally ordered him to leave.

At noon I felt a slight touch of fever starting, with constant yawning, then violent shivering, but decided to resist the attack and take to my bed only as an extreme measure. Three natives from Gorendu called in, and peering into Olsson's room and not hearing Boy's gasps, asked if he were still alive. Again the Papuans asked to take Boy away with them, though I knew not the purpose of their request. I could not see what importance he could hold for them; obviously they did not fear him as an enemy, or they perhaps wished to make of him an ally — too late.

After lunch I showed Olsson a huge log brought in by the tide and scraping against our dinghy, as I wished him to dispose of it. I returned to the hut, to paperwork, heard Boy crying out, and looked into his room. Poor fellow, he was writhing upon the floor in pain and I rushed to raise him in my arms — possible only because he had grown so thin during the last weeks that he was hardly heavier than a child. His cold and bony hands clung about my neck; his panting breath, sunken eyes, pale nose and lips, all convinced me that he would not have to suffer much longer. I laid the poor man on his bed and returned to my work. A little later the sound of some object falling to the floor and a breathless cry sent me to lift Boy back to bed again. His chilled hands held mine for a time and it appeared that he wished to speak, but lacked energy to form the words. His pulse was very weak, and his hands and arms became every moment colder.

I left Boy in bed and went to the beach where Olsson struggled to free the boat from the drifting log. I told Olsson that Boy would die in a few hours; the news appeared to shock him despite weeks of expectation of this event. Together we returned to the hut to find Boy again rolling upon the floor clutching at his own arms, while we stood as helpless witnesses to his agony. I pressed chloroform-soaked cotton wool to Boy's mouth and nose, and for a few minutes he appeared eased and even mumbled a few words.

Olsson stood by, suffering in his helplessness and asked repeatedly what we could do. I explained that during the night we must dispose of Boy's body in the sea, and that he should immediately collect and place appropriate rocks in the dinghy to weight the corpse.

My suggestion was not welcomed and I needed to offer a convincing argument. I stressed the haste necessary in disposing of the carcase before decomposition began in such a climate as prevailed. I did not intend to hold any burial ceremony in front of the natives; to dig a grave in the coral bed would prove nearly impossible, and too shallow a grave would allow access for the natives' dogs. The two final reasons offered left Olsson in no doubt as to the wisdom of my decision, but still I followed him to the beach to be sure that enough rocks were collected.

On returning to the hut I was met by only silence in the darkness. The gasping had ceased, and when I approached and took up Boy's hand, could feel no pulse. I placed one hand to his mouth and the other upon his heart, but neither breath nor beat could be felt. Boy had passed away alone as he had lived all his life. I lit a candle, illuminating Boy's body lying in his customary position with legs curled and arms folded. While Boy was alive, Olsson had constantly criticised him and assumed an unfriendly attitude, but now he was suddenly depressed and talked of "God's Will". Inexplicably we both found ourselves whispering, as if afraid we might waken the dead man.

When I explained to Olsson that I intended to open Boy's skull and retain the brain for experimental purposes, the man nearly collapsed and pleaded with me to change my plan. However, I found that I lacked a storage jar of sufficient size to accommodate the brain; fearing that at any moment native callers might appear, I was forced to abandon the project.

Preparations for Boy's sea-burial needed to be speedily made, without attracting the notice of the Papuans. The minute details of such a procedure would take too long to describe, but the main objective was to fit the body into two large bags, leaving space for several heavy rocks. At nightfall we carried our burden to the dinghy, Olsson leading, faltering and finally falling. Boy's body fell on Olsson and I fell on top of all; when we retained our feet we could not locate the corpse. It had rolled away and down to the beach, but we finally dragged it aboard the dinghy. We then packed about 30 kilograms of rocks into the bag. The night was pitch-dark, the tide at its lowest ebb and our task a hellish one to drag the dinghy to the water.

As we launched the vessel, a light appeared at a point perhaps a quarter of a mile away, behind Cape Gabina. Then a second torch flared, and then another and another, until ten might be counted. Eleven Papuan pirogues were moving towards us with the obvious intention of paying the camp a visit and, if they sighted the dinghy, would certainly investigate. The brilliant light of the torches would clearly illuminate the bag containing the corpse, so it appeared we would be discovered and the Papuans would thus hear of Boy's death.

"Could we not hide Boy in the bush?" suggested Olsson. But the bag, now weighted with rocks as well as the body, was too heavy to be moved in the few minutes before the natives would reach us. "Row faster," I called to Olsson, "we may yet avoid them." Olsson moved the oars and strained manfully, but the dinghy did not move —he made further efforts but still to no effect. The dinghy was held fast by the rope which, though loosed from the beach, had not been hauled aboard and had become tangled in the rocks. I caught up a knife to sever the rope and free the craft while Olsson manned the oars once more. The natives, it seemed, were on a fishing expedition; the lights on the pirogues were more distinguishable as they approached closer, and soon voices could also be heard.

We tried to steer the dinghy away from the Papuans' course, and rowed vigorously. At each sweep, we took care to slip the oars gently into the water so as not to attract the natives' attention with their splashing. "If they see Boy, they will think we have killed him, and will then kill us," said Olsson. I did not know if his guess was an accurate one, but certainly preferred not to encounter the natives in that situation. There were 33 Papuans (three to each pirogue) armed with spears and arrows, in a far superior position to ours. However, in spite of being so outnumbered, we did not panic, knowing that our pistols could cause a mass retreat within seconds.

The reasons we escaped notice were the absence of a light on our craft and the natives' preoccupation with fishing. I was musing first about Boy, and later upon worrisome aspects of my work when Olsson interrupted my thoughts, exclaiming that the pirogues were moving away. We pressed ahead at greater speed to a point approximately a mile off Cape Gabina where we lowered the corpse overboard. The body sank quickly and I was certain that sharks would tear it to pieces in a short time.

Exhausted, we rowed slowly for the shore to face the difficult task of beaching the dinghy from low water in total darkness. Finally we reached the camp where ash-covered embers still glowed in the fire and Olsson began to make tea.

## 14 December

As soon as I rose, I ordered Olsson to leave the arrangement of his living quarters exactly as it had been during Boy's life, and not to speak of the Samoan's death to the Papuans. Shortly after this Tui came calling, accompanied by two strangers, one of whom tried to climb the steps into the hut. However, when I authoritatively showed him that his place was in front of the hut, not inside, he descended and sat down in the clearing.

Tui again started the discussion about Boy, and quite excitedly tried to convince me that one of the visitors could cure Boy's sickness if he could but come to Gumbu. To distract attention from the subject of Boy, I decided to divert the men with the performance of an experiment. I took a saucer from under a cup, wiped it with a cloth and poured in some spirit. I left this on the verandah and called my guests to enter. When the Papuans had climbed the steps, I took a glass of water and offered it to one of the men to test, and ascertain its nature.

The natives followed my every move with extreme curiosity. To the saucer of spirit I added a few drops of water, and then lighted it — this had such an impact upon the natives as to cause them to back breathlessly against the wall. I caught up the saucer and splashed the flashing contents about the floor, whereupon the natives sprang away for fear of being burnt. Such was their apprehension of further and more disastrous events that they left immediately.

Hardly a quarter of an hour passed before a larger group of natives appeared, comprising villagers from Bongu, Bili Bili and Karkar — a picturesque gathering of varying age groups. Each native was ceremonially decorated with ear and arm ornaments of the materials most available to the inhabitants of his particular village. The inlanders were mostly adorned with flowers, leaves and seeds, while the villagers from Bili Bili and Karkar wore shells, fish-bones and tortoiseshell.

The people from Karkar had one more distinction: most of their bodies, and particularly their heads, were daubed with dark earth. At first sight this appeared as dark skin, but several had their heads only stained with clay, and the difference in body colour was clearly noticeable. In contrast to the Karkar people, the Bongu men had their skin stained red, and wore red Siamese roses (hibiscus flowers) in their hair and in their leg and arm bands.

Altogether some forty natives formed the group, each one bore some unique characteristic of appearance — a personal style of hair-dressing, if nothing else. Most had colour in their hair — red, black or one of many others — and combs of bamboo made gay with the feathers of cockatoo and other birds. Some of the men had flat ears as in the New Hebridian tribes.

The visit lasted approximately two hours. The natives particularly wished to see the flaming water that they had heard of from Tui, and begged me to repeat the demonstration of "how water burns". I fulfilled this desire and the impression made upon the audience was almost indescribable — the witnesses fled to the bush and begged me, loudly, not to burn the sea. Some of the natives were so shocked that they lacked the energy to run away.

My status had so risen after this performance that the villages of Bili Bili, Karkar, Segu, Rio and others, vied with each other to be my host in the future. Several men from Bili Bili and Karkar remained behind when the others left, begging to be given *gare* (skin) to cover their suppurating wounds. The weeping sores attracted numerous flies and insects and constant swishing of the hand was the natives' only deterrent for these; as soon as the movement ceased, the flies would swarm again upon the wound. I was not in a position to offer comprehensive treatment for the afflictions, but applied medicaments and bandaged them against the flies. From only one such sore I removed a hundred maggots

— no wonder my patient was grateful. A boy of perhaps five years, brought by his father, deserved particular treatment so I carefully washed his afflicted legs and bound them well. The parent was so grateful for my attention that he took the shell ornament from his chest and hung it about my neck.

## 15 December

A new batch of patients came from Bili Bili, one of whom was gripped with fever. My first thought was to administer quinine, but suggested to the agitated sufferer that he should return later, after he had calmed down, for *onim* (medicine). However, he shook his head, explaining that to take medicine was to die. The Papuans were afraid to drink my medicine, but highly appreciated the treatment of their sores.

Boy had left behind a bottle of coconut oil scented with a strong smell of a type of grass. The Bili Bili man complained of pain in his back and shoulder (very likely rheumatism). I gave him the oil with instructions to massage himself. He immediately began to carry out my directions. At first he rubbed his skin with the oil, but stopped a minute later, apparently struck by the possibility of dying from the use of the unknown *onim*. In sudden panic the man fell upon his nearest neighbour, rubbing his skin, then that of the next man and of each in the group with the suspected oil — he seemed not to wish to die alone. The other Papuans were obviously confused as to whether they should be angry or amused.

I discovered that the Bili Bili dialect is different from that of Gumbu, Bongu and Gorendu, and even came across a few words which are entirely foreign to Bongu. The father of my child patient called in, bringing several children whose skin pigment seemed no darker than that of Samoans.

## 18 December

I had no native callers during the morning. My choice of location for the hut had proved to be a wise one; if I had established myself close to a village, I would have had no peace from native visitors.

By accident I discovered the poor condition of my small-clothes stored in the basket upon which I slept. The cloth was quite liberally marked with dark spots which could easily be perforated with a finger — a phenomenon permitted by my carelessness.

It had not occurred to me within the previous three months, to take the clothes from their damp confinement and hang them out to air. I ordered Olsson to take out every item and expose all to the sunlight.

The natives asked, again, about Boy's whereabouts and I answered: "*Boy aren*" (there is no Boy). "Where is he?" they insisted. I was disinclined to lie to the Papuans, but also found it unwise to point to the sea and attempt an explanation, so I merely waved my questioners away. The natives concluded that I was indicating the horizon, beyond which lay Russia, and they gathered to discuss this possibility. The outcome apparently, was a decision that Boy had flown to Russia, though I had difficulty defining the exact meaning of their word 'fly' due to my inadequate grasp of Papuan.

Today I collected implements of some importance in exchange for goods presented to the natives. My acquisitions included eating equipment made from small bones: one called a *dongan* resembled a knife, and was fashioned from a pig's bone; another, a spoon-shaped *shelupa* from kangaroo bone.

## 20 December

By now the hut was quite comfortable but only in fine weather. During the rainy weather the roof leaked prodigiously and caused considerable discomfort.

A family group, St Petersburg, 1882. Maclay (right), his brother
Mikhail, their mother and a small relative.

LEFT: Margaret Miklouho–Maclay, about 1883.
RIGHT: Alexander Miklouho–Maclay, the traveller's older son,
St Petersburg, 1888.

The biological station, Laing's Point, Sydney.

Nikolai Miklouho–Maclay.

The cabin at Garagassi, Port Konstantin, New Guinea, 1872.

Gorendu village, Maclay Coast, New Guinea, February 1872.

Gumbu village, Maclay Coast, February 1872.

The men's house in Bongu, Maclay Coast.

The house at Aiva, Papua–Koviai, 1874.

LEFT: Saul of Bongu, 1877.
RIGHT: A corner in the house at Bugarlom.

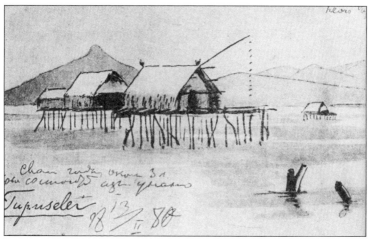

Tupislei village, south-eastern New Guinea, 1880.

A Bili Bili *vang*.

Natives from Bongu called, quite convinced that I had given Boy magic powers enabling him to fly to Russia. They seemed to regard Olsson and me as supernatural beings.

## 25 December

After three days of fever, during which I spent only a few hours of daylight in bed at times of extreme weakness and fatigue, I felt a little better, but still needed to take quinine. Although the fever symptoms had improved, I was left with a feeling of great weakness, with legs like lead and bouts of dizziness.

Olsson was very bored, the long solitude almost crushing such a sociable and talkative personality as his. He often talked to himself, alleviating the situation to some degree. The isolation had quite a different effect on me as I enjoyed every moment of silent solitude. Being alone helped me to concentrate on my work, to think through and to clarify many problems in my study of nature.

Our situation had made a distinct change in Olsson and left a considerable mark upon his personality. Before our sojourn he had been an energetic and enthusiastic young man, but had become sullen and even provocative, complaining without cease. Apathy had grown in him — he slept eleven hours each night and an additional two hours after lunch, yet constantly complained "*das Leben sehr miserabel!*" (life is miserable).

The absence of meat had become noticeable. We had lived on vegetarian fare for three months and had grown weak, both from this diet and from periodic bouts of fever. Nonetheless, my abhorrence of tinned food prevailed and I chose to remain vegetarian. I planned, when more familiar with the natives, to supplement our food by hunting — although there are numerous wild pigs in the jungle, I dislike the meat. The previous day Tui had presented each of us with two great pieces of this pork and I gave my portion to Olsson, who had such an appetite for it that he finished all without delay. At the end of the meal he not only chewed the bones, but also consumed the animal's skin (it was an old boar) and I mused as I watched this performance — man, without doubt, is a cannibal.

The dinghy caused considerable annoyance as there was no means of anchoring it safely.

My hands had become rough but my skill with the axe prodigious, although using my large muscles so regularly caused a failure in my ability to do precise work such as drawing. Not only bearing the bulk of the domestic work but also taming the rugged environment, my hands were the tools of survival in such a situation. The skin of my hands had cracked and blistered and my right hand had developed and increased in size — an unusual phenomenon in an academic, and caused, of course, by the constant use and thus rapid expansion of the muscles. The fingers had grown strong and even the thumb had developed.

My hands have never been soft, but had become quite covered with cuts, blisters and burns. Old wounds healed, but new ones were added almost daily. I had always considered my finger-nails were strong, but were proved insufficiently so to confront such hard work without cracking. I had not compared my nails with those of the Papuans as the difference would be so great. The natives employ their nails in performing many tasks for which they lacked adequate tools. The thumb nail was particularly strong, often pared away at the sides and the central part allowed to grow rather long. The other nails grew on the same pattern and altogether gave the appearance of talons.

## 27 December

While my Papuan visitors were busy inspecting their faces in mirrors they had received from me and plucking occasional hairs from their chins, I peered into a *goon* (bag) hanging from a native's shoulder. The contents interested me, comprising as they did the owner's most personal possessions. Apart from two large *dongan* (a sharp human, animal or cassowary bone used as a cutting implement) there were a number of other bones and tools. Inside a hollow bamboo tube were four specially polished and sharpened bones, which could equally well serve as knife, needle or nail. In the *goon* was an *arur* (sea-shell) with one serrated edge, convenient for gouging coconut meat from its husk, and a piece of coconut shell for use as a spoon. I saw there, too, a nail (likely a gift from me in the past) which had been honed to a fine point for piercing, and was well kept and sharp as were all the tools.

The Papuans were highly skilled in plaiting and braiding grass into bracelets (*sagyu*) and headbands (*diu*), but surprisingly did not utilise their talent to make mats, despite the plenitude of pandanus leaves. I could discover no reason for this except to surmise that there was no need for matting — or that the necessary patience was lacking. Baskets, however, were cleverly woven from palm fronds and resembled those made on Polynesian islands. The natives treated these baskets with care for certainly it was no easy matter to manufacture another, lacking as they did the aid of sophisticated tools. Half an hour's toil, for example, would be needed to cut a tree 14 centimetres in diameter. Body adornments were laboriously fashioned with shell or stone implements. Although stone-age tools only were used, the huts and canoes were strong and well-made as well as attractively decorated. The ornamentation often differed in style and size, and I decided to sketch the varying designs used on the Papuans' canoes.

## 28 December

I stopped a pirogue proceeding from Gorendu as I recognised Tui's son, Bonem, standing upon the deck in ceremonial attire. His wild hair was stuck with feathers and red Siamese Rose blooms; armed with taut bow and arrow, he made an impressive picture. Swaying with the movement of the rolling craft, the Papuan was arched over the water in an alert attitude, in readiness to release the arrow. Long leaves of red and green *Colodracon* placed in his waist belt and arm bands completed his ceremonial dress, the belt being a new one of predominantly red tones.

The Papuans gratefully accepted an invitation to call on me, thus providing me an opportunity to sketch the decorative effect of the young man's hair adornment. A wreath of scarlet flowers circled his head and in front was thrust three small combs, each with a feather behind it, keeping the circlet of blooms firmly upon the hair. A fourth and larger comb held a long cock's feather, curling backward. As I wanted to sketch without interruption, I distributed tobacco and sent the other natives to the kitchen to smoke it. On finishing my task, I granted the Papuans' wish for a mirror and a queue quickly formed for the purpose of adjusting hair dressing and adornments.

Bonem took the combs and flowers from his hair and used the larger comb to tease out those locks that had become flattened. After these attentions the hair formed an enormous crown, with two braids falling upon his shoulders at the back. Replacing the comb and flowers, the young man looked in the mirror, smiled in satisfaction at what was reflected there, and passed the glass to the next in line. (I mention these details of how the Papuans' hair rose in such a bushy style to correct the false reports of some earlier explorers who made only brief contact with the natives.) The tightly curled hair, when pressed close to the scalp, becomes so matted as to appear as a solid mass, thus misleading earlier reporters who came to the false conclusion that the Papuan race contained deviations in physical characteristics. After peering their fill in the mirror, my guests returned to their pirogue calling "*E meme*" (the meaning still a mystery to me).

Olsson had the fever again, which was apparently becoming a chronic affliction.

## 29 December

I went to Gorendu, whose inhabitants had not brought me fresh coconuts for some time. "We did not bring nuts," it was explained to me, "because *tamo russ* (Russian men) cut so many of our coconut trees." The Papuans were exaggerating the situation, as even if some trees had been felled, this would have been accidental, so I asked to be shown some examples. The men willingly led me to some fallen trees at a short distance from the village. "You may eat the nuts, but never cut the tree," they explained. They were right, so I held my peace.

*1 January 1872*

A tempest howled through the night and sporadic bursts of rain, accompanied by a wild wind, continued throughout the day. Lianas and other vines, cut at the base during the clearing operations but still clinging aloft, were blown to the ground by the storm, and one such fell crashing through the roof of my house, breaking the thermometer used for measuring water temperatures.

*2 January*

During the night, a huge tree near the house, its bole already severed by the working party, was blown down amid great noise, and fell in such a position as to bridge the creek with the upper section of its trunk. It cost me considerable time and effort to clear the area of fallen timber.

*3 January*

On his return from the plantation, Tui brought a piglet, killed by a dog that had not had the opportunity to devour its prize. The inadequacy of meat in our diet and Olsson's craving for the same, forced me to accept Tui's gift. A poor, skinny creature, it was nonetheless of interest to me as a specimen of its kind, representing a rare variety of its species. It had dark brown and reddish stripes covering much of its upper body, while chest, belly and legs were white. I made a sketch of the pig, took its head off to preserve by taxidermy, and handed the rest of the animal to

Olsson who was anxiously waiting, knife in hand, to prepare it for eating. Looking at Olsson, first butchering the piglet and later eating it, I realised to what a great extent the human is a cannibal — meat remains his most favoured food.

A few days ago, after inspecting my collection of Papuan hair, I reached an interesting conclusion — the manner of hair growth forms a significant racial characteristic of the Papuan race. In my earlier comments, I had expressed doubts regarding the theory of Papuan hair growing in tufts, but had never taken the liberty of peering into the bushy growth on the heads of my friends. Looking at neck growth, however, I saw no trace of such tufts and each hair was seen to grow individually, but I had no chance of examining this more closely.

After lunch I rested in my hammock, rocked to sleep by the wind, until a voice calling woke me up. A Papuan called Kolle had come from Bongu with his young son Syroi whose head had been shaved to the skin. I carefully examined the boy's scalp, utterly absorbed for so long that the natives became suspicious of my behaviour, grew restless and left in great haste.

Later in the day a group of Papuans from Gorendu called and provided another opportunity to continue this research. My friend Lalu asked me for a mirror and, upon receiving this, began to pluck hairs from his moustache and eyebrows, concentrating chiefly on those grown grey. Taking up a pair of tweezers I offered my help and noticed great appreciation on Lalu's face. As I plucked each hair I observed it closely, finding a thinner and weaker growth than that of the average European.

4 *January*

A refreshing wind had been a common phenomenon during the past fortnight, most noticeable between 10.00 a.m. and 5.00 p.m. During October and November such winds are rare in the area.

Olsson persuaded me to go fishing but, as I had anticipated, we caught nothing. Villagers from Gorendu and Bongu were also afloat in their pirogues, but their lights were extinguished and the vessels sped toward the beach where they were engulfed in the darkness. The Papuans had women aboard, which necessitated the rapid departure — we heard the distant female voices as they disembarked upon the beach. With male crews only, the pirogues made out to sea again; about a dozen vessels surrounded my dinghy and each Papuan presented me with a fish or two. The presentations made, the craft moved away and the fishing was resumed.

Each pirogue was heaped with bundles of dry reeds; a Papuan standing in the prow illuminated the surface of the water by lighting such a bundle, using it as a torch. Another man alongside the first, bore a sharp-pronged *yur* (harpoon) about nine feet in length, and at each thrust of this weapon invariably drew several fish from the water. Occasionally a miscalculation resulted in the loss of the spear, but even with three-quarters of the shaft above the water the *yur* stayed vertical and afloat. A third Papuan on the vessel then manoeuvred the pirogue within reach of the errant weapon.

### 7 January

Showers prevailed all day accompanied by a chilliness in the air. I suffered two bouts of fever during the day, the morning attack worsening despite my warm clothes (two flannel shirts, two pairs of under-drawers and fur about my knees and shoulders), and I continued to feel colder and colder as well as experiencing such fits of dizziness that I found it possible to write only by supporting my head in my hand.

For the second day in succession I was unfit for any work, and stayed in my bed until about 6.00 p.m.; then feeling slightly better I rose. However, only half an hour later the fever symptoms returned. In the previous three and a half days I had suffered three attacks of fever and swallowed four grains of quinine. The guardians of New Guinea are not native warriors, excessive tropical heat, or inaccessible jungle. No, the most loyal protector of the natives against intrusion must surely be the 'cold fever' that flames suddenly into soaring temperatures, and which awaits all newcomers here. It might appear with the rising sun, accompany the afternoon's heat, or hide in the first shadow of dusk; it may visit on a rainy night, or in moonlight, but come it will — to even the most cautious. The physical symptoms might pass unnoticed at first, but soon the victim will realise his legs seem made of lead and his thoughts distracted by a fearsome headache. Finally, the shivering fever will come, muscles will stiffen, and the joints become scarcely movable — strange hallucinations visit as the temperature moves up … up … up.

So severe was my attack, my hands so a-tremble, that my diary could not be written. At only 9.00 a.m. my limited energy would suffice only to crawl back to my bed.

*8 January*

Fever

*9 January*

Fever

*10 January*

Fever

*11 January*

The fever of the previous five days had completely exhausted me, but at last it began to abate. I suffered only one attack yesterday and one mild attack today; despite this improvement my knees still trembled. It might seem foolish to describe my illness in detail, but such information may serve to assist any European who comes and finds himself trapped in this area. The main pain suffered was from headache, accompanied by distaste for food.

Tea and taro, my substitute for bread, were all I took and exhaustion was certainly aggravated by lack of food. I had not the energy to stand and did not feel inclined to call Olsson for help. From my bed I crawled to the floor and crept to the verandah three times daily to record my meteorological data. During my illness I was in a trance-like state and did not take regular doses of quinine — a possible explanation for the length of the attack. While taking the medicine, my hand holding the spoon trembled to such an extent that I had to steady it against the bed in order to direct spoon to mouth. Yesterday the dizziness was so extreme I was unable to sit erect in a chair and my forehead and eyes were greatly swollen; but these symptoms subsided and I was able to move about.

My neighbours had called regularly during the five days of my illness and during these visits I made great efforts to appear on the verandah, not wishing to disclose my indisposition. To curtail the callers I made no conversation and passed gifts of tobacco. Olsson's nagging and complaining often drove me to anger as his chief worry during my illness was for his own fate should my fever continue; his assistance was negligible. When ill I prefer to keep to myself, but the servant took advantage of this and ignored me entirely. During the five days of fever he did not once offer help, even to get tea, and I was forced to issue orders.

At noon men from Bongu came with an invitation to visit their village. One told me he was hungry so I returned to him a coconut he had just presented me. He peeled the coconut husk first with an axe, and then used his *dongun* (a bone knife). He asked for a *tabir* (a wooden dish) but, having none, I gave him a plate instead. Holding the nut in his left hand, the man struck it with a stone, splitting the fruit into two identical halves, and letting the milk drain into the plate. Another native then seated himself beside the first, and both men took *yarur* (shells) from their bags. These they used to shred the coconut meat into long, thin strips, letting these fall into the plate of milk. When the plate was filled, the empty nuts became cups and the *yarur* became spoons. The delicacy was prepared with such ease and the implements so simply made; it was the most delightful way of serving coconut I had ever seen. The Papuans called this dish *monki-lya* and it played an important role in their feasts.

Although misty rain was falling, I accepted the invitation to Bongu. Confident in the improvement of my mastery over the Papuan language, I hoped to learn many details of village culture still hidden from me. I made the trip to Bongu by sea; however, as the beach was open to the rising tide, I risked losing the dinghy if I left it unmoored on the sand. The natives indicated a nearby *subari* (a large tree *Calophyllum inophyllum*). Its trunk leaned across the water providing a suitable berth, and in the absence of an anchor I utilised a rock to secure my rope.

My hosts, chest deep in the sea, carried me from dinghy to shore and a small boy was sent running ahead to announce my arrival to the village. I was accompanied by about twenty-five Papuans along a well beaten path, unseen from the sea, towards Bongu; so well concealed in its surrounding greenery as to be indistinguishable by sight or sound from only five yards distance. I passed the first hut before I realised we had arrived, and in a few steps I gained the central clearing and its group of huts.

Earlier in this diary I referred briefly to the Papuan hut; sturdily roofed, most had low walls and a small doorway raised from the ground. The interior was dark, being without windows; the sleeping platform provided the only form of furniture. Apart from individual huts, however, the villages had other buildings of communal character; the *buambramra* were much larger and taller, resembling barns. These *buambramra* were often built without walls at front and back and the entire building consisted of a roof rising directly from the ground on two sides. The shelter thus formed accommodated on one side a long platform for sitting or lying on, and on the other side storage for large dishes and other collective ceremonial material used by the community. Later I learned that the *buambramra* were for the use of village males only — an exclusive club of which Bongu had five, one for each clearing.

I was conducted to each in turn, in every one a group of Papuans awaited me, and in each I left behind tobacco and nails for the men and red cloth for the women (again they were hidden from me and none were to be seen). Bongu village was about three times the size of Gorendu, but the system of architecture and the style of ornamentation were identical. The huts were situated in small cleared spaces under coconut or banana palms and were connected by a system of short footpaths.

After inspecting the entire village I sat upon a *barla* (platform) in one of the *buambramra,* and a group of some forty Papuans gathered about me. The base of the roof under which I sat was supported on three solid, foot-high poles close to the ground. Another sturdy row of much higher poles supported the main beams as they rose to form the 'A' shape of the construction. The building was 24 feet wide, 42 feet long and 20 feet high in the middle. A thick network of saplings and crossbeams strengthened the whole, sufficient to withstand, in my estimation, ten years of storm and rain. From the wall above the platform hung various weapons; on the opposite wall, shelves held wooden and clay dishes, and above these hung pig jaws and fish heads — relics of past feasting.

As I completed my visit to each *buambramra,* having conversed with the natives and questioned them, I left Olsson and a Papuan to accept the gifts presented by the villagers — mainly sweet potatoes, bananas, roasted or smoked fish and sugar-cane.

One *buambramra* possessed a rear wall built of bark, decorated on the upper part with a painting composed in red, black and white of stars, sun-fish and human figures. I wanted to sketch this for my records but was prevented by rain.

Eventually, in one *buambramra* I discovered something I had long hoped to see — a group of carved wooden figures, *telum.* One of these, about two metres in height, was placed in the centre of the shelter; another, one metre and a half high, was situated behind the platform; the third, obviously old and slightly damaged, lay upon the ground. While sketching these, I talked with the villagers who asked if there were *telum* in Russia, and what were they called.

In another *buambramra* I noticed several figures carved into a thick plank hanging high in the roof — too high for me to closely observe the details. I offered to exchange up to three knives for a small *telum*, and the Papuans were quick to bring an old and partly spoiled figure; but I did not accept this immediately, hoping for a better one. The sun was setting as I returned to the dinghy, and the natives called after me, in farewell, "*E-meme, e-meme.*"

When we arrived home and began to unpack the gifts received, Olsson set up a complaint against our friends from Bongu. "They don't give much, do they? The coconuts are old, the fish as dry as wood, the bananas are green … and still no chance to see the women."

## 15 January

A storm borne upon a south-west wind roared through the night and the jungle about us echoed with the crashing of trees which I feared at any time would land on my roof. Despite the noise, such a night — cold, refreshing, without mosquitoes — made for excellent repose.

A great crashing wakened me at approximately 1 a.m., and within seconds I was aware that something of great weight had fallen on my roof. From the doorway nothing could be discerned in the impenetrable darkness and I returned to my bed, and was soon asleep. I was wakened early by the thunderous roar of great waves beating upon the beach, and although at 5.00 a.m. it was not fully daylight, there was enough light to silhouette a huge tree, felled by the storm, in front of the hut.

As was customary, the tree had carried with its fall festoons of liana, an entire network of parasites fastened about its trunk and branches, and at least part of a neighbouring tree. Some hours with an axe were necessary before I at last cleared a way to the creek.

The entire day was spent on domestic tasks. Olsson, suffering from fever, could not rise. I must fetch the water, light a fire, make tea and then return to clearing the fallen timber from about the hut. Having made my meteorological recordings and administered to Olsson, scant hours were left for work at the microscope — even these were interrupted at 10.00 a.m. by the necessity to chop firewood. For lunch I cooked rice and baked sweet potatoes in the ashes of my fire.

A proposed rest after luncheon was disturbed by the arrival of a group of Papuans who remained until 3 p.m. One visitor drew my attention to the dinghy, partly submerged and scarcely visible above the waves, and I had no alternative but to immediately begin bailing the water from the disabled vessel. As I set my drenched clothing to dry, it was already 5.00 p.m. and time to prepare the evening meal — again rice. Cooking bores me, I detest it.

The rain began again as I sat at my meal, necessitating a hasty rescue of my clothing hanging outside to dry. Dusk was falling and my lamps also had to be made ready. Even to drink tea required troublesome preparations; the sugar supply had failed weeks before and lack of it rendered the drink savourless for me, so it was necessary to utilise sugarcane. The outer husk had to be peeled before the canes were cut in pieces ready to chew, and as I drank the tea, I sucked the sweetness from the cane.

At 8.00 p.m. I sat down to my diary knowing that within an hour a trip first to the sea, then to the creek, would be necessary to record water temperature readings, tide heights, wind direction and speed, in the diary set aside for this purpose. Only when all this had been done could I go peacefully to rest.

The smallest detail was recorded of this past day to serve as a reminder of my difficulties, in case a temptation to self-criticism should arise when viewing the New Guinea sojourn in retrospect.

*17 January*

My intention was to re-visit Bongu and to complete my sketches of the *telum* — the wall-painting on the *buambramra*. On the way I encountered Tui heading for Garagassi. He joined me and as we passed Gorendu, our party numbered also Bonem and Digu. We made our journey along the sand of the shore, and as it was high tide, the waves lapped to the very edge of the jungle — a green and compact wall.

On our arrival I busied myself with the task at hand, recording the details of the aforementioned painting on the upper part of the back wall of the *buambramra*. For the first time during a visit to any village the women did not run into the jungle, but hid in the dark corners of their huts, and remained visible to me as I walked through the village. They wore, at front and back, a small apron-style garment suspended at the waist from a horizontal stick. As we prepared to leave the village, the inhabitants presented bananas and pieces of seemingly roasted meat — pork for me and dog for Olsson. Hungry on my arrival home, I left the pork for Olsson and sampled the other. A few mouthfuls were sufficient for me to find it tough but edible, and though Olsson was at first disgusted at the prospect, he soon finished the portion I had left untouched. The New Guinean dog apparently, is not such a delicacy as the Polynesian breed that Captain James Cook claims is better meat than pork.

*25 January*

The fever tortured me for six days during which I suffered one attack after another while rain fell incessantly.

I went to Gorendu for sugarcane and while awaiting the return of the villagers from the native gardens, I sketched several huts, seeing for the first time how the indigenes store their water supply — in huge bamboo tubes as do many of their contemporaries about the Malay Archipelago.

At last — five months after my arrival — I learned the Papuan words for 'morning' and 'evening', but not for 'night'. The discovery of the word 'good' makes me upset, coming as it does at so late a date — at least twice I have been deluded into thinking I had the correct word, only to find that the term was inappropriate. The Papuans, however, understood my intended meaning.

If a word is not the name of a demonstrable object, it is difficult to ascertain the equivalent of its meaning, though I found the Papuans were aware that as I questioned, I searched for a new word. I would take in my hand an object of certain admiration among the natives, and in the other hand, one of no importance to them. While pointing to the first object, I made happy facial expressions and stated 'good'. Normally the native would realise the meaning of the foreign word, and repeat his own equivalent. Indicating the other object, I made an unhappy face, and said 'bad'. After repeating the process several times, and summarising the results, the correct word should have been obvious. Performing this experiment in New Guinea, I concluded that the native word for 'good' was *kaz*. I recorded the new word, repeated it periodically and employed it for several months before I realised that some Papuans were bewildered by my use of *kaz* to categorise certain objects — I found it meant 'tobacco'.

An intelligent Papuan from Bongu had taught me several words previously, so I turned to him for help with 'good'. Talking to him in the village, I pointed to a new ceramic pot and repeated the world 'good' several times, then took pieces of an old and broken pot, saying 'bad'. The Papuan considered this for a moment, then pronounced *vab* as he pointed to the new pot. I repeated the process using a variety of examples — new and worn shoes, fresh and spoiled fruit and so on — and the result was always *vab*.

About a month later, during which time I had used *vab* for 'good' on many occasions, I discovered its meaning was 'big pot'; *aue* (good), the elusive word I had been searching for, was ascertained some ten days later in a cunning fashion. By serving my Papuan friends a variety of ill-flavoured foods — salt, peppery, bitter — I could listen for the word that expressed their dissatisfaction and heard only *borle* (I found it applied equally to 'bad' and 'ill'). Using *borle* as a key, I easily learned its opposite meaning from Tui.

## 7 February

Tui called, by prior arrangement, at 6.00 a.m. to accompany me to Bongu; for the first time he decided to breakfast with me and after consuming a bowl of rice, we proceeded.

In Bongu I discovered an interesting work combining two figures — a tall, carved wooden *telum*, holding in its hand a small roughly-made pottery miniature. The natives exchanged the piece for three packets of tobacco and though well-pleased, I continued searching for the day's principal goal — skulls. The natives told me that the Russian seamen had taken all, and showed me small and useless European goods received in exchange. By further enquiry, however, I obtained direction from a villager to a grove where some skulls should still remain, though neither my informant nor his companions were eager to help me search for these. When, amidst pig and dog bones all upon a heap, I found a human skull, the natives fell back, murmuring their dissatisfaction and suggesting that I should throw the article back on the heap. I concluded that the Papuans put little value upon the skulls, considering the handful of worthless items exchanged for them previously, and were convinced that the example I held in my hand had been, in life, an enemy of these people. I was surprised to ascertain, however, that it had been, in fact, a *tamo Bongu*.

Visiting neighbouring villages enabled me to exchange goods and to collect supplies of food; the visit to Bongu was no exception. I returned with, among other things, a large quantity of fish, a huge bunch of bananas and carried in addition, two *telum*. Although Digu offered his assistance, a considerable load remained for me to bear. As we proceeded through the jungle, I became hot and breathless, but on reaching the shore I was not only refreshed by the waves splashing my bare legs and by the sea breeze, but quite chilled and soon was shivering and feeling dizzy.

Upon reaching home, I removed my wet clothes and went immediately to bed in the grip of a severe attack of fever; my teeth chattered to such an extent that I was unable to utter a syllable, terrifying Olsson who cried and fell across the bed fearful of his own future. The most serious yet experienced, this bout of fever lasted six hours or more and was accompanied by the sensation of my whole body expanding rapidly, filling the entire room — my head felt like a mountain almost touching the ceiling, hands and legs like great logs. It was with immense relief that I felt these hallucinations recede.

## 8 February

During the night I took 0.8 grams of quinine and repeated the dose in the morning, preventing a further attack of the dreaded fever.

The weather was slightly warmer (29°C) and calm, and the only disturbance was caused by bird and cicada song. The sun breaking through cloud, sparkled upon the greenery so lately refreshed by rain. How splendid, how vivid was the luxuriant growth of the jungle.

The solitude, surrounded as I was by sea and jungle, was a source of great pleasure to me. I am not averse to company but if others are boring or nagging, I prefer to be alone. I felt that had my health been better, I could happily have remained in Papua for the rest of my life, and never return to Europe.

## 9 February

Walking to survey the surrounding area, I became lost in the jungle and, without knowing its direction, I followed a track which led me to a fence of canes. Hearing voices, I peered over and recognised the garden workers as villagers from Gorendu; among them were a large number of women who had removed the greater part of their clothing. Without the apron-like garment, the females wore only a narrow band about the waist, to which was fastened a similar piece passing between the thighs. Immediately I appeared, the women ran to hide among the sugarcanes and did not reappear as long as I stayed in the garden.

The native garden was a recently established one bordered by two rows of sugarcane plants 10 centimetres apart, with the intervening space filled with liana, branches and twigs. Canes from opposite rows were tied together at the top, compressing the mass between and forming an increasingly solid structure as the canes grew upward and formed root systems. The main gate was contrived by cutting a hole at a height of 60 centimetres above the ground, convenient for the natives to step through but inaccessible to wild pigs.

The garden was divided into blocks by a system of footpaths, the soil carefully cultivated to a fine tilth and the raised beds each contained a particular crop — sugarcane, sweet potatoes, tobacco and other local varieties unfamiliar to me. The well-tended soil made me consider the tools available to the natives for such a purpose, and to my surprise only two implements were apparent — a long digging-stick and a narrow spade, both of wood. Within the garden a small fire burnt constantly, principally for use in lighting tobacco.

I still had no knowledge of how the Papuans made fire, though I had often seen natives carrying glowing brands as they moved about, and these would quickly be made into a fire and kept alight if a pause or gathering occurred.

During the evening Tui taught me many new Papuan words, but most escaped my memory. Tui became interested in geography and though I showed him a map of the world, his own concept of this remained unchanged, with his conviction that Russia is no bigger than Bongu or Bili Bili.

## 12 February

What a lucky day! In Gumbu I obtained six good skulls with little effort after I had proceeded thither to sketch a *telum*. The figure was situated in a dark hut, and as lack of sufficient light precluded completion of my work, the villagers helpfully collected a number of *telum* from several huts and arrayed them outdoors in appropriate light. My drawing completed, I opened the knotted scarf in which I carried a variety of gifts — knives, tobacco, and coloured cloth — spread out the offering and announced I wished to have *tamo gate* (human skulls).

At first the natives insisted, loudly, that the Russians had taken every skull and none remained, but I continued my bargaining and offered a packet of tobacco, three large nails, and a strip of red cloth — all for one skull. Quite soon the first skull was brought, shortly after another two, then three more, whereupon I gladly exchanged the promised goods with an extra strip of cloth as a gratuity. I secured the skulls in two bundles, one at each end of a pole, and bore this across my shoulders in spite of the ants crawling from my trophies. I was disappointed that none of the skulls had a lower jaw, these being kept by the living as a souvenir of the dead relative.

## 14 February

For the first time Tui presented me with baked taro.

I was about to begin a sketch of the fifth skull, when mountain villagers arrived to call upon me. I could discern no physical differences between these men and my coastal friends. The visitors were quite severely shocked upon seeing themselves reflected in a small mirror, some stepping back or turning away in fright and approaching the glass again only after some time, and then with extreme caution. At last, however, curiosity gained supremacy and the men snatched the mirror from each other's hands. From one of my mountain visitors I obtained a small ornamented box used to contain lime, in exchange for various metal objects.

After the Papuans had gone, Olsson noticed the absence of a kitchen knife and voiced suspicion of a Gorendu man — the first case of theft thus far; I decided not to let the matter rest, and thus, hopefully, prevent further such trouble. My first impulse was to leave for Gorendu immediately, but I remembered that the dinghy was leaking — traces of woodworm having been detected in its timbers — so the afternoon was spent coating the exterior with tar to render the little vessel seaworthy.

## 16 February

Still busy with repairs to the boat, I received a messenger from Gorendu, breathlessly delivering dramatic news: Tui had been seriously hurt while felling a large tree; the injuries to his head were expected shortly to cause his death and my friend wished to see me once more before he died. I hastily assembled emergency medical equipment and hurried to where Tui lay stretched upon a mat. Obviously pleased at my arrival, and seeing the medical kit, the injured Papuan willingly removed the bindings of grass and leaves from his head. The wound gaping above his eyebrow had jagged edges of torn skin.

I had neglected to bring the curved scissors necessary to clip the hair from about the wound, and I caused great pain to the poor patient as the conventional scissor blades I was forced to use became jammed with thick hair and dried blood. While performing what treatment I could offer, I chatted with Tui and an old man, Bau, who watched as I worked. Eventually I touched upon the subject of the missing knife and the man from Gorendu who was suspected of taking it; both men were distressed and were insistent that the knife would be returned.

On my return from Garagassi after breakfast, I brought the curved scissors and other medical necessities. While treating Tui further by washing the wound, I was watched by a group of natives including the suspected knife thief. As I finished with Tui, I turned to face this man. "Give me my knife," I said. He calmly took out the knife and handed it to me, a gesture which I later discovered was at the request of all the inhabitants of Gorendu.

I instructed Tui to rest, avoid exposure to the sun, and on no account to remove the bandage from his wound. He was in a state of exhaustion, but his face was calm — even expressionless. As I was about to leave, Tui indicated several bundles of *aous* (edible cane) and sugarcane prepared for me, giving the appearance of payment for my services. My offer of tobacco in return was refused, but I left the token within Tui's reach as a reassurance that my medical assistance was freely given, without expectation of reward.

Several times in the past, natives had warned me that the ring-barked trees about my hut might topple in windy weather, and also that the roof of the hut was in imminent danger of collapse. It was suggested that in light of these threats I should move to Gorendu, where the villagers would build me a good hut. Certainly the roof was in poor condition; in several places the moon shone through.

## 17 February

Arriving in Gorendu to see my patient, I found the village entirely deserted except for dogs. The villagers were at their gardens or in the jungle, and Tui must surely have felt better to have gone with them.

## 18 February

Examining Tui when I reached Gorendu today, I found him to be in a far worse condition than on the day he received his injury. The wound was suppurating and a wide area surrounding it was severely swollen. I criticised the man soundly for his foolishness of the previous day and while binding the injury again, I heavily stressed the strong possibility of death in his condition from exposure to the heat of the sun. I intended during the evening to return to the village and examine the injured man again.

At home and about to begin luncheon, I was interrupted by Tui's son, Laley, with an invitation to eat at Gorendu — a menu of fish, taro, *aous*, coconuts and sugarcane. However, I finished my meal at home and only then proceeded with Laley and Lalu to their village. As we crossed a creek upon our journey, Lalu, walking some distance behind, cried out aloud and I made haste to investigate his distress. He had stepped upon a snake he described as *borle* (poisonous), the bite of which men usually died.

Lalu indicated the snake, motionless by the path, and as I stepped towards it both natives cried "*Borle, borle, aka, Maklai moen*" (poison not good, Maclay will die). In order to handle the snake safely, I severed its head; holding it up by the tail, I told Olsson to carry the prize home while I hurried to Gorendu as the sun was now setting.

Whenever entering a native village I announced my presence by whistling, thus enabling the women, unwilling to be seen, to hide themselves, and the natives obviously appreciated these precautions. They were aware from my behaviour that I wished to see only those things they willingly showed me, and at my whistled signal the entire female population would retire to the huts or into the surrounding groves.

Using the last of the fading daylight I dressed Tui's wound, then seated myself beside him in company with a group of men from Bongu and Gumbu. Tui explained that at the sound of my "phew, phew" (trying to express the whistling sound) all the *nangeli* (women) ran away, and that was bad because "*Maklai tamo bilen*" (good man). Soon after he had spoken I heard the sound of a woman's voice and turned to confront an elderly female smiling in friendly fashion — it was Tui's wife; old and ugly, with flat and pendulous breasts and dressed in a short, skirt-type garment fashioned from yellowish fibres. It was certainly very dusty but served its purpose well in covering most of the body between waist and knee. The woman's hair hung down in greasy clots, as her forehead has been rubbed with oil. Smiling warmly, my welcoming hostess inspired me to rise and shake her hand, which gesture pleased not only her but our audience as well. Encouraged by this exchange, from the huts and jungle came women of all ages, each to be introduced by her husband and to shake my hand, the girls in very short skirts, shyly hiding one behind another and giggling loudly. Each woman in her turn presented me with a bundle of *aous* and sugarcane. We all were delighted with our first social contact and at last the natives were released from the burden of hiding their women at my every visit.

The men grouped about Tui lay upon the ground, smoking, chatting and often addressing remarks to me (my understanding of the language had improved, though I was still not confident in speech) while the women gathered around Tui's wife, busily cleaning taro. Many of the young women, among them the wife of Tui's eldest son Bonem, were very pretty. Instead of skirts, the youngest girls wore a fibre apron at front and back, leaving hip and thigh exposed.

So many gifts did I receive from the women, that I accepted the services volunteered by two men to carry them to Garagassi. The darkness was descending so I hurried home, travelling part of the way through a shower of heavy rain.

*19 February*

I found that Tui's wound had deteriorated; unable to sit, he had kept moving about in the sun. He thought of offering me some taro but realised that the fire in his hut had died out. Laley was sent to look for some but returned ten minutes later, saying that no fire could be found anywhere. Since there was not a soul in the village except the three of us and the huts closed with bamboo, Tui asked his sons to check to see if a fire could be found in any of them. Some girls appeared and helped Laley look through the huts but no fire was found. Tui felt upset for not being able to cook taro and to smoke. He hoped, however, that the people would soon return from the gardens and would bring some fire with them. Now I felt sure that Papuans had not yet discovered the way to make fire.

A group of women returning to the village sat near us and curiously observed me and my clothes. This was understandable since it was the first time they had seen me in close proximity. I observed them in return. Some of the girls had their hair cut very short; they kept it smeared with ashes or lime to deter insects and to make the hair lighter. The old women kept their hair long, arranging it in *gatessi* (locks of hair at the back of the head) smeared with black earth. Coming back from the gardens, the women and girls carried large bags on their backs, supported by a band across the forehead. Burdened by the weight of the bag, they bent forward to keep balance.

Like their men, the women also had their nasal partitions pierced. In their ears, apart from a main hole for a large ring, there was another one on the upper part of the ear.

Through this hole was tucked a thread which, passing over the top of the head, went through a similar hole on the other ear; hanging from each end of the thread were two dog fangs, almost reaching the shoulders.

Above the entrance to one hut I saw a large beetle tied by a string and trying desperately to break free. Laley, Tui's seven year old son, told me that he had brought the beetle to eat but that I could have it for myself. The specimen was an unknown species and I took the offer. While I was busy untying the beetle, Tui pointed to a large spider, explaining that people of Gorendu, Bongu and Gumbu ate *kobum* (spiders). As food for Papuans, one may also include butterflies, grubs and other insects.

## 20 February

As I approached Tui's hut this morning, I saw, while still at some distance, a group of villagers assembled. I was surprised to discern among them women whom one might expect, at that time, to find working in the garden.

Immediately upon arrival, I realised the cause of the unusual gathering — Tui lay almost motionless with forehead, face and throat most grossly swollen, and eyelids puffed like mushrooms. The poor man could speak only with extreme difficulty and the assembled Papuans obviously assumed death to be imminent. On examination I discovered Tui's condition was caused by inflammation of the wound and I returned immediately to Garagassi for everything I needed to make a poultice.

Tension gripped the Gorendu villagers as they awaited my return, and I began my treatment of their countryman. I applied a compress of flax seeds, which I continually renewed and was soon rewarded with a considerable quantity of pus oozing from the wound, making unnecessary the use of my scalpel already prepared for opening the infected area. I persisted with the flax compresses, changing these repeatedly for some hours while the villagers watched intently from a distance. Some sat, some lay upon the earth, but all made themselves comfortable in obvious expectation of the process they watched being a lengthy one.

During a pause in my medical duties, I distributed gifts among the women; a strip of coloured cloth and a spoonful of glass beads for each — and found it an easier and less noisy task than that of presenting gifts to the men. Immediately upon receiving her share, each woman left smiling or giggling and made no attempt to ask for more.

The Papuan host was by custom the person who cooked the meal for a guest, but Tui's wife and daughter-in-law performed this task for me while Tui lay ill. I carefully watched the preparation and subsequent consumption of the repast, and was much surprised at the quantity eaten. It is not hunger which drives such people to take great quantities of food, but the necessity to compensate for the lack of meat in their daily diet. Even the children partook to such an extent that after a meal, they scarcely could move.

## 21 February

Though feeling far from well, concern for Tui forced me to travel to Gorendu where I found the swelling considerably eased after the previous day's ministrations of compresses. Further subsidence was achieved as I pressed the area of the wound and brought forth more pus.

Not a single woman was to be seen about the village; realising that Tui's condition had improved they went to the gardens, and once there usually stayed working the entire day.

In Papuan society the woman is a more vital member of the community than in European society — in contrast to our way of life where the woman toils for the man. Every Papuan girl was sufficiently sure of attaining marriage as to care almost nothing for her appearance.

Feeling ill again, I went immediately to bed upon reaching Garagassi.

## 22 February

Passing a village hut I was prompted by curiosity to pause and investigate how the Papuan spent his idle hours. A man seated within was faced by several dishes fashioned from the shells of huge coconuts, one of which had a hole in the bottom stuffed with grass. Placing one dish upon another, the native poured a dark green liquid from a third dish, filtering this through the grass into the bottom dish. On questioning the man as to his purpose I was handed a piece of root. "*Keu*" said the Papuan and indicated by pantomime of head and eyes that I would sleep if I drank the liquid.

I was later informed that *keu* was a highly intoxicating drink made from the leaves, stems and roots of a local plant *Piper methysticum*. The roots were first ground between stones, and then chewed; this task often being performed by boys too young to enjoy the privilege of drinking *keu*. The chewed pulp was then filtered and mixed with water before being consumed out of particular, highly decorated and engraved coconut cups.

Even though I had not seen the leaves of that *keu*, I assumed it was most likely to be *Piper methysticum* or the Polynesian *kava*. I had thought earlier that *kava* would be unknown to the natives of New Guinea.

## 24 February

Tui could not be found in the village and I proceeded to the garden to find him sitting in full sun, in spite of his condition, watching his family at work. I sent him immediately back to the village, but lingered myself to observe the cultivation in progress.

The well-kept garden was, as earlier described, stoutly fenced and neatly divided into small blocks of well-tilled soil. The excellent preparation of the land was due solely to hard work with primitive implements — one a pointed digging stick about two metres long and called *udya* and the other a narrow-bladed spade close to one metre in length.

The cultivation of the soil was a collective effort — a line of men simultaneously plunging the *udya* deep into the earth, turning the resulting strip of sod before stepping back to repeat the movement. The first row of *udya* workers was followed by another, using the stick to break the clods of earth; then followed the women using spades (*udya-sab*) to form plots and break the soil further, at times crumbling it in their hands.

## 26 February

In Gorendu I collected another skull, this one complete with lower jaw. I came across the villagers from Koliku-mana and received an invitation to visit them; amongst their number was a young woman of singular good looks in comparison with others I had seen.

*27 February*

I rose, of necessity, very early, packed my full day's ration of cooked beans and taro, and proceeded to Gorendu to meet Bonem and Digu, who would accompany me to Koliku-mana. Tui's condition was improved and after completing his treatment, I enquired after Bonem.

"Gone to Tengum-mana."

"Where is Digu?"

"Gone with Bonem."

"*Tamo borle*," I cursed.

I was furious at my ignorance of the road to Koliku-mana; though I knew the direction by compass, the treacherous jungle footpaths could lead me seriously awry. It was sometimes impossible to follow the track, and only by moving zig-zag left and right could it be located again. It often happened that a clear footpath one followed would suddenly end in a ravine with water flowing far below and a solid green wall of jungle on the opposite bank — where next? The path thus far could be well trodden by many feet, but nonetheless ended at such an impasse without trace of a further track.

Actually, the footpath might seem to end, but not the track. The natives would proceed down the ravine over fallen tree trunks, climb a tree upon the bank to grab the branch of another tree on the opposite bank, then continue via thick branches to locate a tree stump, and thence the track became evident again! At times, a path following the course of a creek might disappear, and the traveller must wade up or down the stream for a hundred or two hundred paces to locate it.

Unwilling to acknowledge that I had been tricked, I took out my compass and announced that I would journey alone. The natives, impressed with the instrument, backed away but not so far that they could not see the movement of the needle. I consulted the compass for the sake of appearance and, manifesting confidence, I chose my direction to the astonishment of the onlookers. In fact, I had decided to go first to Bongu and there find myself a guide.

I was perhaps halfway to the village when I heard familiar voices calling — the Gorendu villagers had, after all, sent two men after me — not, as I thought, to guide me, but to dissuade me from going to Koliku-mana. Seeing, however, that I was not to be swayed, the men turned back to Gorendu and I continued on my way. Later, I heard pursuing footsteps and was overtaken by Laku armed with spear and axe, offering to guide me to Koliku-mana. The Papuans so lacked confidence in me that I could not be permitted to walk behind any of them — thus my guide must walk behind me and called directions from there.

We emerged from the jungle to meet the sea coast; at a distance of some twelve metres below lay a picturesque bay into which we must descend. The track there swung in a left-handed southward loop, almost in the direction from where we had come. If alone, I would have most likely gone astray many times before this juncture; but if by some chance I had been able to get this far, that point would surely have brought disaster.

Laku, coming to a large tree, paused and indicated our path of descent before beginning a rapid but nonetheless cautious journey downward, by the thick network of roots which formed an almost vertical aerial ladder upon the cliff face. Several times as I climbed, I found myself in the precarious position of having hand-holds, but nowhere to place my feet for some seconds; invariably however, I eventually found some support, at times as small as a root, or a crevice, being aware at all times that failure to do so would result in a fall into the abyss below. Having reached the beach we followed the sea for perhaps five minutes, then re-entered the jungle which was of particular luxuriance and slowed our progress considerably.

Once more I heard the crashing of an advancing human behind us, and we were shortly joined by two men from Gorendu — the same two who had tried to dissuade me from the journey, and now eager to travel with us to Koliku-mana.

Away from the shore, the jungle track climbed steadily upward and having negotiated this for some time, I was near to exhaustion as was Laku seemingly, as he stopped in a clearing to rest. Pointing to the distant hills, the Papuan indicated where the huts of Koliku-mana could be detected far away.

A system of undulating foothills extended towards the mountains gradually becoming steeper and more rugged, showing here and there against the dark greenery of the undergrowth the bare earth of the serpentine foot-track we would traverse.

The sun beat strongly down, but its ferocity was scarcely noticed in my absorption with the panorama spread before me to the mountains and below me to the sea. Presently the path passed a large native garden situated on a particularly steep slope, but well kept and effectively cultivated. Along its border was a row of sugarcane. The calls of my guides over the border brought forward a young woman to converse with them. The natives stood in such a way as to hide the woman completely from my gaze until she reached the fence. The men then suddenly stepped aside leaving me facing the woman scarcely metres away — an expression of fear and horror accompanied her first sight of a white man: mouth half-open and gasping for air, and finally clasping her sugarcane for support, the poor woman was a sight to reassure my guides that their prank was a success; and only then did they made their explanations. I presented the victim with some red cloth and we moved on.

The terrain inclined more and more sharply until coconut palms and the roofs of some huts came into view. By way of the track I reached a clearing which accommodated the village of Koliku-mana.

Two native men, a boy and an elderly woman came forward to greet me. My guides from Gorendu were anxious to present a favourable account of me to their neighbours and thus glorified my attributes; they gave an account of Tui's dramatic recovery and elaborated upon the 'miraculous' equipment kept in my *tal*, and so on.

After resting myself and distributing gifts — tobacco for men and cloth for women — I inspected the huts and their environs. The village, situated on a small plateau high on a ridge but surrounded entirely by thick vegetation and coconut palms, boasted little outlook upon the surrounding country. The huts were almost identical to those of the coastal villages but slightly smaller — chiefly because of limited space on the mountain plateau and the difficulty in such rugged terrain of transporting building material.

There appeared to be no physical differences between the mountain-dwellers and their coastal brothers, but they could be identified by a noticeable lack of ornaments compared to the lowlanders. In one *buambramra* I saw a *telum* and sketched it, then went to the next group of huts situated on higher ground from the others. While a meal was being cooked for me, my companions and I asked local natives about *mab*, a species of cuscus which, according to the Papuans, was often seen in the mountains. The locals showed me only a broken skull of one and the lower jaws of two others.

The natives brought a *tabir* (wooden dish or bowl) for me and each of my companions. The food was perfectly cooked. As we began to eat the natives walked off leaving us to consume the food alone. I was able to eat only a portion of the food since the meal was huge. The remainder of the meal was wrapped up in banana leaves for me to eat *mondon* (afterwards) even though I objected to it.

From a clearing amongst the trees I was shown, among other things, the position of Englam and Teñgum-mana, villages I intended to visit. The natives of Koliku-mana were particularly hospitable – at my departure a woman came from each hut and placed an *ayan* (yam) at my feet, and I left after issuing an invitation to the Koliku-mana people to visit me at Garagassi.

At about 3.00 p.m. the sun was still fierce. Travelling down over open hills was especially tiring and moving through the shade of damp jungle felt chilly. As I reached the sea it became windy and cold; I hurried up, but did not escape an attack of fever. On reaching Bongu, without saying a word, I headed straight to a large hut and after taking off my wet boots, stretched out on my *barla* to sleep. When wakened during the night, I felt well and set off for home — it was a fine moonlit night.

## 28 February

I made my way to Gumbu in the hope of finding more skulls, but still exhausted from the previous day's march, I was forced to sit and admire the scenery for a time. A native running at speed along the beach interrupted my rest, however, as he approached gesticulating with one hand and holding a bow and arrow aloft with the other. Villagers advancing to meet the messenger greeted him with some excitement, which mounted higher as another runner, then a third and a fourth, appeared on the beach. The men, as they sped along the sand at equal distance one from the other, displayed not only the skills of warriors, but athleticism as well. The first messenger passed me and the gathering of natives without pause, and continued towards the village. As he passed he beat upon his chest with his right hand, threw back his head and thrust out his tongue (the native indication of death) calling "*Maragum-Gorendu!*"

The next runner came by and the grouped natives ran to the village. I followed and we had scarcely reached the first group of huts when the sound of *barum* (drums) arose, in an unusual tempo. I had earlier witnessed the passing of messages — death, the commencement of ceremonies and so on — but the sound I now heard was different from that of previous occasions and I knew it could only mean war.

From the huts, arms were brought forth and heaped in the clearing. The atmosphere was tense, yet I could not grasp the circumstances, so I stopped a hurrying group of men to ask what had happened. The men from Maragum had attacked Gorendu I was told; several villagers had been killed, and among them was

Bonem. The attackers had also gone to Bongu and could be soon expected at Gumbu, and perhaps *tal* Maclay.

Maragum-mana was a large village with which my neighbours had long maintained hostile relations. During the past weeks I had noticed quantities of weapons, mainly spears and arrows, in Gorendu and realised then that the natives had been expecting the attack for some time.

At Gumbu, alarm ran high — the villagers spoke loud and fearfully. Arms were being prepared, the women and children cried aloud, and the dogs howled. I hurried home, upset and almost angry at some foolish tribesmen and their warlike notions. A few words of explanation to Olsson were sufficient to incite panic. He insisted that the dinghy should be made ready in case of attack, for we should obviously be grossly outnumbered and must cross to Bili Bili Island for escape. In order to calm him, I agreed with the servant's theories, but stressed that there was no necessity to move any gear as one shot from the rifle would disperse any invaders in panic.

Although all guns were prepared and loaded, I decided to wait calmly for the intruders and stretched out on my bed. I was soon asleep, confident that Olsson would surely wake me in the event of any emergency, but was actually disturbed by sounds from the bush followed by a cry from Olsson. "Here they come, Master, tell me what to do. Please tell me what to do." The poor man was in such panic that he spoke half in German and half in Swedish.

I ordered him to barricade the door with boxes and to be prepared to reload the pistols and rifles should shooting become necessary, but before my terrified servant could obey my instructions, he had to control the trembling of his hands. As we prepared for a siege the noises from the jungle grew louder.

On the verandah, flanked by two pistols and a rifle, and carrying a double-barrelled rifle loaded with small pellets, I sighted the first Papuan approaching from the direction of the creek. It was difficult to trust my eyes, for instead of spears and arrows the visitors carried coconuts and bananas, unlikely burdens for Maragum villagers. The confusion lasted but a few seconds as I soon recognised my friends from Bongu; they had come to reassure me regarding Maragum *tamo*, as the entire affair had been false, occurring thus: the Bongu women in the fields that morning had seen several warriors moving hurriedly and immediately deduced that they were the potential quarry. As they ran to escape, they cried and screamed until they reached the garden. Several men, realising the mistake, began to beat the women in an effort to silence their alarming noise, but succeeded only in adding the sympathetic cries of other women and children. The sounds caused concern in other villages and the opinion was that the men of Maragum-mana were massacring the women and children of Bongu. The news of the 'massacre' spread rapidly from village to village.

Though all appeared safe, my visitors were still worried that the warriors who had been seen were actually Maragum *tamo* and could yet attack without warning. Pleased to ascertain that I was prepared to resist any aggression, the villagers requested that their women and children be able to seek protection with me should the need arise. Encouraged by this confidence, I decided that the time had come to demonstrate the power and effects of firearms — a step I had hitherto hesitated to make for fear of causing irreparable alarm. In the present situation however, such an exhibition of power could only increase the natives' confidence in my ability to support their defence.

At my command Olsson brought me a firearm and I fired a shot. Terrified by the dreadful report, the Papuans fled with their hands pressed against their ears; they returned fearfully, with exhortations that I put the rifle in its usual place and use it only if the Maragum *tamo* should come. The natives referred to the gun as *tabu* — presumably in imitation of my early use of the word 'taboo' when indicating items in my possession which I wished them not to touch; and thus a Polynesian word found its way into the Papuan language.

## 1 March

Men from Gumbu called in the hope of persuading me to join them and a party of warriors from Gorendu and Bongu in warfare against the Maragum men. They promised to obey me implicitly. "When they hear Maklai is with us, the Maragum men will run away to the hills," they boasted.

Koliku-mana men also called in the company of Tui and Lalu and the assembled warriors talked much of their assured success over Maragum men with Maklai to assist them. This unwarranted high opinion of my influence I found to be discomfiting. It seemed I was to be involved in their tribal conflicts whether I would or not. Afternoon rain made it necessary to postpone a proposed trip to Bili Bili Island until a period of more suitable weather.

As I sat by the coals roasting *aous* and bananas for my evening meal, the usual silence was shattered by a sudden and frantic beating of drums. The same thought occurred simultaneously to Olsson and me: "The Maragum men are attacking Bongu and Gorendu." Prolonged and wordless human cries rose and diminished from time to time in the darkness; aware that anxious wakefulness would be useless I went to bed and slept, despite a crescendo of sound.

## 2 March

The sounds of *barum* and other instruments, the voices of the villagers all intruded upon my sleep, and at dawn a cry from close quarters wakened me entirely. In the pale dawn light I could discern Bangum from Gorendu standing below my verandah — his mission was to extend an invitation from the villagers of Gumbu, Bongu and Gorendu, to attend their ceremony. Such an opportunity could not be rejected and I hastily dressed myself and followed Bangum. My first encounter in Gorendu was with Tui, pale from a sleepless night and requesting attention to his wound which was paining him. The dressing completed, my patient indicated the seaward footpath and advised, "Go, drink *keu*, and eat *ayan* and *buam*."

The path led to a clearing encircled by huge centuries-old trees and a party of some fifty natives there assembled, although near to exhaustion from the night's festivities, continued the ceremony. The scene was not only valuable as an example of a characteristic Papuan celebration, but was also picturesque. The first light of morning had not penetrated the darkest parts of the jungle, but one side of the clearing was open to the sea and bathed in light. Placed as it was upon the crown of a steep slope, the ceremonial ground seemed almost to touch the sea, and great branches of the surrounding trees sharply silhouetted against the brilliant horizon provided a setting fit for the finest theatre.

Grouped about glowing fires and never far from the wooden *tabir*, the natives (some still on their feet) drank the final dregs of *keu* from their small cups. Others, much intoxicated but not entirely overcome, lay about upon mats and gazed blankly from unseeing eyes. Others, quite unconscious, lay prone or supine upon the earth utterly motionless and reminiscent of great fallen logs. The *keu* had left its marks, to a greater or lesser extent, upon each of the revellers, and though the night of ceremonial activity was nearly at an end, the noise continued. The men still conversed animatedly; those intent on prolonging the evening's excitement blew native tunes on bamboo pipes of some two metres in length, or evoked a sharp whistling melody by blowing into hollow nuts. Propped against the encircling tree-trunks were the natives' weapons of war — spears and arrows.

The scene thus presented before me was filled with the originality of the native environment and I was impressed with its feeling of profound purity — a precious reward for the effort, patience and suffering of the explorer. Such an experience, with its extreme beauty and excitement, would thrill not only an ethnographer, but also a student of the arts. What richness was to be seen in the play of early morning light upon the posed bodies and shadowed exhausted faces, in contrast to the sun-gilded tree-tops.

As the daylight grew stronger I was able to recognise familiar faces from neighbouring villages. The insistent shrilling of bamboo pipes signalled the commencement of the morning meal and the sound, as usual, irritated me with a longing for its immediate and permanent stop. The natives, men from Gumbu, Bongu and Gorendu, clustered about a large wooden dish and began to eat. One of my hosts scooped a portion of a yellowish mess, *buam* (delicacy dish made from sago palm and other ingredients), and handed this to me. I found it to be delicious. The next course consisted of cooked *ayan* with *orlan* sauce of such strange and bitter flavour that I could not swallow more than one mouthful. A banana leaf was provided for use as a napkin and bamboo stems served some as forks, though many used their hair-combs for this purpose (the Papuan language has only one word for both comb and fork). The *yarur* served as a spoon and completed the range of eating utensils used.

Upon my departure from the ceremonial ground I was presented by my host with a small parcel of *buam* for Olsson, and offered a pressing invitation to return for luncheon. It was only then that I realised the feasting had hardly begun, for upon the narrow pathway I encountered Tui at the head of a column of men, each bearing yet more food. Tui, and behind him Bonem, bore between them a long pole from which was suspended a cargo of *buam* wrapped in leaves. Next came men carrying coconuts, pairs of natives bearing baskets of *ayan* slung from saplings, and finally six men who bore a large pig with its legs tied together across a stout rod. I stood aside from the footpath to allow the feast-bearers right of way. Glancing back towards the clearing I saw the natives unloading the food, to be exhibited for a time before being eaten at the midday meal. The consumption of the last morsel of this repast would signal the end of the ceremony, begun with such noise the previous evening.

The native women took no active part in such festivities and although they helped in the preparation of some foods, took their repast apart from the revellers. On occasions when such female participation was evident, it was of a discreet nature, implying that the presence of women and children on the ceremonial ground was considered improper. I witnessed just such an event in Gorendu during which the men feasted but the women and children remained in the village, cleaning *ayan* for the consumption of the revellers.

On my return to the ceremonial ground for luncheon I was aware of a dramatic increase in activity. Natives were busily carving pig meat in the area reserved for food and, in doing so, were using to excellent effect the steel knife they had so recently acquired from me; along with their traditional bamboo and shell utensils and the skilful tearing movements of their hands. At a distance from the pig, two lines of some thirty-one pots were formed; in between, wood stacked in preparation for a fire awaited kindling. Five larger pots particularly used for the preparation of *buam* stood close at hand and a group of natives cleaned and peeled the *buam* in readiness. Others shredded coconut meat and the Gorendu villagers, as hosts, were busy bringing water in bamboo tubes and stacking extra firewood.

A particular form was observed in serving the guests at the ceremonial meal. Tui called each man by name, appending *tamo* to each and adding the name of his village. The guest thus called then received a portion of meat which he carried to one of the pots (each man's food was cooked in a separate pot). "*Maklai tamo russ!*" At the call I approached Tui, to be served with some cuts of meat upon a large leaf. An acquaintance from Bongu kindly indicated the food pot reserved for me and seeing my lack of eagerness to set about the cooking, offered to perform the task for me. The bottom of the pot was lined with large leaves and the native placed on these first some *ayan* and then the pork. Two natives supplied the *ayan* from a great basket which they dragged about between them; when the pot for each guest was filled they stood back to make way for our hosts carrying water in long bamboo containers

110

— each pair of rods containing both fresh and sea-water. Into each pot of *ayan* was poured a mixture approximating two thirds of fresh water and one third seawater, then covered with a bread-fruit leaf and *gamba* (coconut shell). These last operations were performed by a young man from Bongu, his chief duty being to light the fire beneath each pot.

Each step in the preparation of ceremonial food was precisely planned and carried out exactly according to these rules of custom. Even the size of the fire must have been according to protocol, being some 80 metres in length and banked on either side by a row of pots. The firewood must have been carefully selected for it was soon well alight and burning steadily around every pot.

In reference to their musical instruments, the Papuans use of the word *ai* appeared to be one of general meaning. The main instrument was a bamboo pipe about two metres in length, carefully hollowed out, and when blown by a Papuan musician could project a howling note for a distance of two kilometres. The native name for this pipe was *ai kobray*. Another instrument, *orlan ai*, consisted of rows of orlan shells threaded upon numerous strings attached to a stick; when shaken, the shells striking one upon the other produced a musical sound. *Munki ai* was made from a coconut shell pierced with a number of holes; by covering different holes with his fingers as he blew, the musician could alter the note he produced; he could also achieve this result by blowing in turn into different holes.

Irritated by the volume of the Papuan music, I went to the village to see what was in progress there. The women, using their bamboo knives with skill, were still preparing *ayan* for the feast. For the first time I witnessed the sharpening procedure of this tool – effected simply by breaking off the dulled portion of the cutting blade and thus producing a fresh sharp edge. The previous day I had proved the efficiency of such a bamboo blade when it removed some flesh from one of my fingers.

During the day the natives often addressed me as 'Tui' and my

Papuan friend as 'Tui Maklai', and my attempts at correction brought the explanation that my care of Tui during his illness obliged him to do anything for me that I should wish. For this reason, custom ruled that I should be called 'Tui' and he, 'Maklai'. A similar system of name-exchange is practised among Polynesians.

Due partly to the heat and partly to the loud music, I suffered from a headache and made it known to Tui that I must leave. The food in my pot was just then cooked, and although Tui was insistent that I should stay to eat, we compromised and I took the pot with me in order to share the feast at home. The scalding pot was wrapped in bread-fruit leaves and placed in a basket.


## 3 March

On arriving to visit me, Tui showed puzzlement at seeing in my hut the empty basket in which I had carried my share of the feast from Gorendu. He picked it up and hung it outside on a tree-branch instructing me as he did so, that should anyone ask about the basket, I must answer, "*Bul* (pork) and *ayan* from Tui of Gorendu." At last I understood the meaning of many of these small baskets hanging from trees in the villages — whenever I had made enquiries about these, the response was the name of another villager.


## 4 March

I reinforced both doors of the hut with planks, nails and ropes, then lined against this some palm fronds, *à la Papua* style, before raising anchor about midnight and setting off for Bili Bili, an island some fifteen miles from the mainland. With help from the land breeze I had expected to be there on time so that I could return in the afternoon, making use of the north-west wind blowing towards the mainland at that time of day. However, the land breeze failed to carry us forward as expected — there was no urgency to hurry though as we had a good part of the night ahead of us. At dawn, as the breeze increased, we picked up speed. The morning sun revealed an impressive scene of the mountains which, across the stretch of water, looked interestingly high. After observing the configuration of the ranges, I looked for the most convenient spot for landing. Beyond Male, but not as far as Bogatim, a break appeared in the line of coastal ranges. The rain had stopped at daybreak and a temporary calm set in before the north-westerly wind arrived; usually about 8.00 a.m. and lasting barely a few hours. Expecting the north-westerly's arrival, we kept rowing, rather an exhausting task after a sleepless night.

We finally approached the south-eastern shore of the island consisting of a high coral reef against which crashed the waves — a spectacular sight. Some natives who recognised me ran along the beach, indicating that I would have to go around the island for a more suitable landing spot. On a sandy beach lay large pirogues, drawn up such a distance from the water's edge that it looked as if they were in the village next to the huts. Behind them towered a row of coconut palms whose lighter green colour contrasted with the darker background of the jungle.

As we were about to land, native hands reached for my boat and quickly drew it up on to the sloping beach. Leaving Olsson in the boat to guard my things, I made for the village accompanied by the entire male population. No women appeared; wishing to meet them and to relieve the men of the inconvenience of hiding their women, I asked that they should come out to receive the gifts I brought for them. On hearing that the women from Gumbu, Gorendu, Bongu and other villages no longer needed to conceal themselves from me, village elder Kain, who used to visit Garagassi occasionally and knew the Bongu dialect, was able to persuade the inhabitants of Bili Bili to accept my suggestion. At the call of their men, several old, almost naked women appeared from the huts — ugly souls. I was told that the majority of women were at the gardens on the mainland but would soon be returning.

Having distributed tobacco to the men and cloth and beads to

the women, I asked to be shown their *telum*. I was led to one of
the huts, but it was so dark inside that I had to persuade the natives
to bring the *telum* outside. This gave me the opportunity to see for
the first time a *telum* representing a female figure. After sketching
it I went inside a wide *buambramra* in the middle of the village,
with corner posts curved in the shape of *telum*. Having sketched
them in my album I made a tour of the entire village and went as
far as the opposite side of the island. The view from there was
beautiful even though the summits of the ranges were covered
with clouds. On my return to the village I found myself
surrounded by women and children who had just returned from
the gardens. They all pleaded for beads and red cloth like those I
had earlier given the elder women.

The women here wore more ornaments of shells and dog
teeth than the women in the mainland villages, but their clothing
looked shorter and lighter. For girls below thirteen years of age,
the clothing consisted of little more than a girdle with a small
brush hanging in the front and one slightly longer at the back.
Ornaments consisting of seashells and large black and red peas also
hung from the girdle. Their ears were pierced in several places. The
women of Bili Bili are very resourceful and active, often engaged
in making clay pots used to barter with throughout the coastal
villages by their fathers or husbands.

Before departing I thought of quenching my thirst and asked
for a coconut which the natives here call *niu* and was given several.
I wrote in my notebook nearly two dozen words of Bili Bili
dialect that sounded considerably different from the language of
my neighbours, even though there are occasional identical words.
Many of the Bili Bili inhabitants knew the Bongu dialect.

Lightheartedly I told them that I might come over and live in
Bili Bili. My words quickly spread round and the inhabitants
began talking of how Maclay would come to live in their village
and how the people of Bili Bili would be better off than the
people of Bongu, and so forth. As I was about to leave, it began to
rain heavily so I decided to stay overnight in Bili Bili, to the

delight of the local inhabitants. I was provided with one of the larger pirogues where I could sleep in its roomy cabin.

These pirogues are worth mentioning because of their construction. Some of them are up to 35 feet in length, hollowed out of a single tree trunk. To keep the vessel balanced, a long plank is attached to each side of the hollowed out trunk; flexible cane ties the planks to the pirogue. The prow and stern are finished off with a curved board which is also carved. On one side of the pirogue is an outrigger attached to the vessel by two crossbars. On the crossbars sits a platform whereon in the larger pirogues a cabin is erected, about 6 feet wide and some 15 feet long. The cabin's walls are made of split bamboo and roofed by plaited leaves of sago palm. The mast parts the cabin into two halves, each containing two long benches so that people can lie down. Included also is space for two more people to lie on the cabin floor. The cabin can accommodate about eight natives during the night, in need of shelter from bad weather. If required, half of the cabin's walls can be pulled down; even the roof can be removed in a short space of time.

Everything in the pirogue was planned and constructed for convenience — it seemed that no space was wasted. Beside the mast at the height of the seat, rested a flat box filled with earth where one could safely make a fire if it became necessary. The cabin was to provide me with accommodation for the night. I found it very convenient, lighter and cleaner than the village huts. I even thought of the idea of using a similar pirogue for my future tours of native villages along the coast.

Kain, who was master of the pirogue and my good friend, brought me a large *tabir* with steaming taro and some coconut. The rain had stopped before sunset, giving me an opportunity for another tour of the village. In the corner of one hut I saw a crocodile skull; I was told the species inundated the local sea.

I was given the opportunity to see the making of clay pots for which Bili Bili was well known along the coast for miles. Every village family took part in the making of pots and in almost every hut, women were seen making them. I observed the entire production process, beginning with the mixing of clay to the firing of the pots. The implements used for making them were a few small boards and a pair of round stones that looked flattened on both sides. With the help of a small piece of wood, the upper rim was made first, then the clay left to dry in the sun. Once it was hardened, the rest of the pot was gradually added and then smoothed out. The shape was obtained by holding the pot between the knees — a woman would insert her left hand with a round stone into the pot to shape the internal surface of the pot wall, while at the same time her right hand held a similar stone striking a corresponding place on the pot. After being made the pot was left to dry in the sun and later baked on an open fire that served as an improvised kiln. The pots were almost identical in shape but varied in size. There was scarcely any ornamentation on them except for some occasional markings, often made by finger or nails.

Around sunset I made another tour of the island. I soon felt at home as I grew familiar with the pathways on that part Bili Bili. The island was covered with jungle as well as some beautiful old trees and a very impressive cluster of palms. The shoreline, sandy near the village but sloping precipitously in other places, often consisted of coral limestone. Here and there I noticed deep caves into which seawater poured with a roar. The view of the ranges and open sea, the beautiful trees and the persistent sound of the waves, were so pleasant that for a moment I thought I should indeed move onto the island. I even sighted a cosy spot where I could erect my hut.

There was something that did not draw me in — the island was small and overpopulated. However, I felt pleased when I went for a walk that no native ran after me to see where I was going; none even talked about it. The people were too busy with their work. On the mainland my neighbours were far more inquisitive, even suspicious. Living on a small island had a strong impact on the behaviour, activity, and way of life of the whole community.

Not having suitable ground for cultivation, the natives of Bili Bili obtained their food from neighbouring coastal villages — Bili Bili residents were considered to be craftsmen of pots, wooden vessels and pirogues.

Passing by a hut on my way back to the village, I was approached by the hut owner who wanted to give me a gift. The man seized an unfortunate dog by the hind legs and after hitting its head against a tree, placed the animal with its smashed skull at my feet. He managed it so quickly that I had no time to prevent him. Accepting the gift and not wanting to offend the native, I asked him to prepare the food either by boiling or roasting the dog. He later presented me with a *tabir* filled with chunks of boiled dog. I passed on the pieces to the natives gathered around me and left a good dishful for Kain, some for Olsson, and a little piece for myself.

At dusk the entire village population, of both sexes, gathered together. Among them were many children, some of whom their parents wished to rename 'Maklai', but I declined my consent.

### 5 March

I was attracted by the shape of a head (looking very pyramidical with a receding forehead) of one child whom I saw while he was being nursed. It was possible that such a shape had been given to the head intentionally, but I failed to find any evidence of artificial deformation. Such conical heads are not often seen in Polynesia.

Having had an excellent night, I walked to the eastern shore of the island to look at the summits of Mana-boro-boro, the name the natives use when referring to the Finisterre Ranges. The mountains are best visible at sunrise; around 8.00 o'clock in the morning, clouds gather and settle on the summits for the rest of the day. While observing the ranges I was joined by a group of natives, including. Kain. I told him that as soon as the wind picked up, we would set out for home. While waiting for the wind I occupied myself with compiling a vocabulary of the Bili Bili dialect which differs considerably from those of my neighbours. Although very courteous, the natives were rather anxious for me to depart soon. They were accustomed to being alone on their island and visitors rarely came their way.

As soon as the breeze was felt, I gave a sign and a group of men promptly hauled my boat into the water. I raised the flag to the admiration of the natives who uttered a loud "*Ae*" and called out that they would visit me soon on the mainland. The reason for the visit was that after I treated a boy from Karkar who had a large wound on his leg and who recovered after receiving some lead ointment, the news of his recovery spread around – many sick people on Bili Bili wanted my help also, and I told them to visit me.

At about 2.00 p.m. we were already in sight of Cape Garagassi. As soon as I landed I went to my hut which I had never before left for so long. The place seemed in order but before I could undo the ropes that protected the door, scores of men appeared from behind the bushes, asking where I had been — they were concerned that I might have gone back to Russia. After dinner we unloaded the gifts from Bili Bili; 50 coconuts, 4 bunches of good bananas and some sago. The tobacco and nails paid well.

## 6 March

As I went out on my verandah this morning, I saw a snake on my table writhing slowly and beautifully. I seized the right moment and caught him quickly by the upper part of the neck, then placed the reptile in a jar filled with alcohol. I held the reptile until it had swallowed some alcohol and slid to the bottom of the jar.

Tui arrived and we had a long chat about Bili Bili, Karkar, Maragum-mana, and so on. From the information he gave me I learned the names of some objects in dialects of nine neighbouring villages.

Among the coconuts brought from Bili Bili were many that had sprouted. I took these and planted them in front of the hut. I asked Tui about coconut palms at Gorendu — do the trees belong to the village community or single individuals? He informed me that some coconut palms there belong to individuals while others belong to the community.

The evening felt still and dark. I stayed for a long time on the shore, sitting on the trunk of a large tree which hung over the water's edge. The water looked very calm; by following the movement of a multitude of luminous creatures in the sea, one could see how they moved individually and at different speeds. The scene appeared much different from what it does when observed during night from a ship, as the latter's movement and the presence of light upsets the sea life.

## 7 March

Domestic duties again! The white beans were getting spoiled. As I lay them out in the sun to dry, grubs came out from the peas on the white canvas underneath. It took Olsson a few hours to sort out bad from good beans.

At evening when I went to Gorendu for some *ayan*, I found Tui ill again, he had been moving around in the sun during the day, causing a painful abscess on one of his ears. I went back and brought with me a lancet to open the abscess and let pus out. Afterwards Tui told me he felt much better.

Going home in the darkness and stumbling over vines along the pathway, I felt I was becoming Papuan. I thought of it earlier in the morning also, when, feeling hungry during a walk through the jungle, I caught a large crab and ate it raw.

## 8 March

The boat leaked again. It took on almost a bucket of water an hour.

## 9 March

I called at Gorendu where I was provided with breakfast of *ayan* and sago. During February sweet potatoes come to an end, and in March sugarcane disappears also. I was told that soon there would be no *ayan*, but instead *baou* (taro) would appear followed by a species of bean.

## 14 March

The day began with a violent headache, even the slightest noise felt unbearable. The loud cry of a black cockatoo was suddenly heard. I waited a few minutes for it to fly away but losing patience, I went out of the hut with my gun. The bird was perched almost straight above me on a branch about 100 feet high. I thought to frighten the cockatoo into flying off, thus relieving me from its intolerable sound, but I shot it instead. The unexpected and rare quarry made me forget about the headache as I went on dissecting the bird. It measured from the tip of one wing to the other, a metre.

At about noon the headache overcame me completely and I had to lie down. I rested without taking any food until next morning.

## 15 March

At evening on my visit to Gorendu, I saw the results of a big feast the natives had had earlier at Bongu. They had eaten so much that they hardly moved; so overloaded with food, they were unable even to talk. They had barely any strength left in them to stretch on the ground near the fire. I shall never forget that scene.

## 16 March

People from Koliku-mana brought me a pig in return for a gift I gave them, a small mirror with a wooden frame. There were ten natives and I had to give something to everyone, so I handed out to each a small packet of tobacco. My stocks of it were dwindling fast for whenever I met the natives, they asked: "Tobacco, tobacco".

The rumours were still going on about a possible attack from Maragum-mana. I had grown so tired of them that I sometimes wished the attackers would really come.

The natives accepted my presence so heartedly that I felt reluctant about using firearms. Every morning I went out into the forest in search of fresh food. I did not hesitate to eat even a cockatoo and recently I tried the meat of a crow. The natives were very scared of the sound of a gun being fired and were pleased that I did not fire in the vicinity of the village. They were very pleased, however, when they occasionally received from me bird plumage to use for decoration.

### 29 March

My watch stopped yesterday. Intending to get up before daybreak, I retired early to bed. I woke up in the dark assuming that I must have had a long sleep and that it would be time to leave soon. I made tea and cooked some *aous* and bananas in the hot ashes. After breakfast I waited in the dark but no sign of dawn appeared. As I found later, I must have had my breakfast about midnight. It is very inconvenient without a watch.

At Gorendu I met Tui ready to accompany me; we set off about sunrise. First we climbed to Gorendu-mana, then headed south-east through the jungle. We reached the crest of a low ridge covered with tall but open forest, making it easy for us to move through. There were scarcely any birds to be seen, not even the sound of them. After about one hour's journeying, we reached another slope of the ranges covered with tall *unan* (species of grass). From there a beautiful panorama of hills opened out; dark jungle covered ridges and mountains — here and there appeared a light-green grass area covered with *unan*. The distant summits of the higher country were covered with clouds.

Tui hurried ahead down the slopes of the ridge, without giving me much time to admire the view. We descended into a swamp where the tall grass was replaced by reeds and ferns. Distant murmuring sounded ahead of us. Tui explained that we were approaching "big water".

We made our way to the river flowing from south to north for a considerable distance, separating the low coastal ranges from the higher part of the country before meeting the sea near Gumbu. The riverbed looked very wide but dried-up due to lack of rain. It was split into several channels of varying size, forming numerous islands covered chiefly with boulders. The river appeared to be as wide as the Neva at the Petroplavlovsk Fortress, and I counted five channels that had to be crossed in order to reach the other side. In attempting to cross the first of these channels, I felt a strong current pushing me downstream and it was only with the help of Tui's spear, which he held out to me, that I was able to cross onto the shore. We gave up going any further because of the strong current and depth of the water, and I do not swim.

The view from the river bank looked most impressive. I regretted that the hot sun prevented me from making a drawing of the scene. The stones on the little island looked very large, being the remains of a torrential thrust of current during the wet season. Tui told me that there were plenty of fish in the river; the people from Gorendu and Bongu often came here for a good catch.

We set off towards home but by a different route, worn out from travelling through rugged bush and hungry. Tui wandered out into the forest, presumably to cut some bamboo. I waited for him and called out, but, as he failed to return, I headed home on my own. Being no track to follow, I lost my way in the dense *unan*, far higher than myself — moving on was exhaustingly slow and painful. I reached the Garagassi area and known tracks, only with the help of my compass.

## 30 March

After mounting skeletons of a grey crow and red parrot, I made a meal from the meat of both birds. The weather felt as fine as yesterday, about 29°C in the shade; infrequent here. In the evening natives from Gorendu arrived to catch fish near my hut, after asking for my permission to do so. Tui and Bugai sat near me, sending the younger men to do the fishing. At their suggestion Olsson sang them a Swedish song.

Catching fish with lights is very interesting so I sat for a while observing the scene. A native uses all his limbs when fishing. His left hand holds a torch, swinging it in the air; his right hand holds a harpoon to be thrown at the fish; the man stands on his right foot, using his left foot to remove the caught fish from the harpoon. When their fishing was completed, the natives presented me with some of their catch.

## 31 March

I measured out rice and beans to keep us for five months. The rations were small but would help us not to depend on natives for food. In addition, I daily obtained fresh meat by hunting so our life looked reasonably secure.

During the last few days the weather began to change and a light breeze took the place of the north-westerly wind. There was less rain in March than during the preceding months. Black clouds have been building up in the last few days.

There seems to be a shortage of food in the village.

## 2 April

Around 3.00 p.m. I suffered a strong attack of fever and had to lie down throughout the whole evening. During the night we had a most impressive storm, the lightning frequently lit up the surrounding trees, sea and clouds. The storm engulfed a large area

— distant thunder could be heard almost simultaneously with one clap exploding directly overhead. During all this, my fever attacks continued. It felt draughty in the hut. The roof leaked just above my head, with water dripping on my face. I feared that a gust of wind might tear away the roof. Badly needing some sleep, I took a small dose of morphine.

## 6 April

I was about to set off on a trip to Tengum-mana by boat for an overnight stay, when a storm broke out and the trip had to be postponed.

## 7 April

The mountain village of Tengum-mana was of special interest to me for it is the highest village in the ranges called Mana-boro-boro. I had previously seen some of the villagers from there during their occasional visits to Garagassi. Leaving Olsson to mind the hut, I slung a small haversack over my shoulders — the same haversack I used in my student days at Heidelberg and Jena when I toured parts of Germany and Switzerland. I also packed a light blanket but on the way I became tired and handed some of the gear to Digu to carry for me.

The sun was already setting when we reached Bongu. Most of the villagers there were preparing to go fishing, but some would remain behind because of my visit to make a meal for me. There were also some visitors from Bili Bili and Bongu — we all dined together. The Papuans did not think of lighting any additional fires apart from what was needed for cooking food, and even these were about to go out. The people sat and ate in the dark. Perhaps there may have been difficulty in obtaining a sufficient supply of wood with stone axes. Now and then the people lit a bundle of dry coconut leaves, illuminating their surroundings for a minute or two.

The natives have the good habit of keeping quiet when eating. Bored with sitting in darkness, I walked to the shore to observe the fishing. A native holding a bunch of lit coconut leaves led us to the beach where a dozen or so bright lights were seen on the pirogues, illuminating the foam from the surf. Behind, the horizon appeared to be covered with dark clouds. Above Karkar lightning occasionally flashed with sounds of distant thunder. I joined a group of people sitting on a large tree trunk that had been washed up on the beach. The pirogues, one after another, came towards the shore. The fishermen were kept busy sorting the catch. Boys about nine to ten years of age stood on the platforms in each pirogue, holding torches while the adults piled up the fish.

Well lit, the boys' profiles appeared typically Papuan, more so than the adults with their profiles hidden behind heavy beards. Three features in the young faces could be observed as being characteristic: the high backward sloping skull with a rather flat-looking forehead, the protruding jaw and upper lip, and the thin neck, especially the upper part.

Each fisherman gave me some fish; one even had it baked for me in hot ashes on our return to the village. When I was about to retire to the *buambramra*, five natives accompanied me, eager to see how I would lie down to sleep. The hut owner Lako already had a fire burning and was cooking the freshly cleaned fish. Inside the hut, its roominess made a strange impression on me. The fire burned in the middle of the room; long planks for beds lay against the right wall; long shelves were erected along the left side on which rested several coconuts; above the plank beds hung spears, bows and arrows. From the roof hung a rope attached to four corners of a bamboo basket containing cooked food wrapped in green leaves.

A few coconuts, some baked *ayan* with fish, spears, bow and arrows and three *mal* (loin cloths) — like most Papuans, that was Lako's complete and movable property. Although unmarried, he already had his own hut, something unusual for a single native man. I made my bed by spreading my blanket over the board, placed my haversack under my head, blew up my rubber cushion and took off my shoes — to the great astonishment of the natives. Half the blanket was under me, the other half covering myself. Six extremely curious natives watched my every move. After I closed my eyes, they sat by the fire, whispering so as not to disturb me. Soon I fell asleep.

*8 April*

During the night I was awakened by my bed moving. Lako, who slept on the other end of the plank, had got up to rekindle the fire. He must have felt chilled from the cold air blowing in from outside for the man wore no clothes. Lako made a small fire underneath his part of the plank bed so that the heat passed between the split bamboo to warm his uncovered body. As for myself, the blanket sufficiently protected me from the chilly night air. I heard Lako get up several times during the night to attend to his fire. Occasionally I was also awakened by crying children from a neighbouring hut. A crowing rooster and Lako's chatter finally roused me from my bed. Unable to find any water to wash myself, I walked to the nearby stream. It was still quite dark, so with a burning brand in my hand I found the pathway to the place where the stream entered the sea. Dark clouds had gathered above Karkar and frequent lightning flashes could be seen in the distance; from the east the dawn appeared.

After washing, I took some water back in a bamboo carrier to make my morning tea. The process of making tea surprised Lako and the other Papuans very much. They grouped around me and began to giggle at seeing me drink hot water, assuming it was *ingi* (food) for Maclay. After tea, I went back to the hut. It was still dark, even though I had been up for about an hour. Having no watch with me I decided to lie down again. When I woke it was daylight, so I hurriedly organised myself for the trip. A problem came up — the Bongu people did not want to spend the night at Tengum-mana and I had planned to stay there until the following day. I decided to let the Bongu men go back home as soon as I had arrived, and I would return the following day accompanied by people from Tengum-mana. The problem solved, seven men, instead of two, set off with me.

Passing over the coastal ranges, rising to about 400 feet, we descended to the Gabenau River. It was a very steep descent as the track went straight down without any winding but, with the help of a spear from one of my companions, I made the descent satisfactorily. We stopped at the river bank; the river's torrent roared by, stones rolling along its bed. I undressed, except for my boots, shorts and hat, and distributed my clothes amongst my companions. Having a cord line with me, I gave one end to a native, instructing the man next to him to take the other end across the river. As the man was crossing, the current swung him slightly downstream from its main course, so the rope, about 60 yards in length, fell short of the bank. I instructed the native holding the rope end on the bank to advance along the bank until the rope reached across the water. As I stepped into the river holding the stretched line in one hand, the water, which covered my shoulders, seemed very cold even though the daily temperatures registered 22°C. The stones rolled by the river current kept hitting against my legs but were not big enough to knock me off my feet. Confident that one could cross the river safely, I crossed the three remaining channels without the use of the rope, moving at a slight diagonal. Occasionally a problem occurred when treading the uneven rocky bottom, hidden by murky water.

On reaching the other bank, I was about to put the rest of my clothes on when the natives informed me that we had to cross one more channel. I heeded their advice even though the sun was uncomfortably burning my bare legs. Instead of climbing up the right bank, we went along the river bed, treading our way through water often reaching chest level. Moving on like this for about two hours, I worried about a possible attack of fever, so took some quinine as a counter measure.

Both river banks, covered with jungle vegetation, were high

and often precipitous. On reaching a large sago palm trunk brought down by the last 'big water', Lako told me to dress for there would be no more water to cross on our way. While I dressed, the natives smoked, chewed *betel*, and looked at my boots, socks and hat — making comments that expressed their curiosity. On a stump nearby I noticed some carved figures, probably chiselled by a stone axe and very much like those I had seen during my last outing to the river.

On reaching the right bank of the river, I was shown a narrow track that climbed very steeply. Only with the help of roots and branches to hold onto was I able to reach a part where the track widened and was easier to traverse. The climb was exhausting and I had to halt frequently in order to catch my breath. A difficulty also arose because of the natives' insistence that I head the column; my stopping often held up the natives behind me, who found the climb far less troublesome. No Papuan wished or dared to go in front of me.

Finally, after passing through a broad garden of sugarcane and bananas, we reached the summit. I expected that a villager would appear, but we had to move on still further. At the call of my companions, some voices answered and soon after a group of villagers appeared — some of whom ran away at the sight of me. It took considerable calling and shouting by my companions to bring them back. They timidly approached me but as I stretched out my hand to one of them, he ran back into the bush. It was strange to see all those sturdy men trembling in fear as each gave me his hand, but quickly withdrew it, afraid to look at me.

After the meeting ceremony was completed we walked into the village; I was first and behind me some twenty-five men followed in a line. My appearance in the village caused panic and fear: the men ran away, the women hastily withdrew into their huts closing the doors behind them, children cried; even the dogs ran off howling, with tails tucked between their back legs. Pretending that nothing unusual was happening, I sat down. After a while the inhabitants began to appear again, one after another, from the darkness of their huts. My understanding of Bongu dialect was of not much use here, and only with the help of an interpreter was I able to explain that I would like to stay the night in the village and asked if I could have a hut. I also asked if I could have two *mab* (cuscus), a *dyuga* (cassowary) in exchange for a knife.

After a short discussion the natives took me to a roomy hut. Leaving my belongings there, I set off to tour the village accompanied by a crowd of Papuans. The village was situated on the very saddle of the range. Through the middle stretched a broad 'street' with a line of huts on each side; steep slopes descended behind them, covered with dense greenery. Near the huts grew numerous tall coconut palms, their vigorous growth envied by the natives of neighbouring villages.

In general the huts were smaller than those seen in the coastal villages. They were all erected the same way — oval in shape and consisting almost entirely of roof since the walls on which the roof sat were barely visible. In front of a small doorway was a semi-circular platform protected by the roof and supported by two posts. On that platform the women sat and worked, sheltered from the sun. While I was busy sketching two *telum* and the villagers prepared dinner for their guests, two boys came in with news that *ingi* (food) was ready. The boys were followed by four natives, each carrying a *tabir* — the first one contained grated coconut soaked in coconut milk while the other three contained *baou*. All the food was placed at my feet. Taking a small portion of *monki-lya* (coconut pulp) and some taro, I handed the rest to my companions who soon indulged in it.

Some distance away rested the inhabitants of Tengum-mana, giving me the opportunity to observe their faces as they chatted with the people from Bongu. Among the locals were some faces fitting the descriptive ideal of 'savage man'. Even an artist with the best possible imagination could not have portrayed them better. I was shown a few broken skulls of *mab* but not a single cassowary. It was obvious that the local people were not very keen on hunting and killing animals, except occasionally when the opportunity arose. My companions told the locals some terrifying stories about me — I could burn water, kill with fire, people could fall ill from my look, and so on. In their fear the local people suggested to the Bongu visitors that it might be wise for them to go back home while I remained at Tengum-mana. I was angry with my companions for trying to frighten the local people with stories about me. Later it dawned on me that by trying to portray me as especially powerful, they were at the same time showing what a friend and protector they had on their side.

Frequently asked if I would stay at Tengum-mana or return home, I repeated "yes" before retiring on the plank bed under a semi-circular awning. My rest lasted about an hour when through my sleep I heard the locals farewell the Bongu natives.

In the morning I went for a stroll around the neighbourhood accompanied by a group of natives. After a short walk we came to an elevated spot whence I heard voices and saw a roof surrounded by coconut palms. This was a second part of the village and above it laid a third part, marking the highest point in Tengum-mana. The view from there would have been splendid but was obstructed by extensive vegetation and greenery. To the north-east in the distance extended the sea; to the east, across a deep valley lay Englam-mana; to the west, after a chain of hills, the stony bed of the River Koli was visible; to the south-west stretched a labyrinth of mountains. When I asked the natives about the mountains I got the impression that the only populated area was Englam-mana while the rest was uninhabited, and that as no one ever went there, no tracks were made.

Returning to the village, I looked more closely at the huts. At the entrance of many of them, hung bones, feathers, dog skulls, cuscus, and even human skulls — but without the lower jaw. A rope was stretched across a space between two trees and from it hung several baskets containing gifts from other villages. Englam-mana is abundant with areca palms and *keu*. I put up my small table and brought out my case with paper and drawing equipment; the natives who had gathered around me then stepped back and disappeared. Not knowing their dialect I kept quiet and tried to sketch one of the village huts. Eventually the natives came back and soon sat down, so quietly that I was able to sketch two portraits. One was of the man I had noticed before, resembling our very idea of 'savage'. The 'savageness', however, is not in the facial lines but in the quick changes of expression, and I succeeded in transferring these lines onto my paper, though not as satisfactorily as I would have liked. The other portrait was of a good-looking native who had a less protruding jaw.

For dinner we again received boiled *baou*, bananas and grated coconut. A local man knowing some Bongu dialect decided to be my guide and kept close to me throughout the whole visit. As the *baou* given me was too hot to be eaten, he took each piece of taro in his unwashed hands and blew on them. I hurriedly moved the *tabir* away and suggested that he eat the pieces himself. The other natives stayed close, watching my every movement.

The local natives were far less clean compared to the coastal people. This was partly due to the difficulty in obtaining water, which had to be carried from the nearby river along a steep pathway. When I asked for some water, the natives, after some lengthy discussion, poured some for me from a bamboo container; it looked murky so I declined the drink.

About 6.00 p.m. when the clouds covered the setting sun, it became damp and cold and soon grew dark. We sat in the darkness just as we had yesterday at Bongu. Sitting by the fire, one could barely make out the outline of people only two paces away. I asked for some light so my guide brought me an armful of palm fronds and lit them. The sudden flame illuminated the group of natives who were sitting opposite me smoking *betel*. Among them was a native elder who often called out orders, which were obeyed. I had seen him earlier talking to the men from Bongu and he attended the meals. Although this elder wore nothing special to distinguish him from the others, his manner made me believe that he was the principal man at Tengum-mana. Such men are present in all villages; as far as I could gather, the largest *buambramra* often belong to them, and the other natives group themselves around it to more easily receive instructions.

I was anxious to hear the local people singing so that I might compare their songs with the coastal natives, but as no one decided to strike up Tengum-mana *mum*, I went to bed.

## 9 April

The people gathered in front of my hut stayed there long after I had retired, engaged in debate, and Minem, whom I understood to be the elder, spoke at considerable length. As I was about to fall asleep, the squealing of a pig was heard outside and I saw a group of natives, illuminated by burning bamboos, tying a fairly large pig to a pole. The animal was intended for me. Throughout the night I heard frequent coughing from a nearby hut. Two natives sleeping on plank beds next to mine often arose to rekindle the fire and place some red coals under their beds. I got up at sunrise and wandered around the village, looking for skulls of cuscus and anything else that could be of interest. I collected two human skulls, each without the lower jaw, and *telum* which the local people called *kariya*. I acquired a *telum* with the help of Minem after promising to send the locals some nails and bottles.

After breakfast consisting of boiled taro and coconut, I handed my gear to three native carriers and walked out from under the hut's awning. Gathered in the clearing in front of me was the entire village. The folk formed a semi-circle around two natives bearing a long bamboo sapling on their shoulders, from which hung the pig. Minem the elder, with a green branch in his hand, moved ceremoniously closer to the pig and gave a short speech to the silent crowd. From his speech I gathered that the pig was to be given to Maclay by the inhabitants of Tengum-mana, and that it would be carried by the village men to Maclay's house where Maclay would kill it with his spear; that the pig would squeal and then die; then Maclay would untie it, singe its hair, cut up the meat and feast on it.

Having delivered his speech, Minem tucked his green branch into the vines which fastened the pig to the pole. The people remained silent, awaiting something; it dawned on me that I was expected to say some words. Moving closer to the pig and gathering all my vocabulary of Bongu dialect, I answered Minem and had the pleasure of seeing that he understood my words and was happy with what I had to say. I told him that I came to Tengum-mana not for a pig but to meet the people, and to see their huts and the surrounding mountains; that I would like to have a specimen of *mab* and *dyuga*, and offered a good knife for each (general approval from the people accompanied with the word *essi*); that when back at Garagassi, I would give what I had given to many others — *kanum* (mirrors), to general approval again; that when I ate the pig I would remind myself that the people of Tengum-mana are good people, and if any of them should come to Maclay's house, he would receive tobacco, red cloth, nails and bottles; that if the Tengum-mana men were friendly, Maclay would also be friendly. There was general approval with calls: "Maklai is good — *tamo* Tengum-mana are good." After hand-shakes and calls from the locals of "*E-meme*", I hurriedly left the village as the sun was already rising high.

While passing the last village hut I noticed a small girl trying to loop with her fingers, a length of string with both ends joined. I halted to observe her; smilingly she repeated her play, twisting the string just as children of her age in Europe would do.

Descending from the village over hilly tracks I was supervised by the group of natives accompanying me; all carried spears, bows and arrows. Some carried smouldering fire-sticks so as to smoke along the way — it seemed that they had not yet discovered the way of making fire. Going down, I was taken on a different track from the one I was brought in. The locals knew the route far better than the people of Bongu, and the way seemed shorter and far steeper than the track I came up yesterday. Along the path, near a plantation, was a fallen tree trunk over a metre in diameter. On the side of this, facing the village, were carved figures similar to those I had seen some days ago on a sago palm, though these looked much older.

The carved figures on trees, the similar images at Bongu and on the pirogues at Bili Bili I spoke of earlier, deserve special attention. On the whole they represent the very beginning of script, though still in its ideographic state. A man drawing with charcoal or colour, or carving the figure of his ancestor with an axe, tries to express a thought or portray his beliefs. The figures he creates are not mere ornaments, but have a much deeper meaning. The portrayal of a festive procession at Bili Bili, for instance, was to commemorate the construction and completion of a pirogue. The carvings on the trees are rather crude; consisting of just a few lines, the meaning probably understood only by those people who carved them and by those natives to whom they may be explained.

It was a pleasure to hear the sound of the river. Walking through rough bush the traveller must concentrate on his moves; not let his legs get caught on some vine or stumble over a rock or fall over a tree-trunk concealed in grass, or have his eyes lashed by twigs — all this prevents one from observing the locality. I suddenly realised that we had arrived at the same spot where yesterday we had begun the ascent to Tengum-mana. The view of the river was picturesque.

Stopping to rest and to make a rough sketch of the scenery, I told the natives to go down to the river and wait for me there. The scene, enlivened by the figures of descending Papuans, looked particularly impressive. I counted eighteen men who arranged themselves into several groups to rest. Some lay on the warm sand; others kept busy putting together the fire sticks they had carried, preparing to sit down to chew and smoke betel. Some of the men were bending over the river to drink its muddy water, while others, not parting with their weapons, stood on large rocks leaning on their spears — vigilantly and anxiously watching the other banks. I learned later that the inhabitants of Tengum-mana were in conflict, a kind of protracted war, with the natives of

Gadabi-mana. They were all armed and some had to stay on guard while the others rested.

Lost in contemplation of the picture around me, I forgot to draw. My unprofessional artistic skill produced an imperfect and pale copy of the unique scene. On going down to the river, I took off my clothes as I did yesterday and walked into the water. The sun felt scorching and the stones over which I had to step bruised my feet till they bled.

Two incidents enlivened our crossing. Noticing a lizard sunbathing on a rock and knowing that I collected various animals, a native crept up and threw himself on it, but the lizard slipped away. Then some ten Papuans set out after it, hurriedly pulling reeds, turning stones and burrowing into the earth with their bare hands in the hunt for the creature. One man seized the lizard by the neck and handed it to me, but apart from a handkerchief, I could find nothing to keep it in. While I was tying it up, the lizard bit one of Papuans, drawing blood with the bite, but it did not get away.

While crossing one of the river channels, the natives noticed a large number of small fish swiftly gliding among the rocks. The men picked up some stones and threw them at the fish and to my surprise they hit their targets. The dead or wounded fish were picked up, wrapped in broad leaves and kept for dinner.

Today we had to move further down the river than yesterday, for I intended going straight home and not to Bongu or Gorendu. I reached home about 4.00 p.m. to find Olsson pale and shaking, suffering from an attack of fever because he had not taken quinine in time. I was very displeased to learn that, in my absence, Tui had spent the night at Garagassi (probably invited by Olsson). Groups of natives from Gorendu, with their guests from Bili Bili, arrived for a visit. About forty of them were crowded, chattering, into my hut. I gave tobacco and a piece of red cloth to each visitor. To one of them I gave a mirror in exchange for a pig. I traded some bottles and several large nails for *telum*, and then they left for Tengum-mana, all very pleased.

Having had no food for the last ten hours, I drank tea without sugar and ate baked *ayan* with the utmost pleasure.

## 10 April

Throughout the night I felt pain in one of my legs and when getting up in the morning I noticed a swelling of the leg and three small sores full of pus. This was the price I paid for having crossed the river yesterday. I was unable to put my boots on and the pain of any movement made me stay at home. I asked the natives from Bongu to tie up the pig that I had brought back yesterday, as I did not want it slaughtered immediately.

## 12 April

The two days' rest at home had a favourable effect on my leg. I felt it was in a fit state again and, after Olsson slaughtered the Tengummana pig, I carried a portion of the pork as a present to the people of Gorendu. The pig was too much for two of us to eat, and not wishing to bother with salting it, instead I followed local custom and took half of the meat to friends in Gorendu and Bongu. Although the gift was intended for only three of my friends there, women were called from neighbouring huts to clean and cook *ayan* and *baou* for the whole community to feast upon.

Resting in the cool of a *buambramra* I noticed an old *telum*, its body shaped like a human but with a crocodile head. Later I took note of preparations for the Papuan dish *kale* which I saw for the first time. The dish consisted of grated and lightly roasted coconut ground up with *baou* and *ayan* — all very tasty.

Papuan children are taught early in life to help in the household. Even a one- or two-year-old boy is seen dragging a large piece of wood to the fire and then running to his mother to suck her breast.

I again had the opportunity to see details of how the Papuans prepare *keu*. The beverage is sometimes drunk by women as well.

## 14 April

Several men arrived from Bongu seeking medicine — one suffered from bad legs, another brought me a sample of a pipe that I had earlier ordered from him, and the rest came with coconuts.

Handing me a long bamboo tube, one visitor told me not to show *ai* to women or children. The tube was actually a musical instrument he said, and it would be bad for them to see it. As the natives here kept all their musical instruments hidden from women, the *ai* is always played outside the village, but I have not yet been told the reasons behind this.

## 15 April

The weather is changing with frequent calm periods, a light south-easterly wind, cloudy sky. My hut is so small that unless I carry out strict practices and daily put everything in its place, there would be no room for me to sit. The regular tidying up is very tedious, causing considerable loss of time.

## 16 April

On arriving at Gorendu this morning I was met by two women from another village who were visiting the wives of Tui and Bugai. On her back each carried a large bag with gifts of *baou* and *ayan*. The bags were held by strips around the forehead and the load was so heavy that neither woman could talk or stand without bending forward. Both visitors were made very welcome by the Gorendu women who held their hands and stroked their shoulders. When greeting each other, Papuan women give one another a hand or three fingers. From the shoulders and the chests of the visiting women, and stretching down towards their waists, were lines of tattooed dots in a colour lighter than their skin. But not all women were marked like this.

## 17 April

I witnessed in Gumbu today how, with the aid of a simple shell and splinters of flint, the Papuans made combs from bamboo. The upper part of the comb is decorated with traditional designs engraved skilfully with a splinter of flint. I copied some of the designs. To successfully cut a small comb with primitive tools, a Papuan must spend almost half a day.

Lately I have had to take up regular hunting since our daily intake of food had become inadequate. Normally I had a glass of coffee in the morning with a small quantity of *taro* (boiled or baked) and some beans; for dinner, *taro* and a cup of tea. Hunting is easy here since the birds, still unfamiliar with firearms, are not timid and allow hunters to come very near.

I experimented with the effect of *keu* on myself. After scraping the root and stem of *Piper methysticum* with a knife and cutting the leaves, I placed the scrapings into a glass filled to the brim with water. I left this for about one hour, then strained the wet mass several times through a cloth. The squeezed-out greenish liquid had a bitter but not unpleasant taste; however, I felt no particular effect from drinking it.

## 19 April

It rained heavily all night and morning. My rain gauge showed 480 points.

## 20 April

On arriving at Gorendu I sat on a *barla* waiting dinner; with nothing to do I picked up an arrow I saw on the ground and noticed that its end had been broken. I took out my knife to sharpen it, thinking that the natives who had to rely solely on flint would need to put in considerable effort and time to do the same work. Vangum, who was standing nearby, explained that the arrow had been broken when it was aimed at a *mab*. When I asked if they had killed the *mab* he answered: "No, it is in the hut." I went in, actually climbed in, since the doorway was so small, and in the half-dark noticed something white hanging from the roof — which proved to be the *mab* tied firmly by the tail. Wishing to inspect the *mab* more closely, I asked if the animal could be brought out of the hut. Using a shell Vangum cut the vine tied to the animal's tail, but the *mab* held on with its forepaws; even when Vangum pulled its tail with both his hands, it clung there with its strong sharp claws buried in the wood. Before I could prevent him, Vangum violently struck the forepaws of the *mab* with a stout stick; the animal lost its grip and was pulled down. Holding it by the tail so as not to be bitten, Vangum threw the animal out of the hut where I followed after it. Poor injured animal, its mouth gaped fiercely at each of my movements to show long teeth and a reddish tongue, but it made no attempt to run away. The animal was greyish-white in colour and about 50 centimetres long; its fur was soft and thick but short. Its body was so fat that it had difficulty standing on its short legs which had long curved claws. When it had gathered enough courage the *mab* attempted to run, but it made only a few clumsy movements over the level ground before it gave up. Being unable to run may have resulted from the blows on the animal's forelegs by the stick, or from the arrow wound.

Wishing to acquire the *mab* I offered a knife for it, which the Papuans would normally consider to be a very good price. But when I asked to whom I should give the knife, it turned out that no native could claim ownership. The animal was first sighted that morning by two natives as it descended from a tree in the village area. When they rushed to catch the frightened *mab*, it saw no other escape route and had climbed up a palm tree. Then about half the village had gathered around, taking part in the hunt. One Papuan threw an arrow, wounding the animal in the neck; another native climbed up the tree and threw the animal down. The villagers then decided to eat the *mab* together and prepared a fire to burn off the thick fur. My proposal confused them. Each

Papuan wanted to receive a knife but felt reluctant to say "It is my animal". Instead they said that the Gorendu children would cry if they did not receive some meat from the animal. I felt certain that if I were to take the animal and carry it home, not one native would dare to object but that would be unjust, so I said, "Let the people of Gorendu eat the meat, but I will take the head." Happy at this turn of events the Papuans rushed to help me. With a blunt knife I sawed at the neck of the poor animal, which did not utter even a cry during such barbaric slaughter.

Later, when washing the blood off my hands, I remembered that I should have cut off the fore and hind legs, but the *mab* was already on the fire and the parts I hastily collected were partly charred. I managed, however, to save part of the prehensile tail; it looked much like a long finger covered with warty growths, making it possible for the animal to hold on to the branches.

## 21 April

I made a drawing of the snout, legs and tail of the *mab*, then mounted the skull. The specimen appeared to be different from the one obtained in Tengum-mana which had black fur with yellow spots. After extracting the brain I made a drawing of it. While occupied with all this I heard a rustle. A large lizard about a metre and a half long had found its way under the verandah, scavenging for scraps of *mab* that I had thrown away after mounting the skull. While I reached for my gun the lizard ran across the clearing in front of the house and disappeared into the jungle. I moved forward and heard a strange sound above me. High up in the branches I sighted the beautiful crest of a black cockatoo. The bird must have seen me and flew off with a cry into the jungle. At about the same time I heard the sound of a falling *kengara* nut (*Canarium commune*).

Walking around the tree I saw another cockatoo perched even higher on a branch while biting through the hard shell of a nut. I chanced firing a shot and the big bird, flapping one of its wings, fell to the ground. Wounded, the cockatoo thrashed its wings and clawed the ground. Gripped in the bird's beak was a stick of bamboo about three centimetres in diameter which it shredded into splinters. The cockatoo finally fell on its back, opened its beak wide and gasped. After a prolonged struggle the bird closed the whole orifice of its mouth, using its tongue like some adaptable valve. This phenomenon is also seen in some other birds, and is important during flight. The bird died soon after and I hurried to prepare the skeleton. After measuring the distance between the tips of the wings, I carefully mounted the beautiful crest and pulled out the tail feathers, often used by the natives for decoration. The feathers were very impressive — a dull black colour blended with blue.

In spite of an attack of fever, I went on carefully preparing the skeleton. The weight of the flesh cut off was about two pounds while the weight of the whole bird amounted to four-and-a-half pounds. The minced pieces of bird-flesh provided us with a coconut-cup size each of good soup. I must confess that our crockery was more and more being replaced by primitive vessels that proved to be more practical as they did not break like porcelain or china. I made several cups from coconut shell to replace broken dishes and plates.

## 23 April

Visiting Gumbu I found the natives occupied with the weaving of a large basket intended for catching fish. Their craft-work looked impressive and was sturdily made. The basket was woven out of bamboo in a rather unusual shape, and the several women and girls engaged in its making were using not only their fingers but their toes as well.

Feeling an attack of fever on the way, I hurried home and lay down. The attack seemed stronger than usual. I recovered by about 6.00 p.m. but felt exhausted.

## 25 April

Had an attack of fever again yesterday. The weather was fine throughout the day but it rained heavily at night. No sign of the south-easterly wind yet.

## 26 April

A pirogue from Bili Bili arrived at Bongu yesterday. From early morning today a crowd of natives, with whom I was already acquainted, was lounging about in front of my hut. Among them, however, were four men from the village of Rai located on the south-east area of the bay some distance beyond the river, and it was the first time that I had seen inhabitants from that part of the coast. By their appearance and ornaments, they seemed be no different from other local people.

Kain asked me to sharpen his small axe. Some time ago I gave him a piece of discarded metal from a broken box and he had made a handle, much like the ones Papuans use for their stone axes, and fitted in the piece of iron instead of stone. He fastened it to the handle the same way as he would the stone blade. He had attempted to sharpen it on stone but was unsuccessful — so the axe was brought to Garagassi. Judging by this and similar examples, I felt positive that the natives would gladly take and use European implements without any hesitation.

My guests stayed for a while and before leaving for Bili Bili, asked me about my *taboo* that killed birds perched in the tops of trees and could kill people as well, as the news about it had spread at Bongu and Gorendu. They wanted to see the *taboo* and the way I fired it, so that they could pass on the news among the villages further on. The men from Rai-mana were very afraid and pleaded with me not to fire it, but other braver men in the crowd made them feel ashamed; to settle the matter, I agreed to a demonstration.

When I brought out the gun the Papuans huddled close to

each other like a flock of sheep. Many of them gripped each other's hands, expecting something terrible to happen. As I fired the shot they all collapsed on the ground with their limbs shaking in terror. It was some time after I had put down the gun before a few of them dared to look towards me, raising their heads a little and taking their hands from their ears. It was interesting to observe the expressions of fear on their faces — their mouths hanging half open, their tongues moving but unable to utter any words. Their eyes were wide open and hands trembling as they tried to tell me to take the terrible weapon back into the hut.

Coming out of the hut again I found the natives occupied in discussion, convincing one another that they ought to leave my place as soon as possible. I tried to calm them, explaining that my gun was only lethal for bad people, but for good men like them I had tobacco, nails and much else. Without witnessing it personally, I would have had difficulty in believing such fear of the gun by grown-up men. I noticed, however, that their fear was of short duration and they soon relaxed. After they left I took my gun into the jungle where I came across three natives. One of them was playing a Papuan flute consisting of a single piece of bamboo with both ends plugged, but with two holes on one side, one above the other. Two other natives were hacking with their stone axes at a thick old stump — chips flying in all directions. Out of the rotten wood crawled fat white grubs.

When the chopping was done the Papuans gathered the grubs, hastily pushing them into their mouths with both hands. After this feast the flautist took up his flute again and the others their axes. They all looked happy, cheered by the sound of the flute. At various periods throughout the year, different instruments and tunes become popular among the natives — each connected with the availability of a certain food coming into season and with the gathering and consuming of it. When eating *baou* the natives play *tyumbin* (a bamboo flute) but when feasting on pork they blow on large bamboo pipes accompanied by the beating of *barum* … and so on.

## 29 April

On approaching Bongu I noticed a large pirogue drawn up on the beach. It looked exactly the same as those constructed at Bili Bili. The vessel belonged to people from Graged who, on seeing me, asked me to join them; even though they were meeting me for the first time, they all knew my name. Amongst them and the inhabitants of Mitebog I met some very sympathetic faces. The facial expression of some young Papuans is gentle and soft, and could be envied by many of us from the so-called "civilised" world. My neighbours from the local villages had more severe looks and a less courteous manner. There are transitional types between islanders and the people who live in the mountain villages. While the locals were preparing dinner for me, I turned my attention to the making of large bamboo combs. A simple shell is used as the sole implement and I admired the craft, the skill and the patience of the natives in making them.

A group of boys and girls of about ten years of age, completely naked, were dragging along a dry palm frond to be used for roofing. The girls, with their long torsos and short legs, contrasted sharply with the long-legged figures of the boys.

When the visitors from the islands of Graged and Mitebog were about to leave, I noticed among the gifts they received from the Bongu villagers was not only a large quantity of taro, but also an empty bottle and three nails in the baskets. Thus articles of European origin moved from one place to another, their presence would perhaps lead to misunderstanding should they be "discovered" by some future explorers.

## 30 April

On returning from a successful hunt with six large birds killed in an hour, I went to Gumbu, eager to drink some coconut milk. On my way there I noticed several trees with ancient carved figures. On reaching Gumbu I found not a single soul in the village —

even the dogs were absent. Olsson was very pleased with what I had shot, telling me that he often felt hungry; I often feel that way myself. The pumpkin seeds that I gave the Papuans some months ago are now bearing and Tui and Lalu called in the morning to invite me to visit them for a 'pumpkin feast' dinner. I was surprised that they remembered the name and that the word 'pumpkin' had found its way into the Papuan language.

At Gorendu I found Bonem and other natives making a sail for a pirogue. The work did not look particularly intricate: strings made from plant fibre were stretched at frequent intervals between two posts and one of the men, using a shell implement, cut into a pandanus leaf, trimming off the thorny edges. Perhaps two long strips were obtained from each leaf and these strips were then interwoven between the stretched strings. More men arrived to join the group, bringing with them from the jungle, long straight poles with their branches and twigs carefully removed. The bark was skilfully peeled from the wood in one piece, then turned over and carefully stripped of the outer layer before being beaten on a flat stone with a stick. In the meantime two natives inspired the working men with the sounds of the *tyumbin*.

Tui called on me to learn how the locals should prepare pumpkin for a meal. I cut it up, placed the pieces in a pot with water and then left it to cook. The Papuans crowded around, anxious to see how I liked the food. Even though I dislike pumpkin, I tried to demonstrate my enjoyment of what I was consuming and so let the villagers taste the new food without any prejudice. This new food, so special for the natives, was combined with grated coconut and the whole pumpkin was soon consumed.

4 *May*

The beating of *barum* was heard from Bongu throughout the night. At midday several natives arrived to invite me to eat some pork and enjoy the sound of their singing, and rather than offend my hosts I accepted their invitation.

The village appeared devoid of men; only a few women and children could be seen there. Then in the forest clearing, a prolonged cry sounded from all sides, and people began to call me to take part in the gathering. I selected a place on one side in order to give me a better view of what was going on. Several men were busy preparing the food; other Papuans sat on the ground chewing *keu,* its impact beginning to show in their faces. Most of the natives were sitting down idly engaged in conversation, often mentioning the names *Anut* and *tamo Anut.* I was not able to remember exactly where those mentioned resided but vaguely recalled that they were from somewhere beyond the river or around Maragum-mana, occupying an area that included several villages. I was told by my neighbours that those people wanted to attack my Garagassi hut since they had heard that I possessed many knives and loin cloths, and that there were only two of us living there. Confident that this was impossible without the approval of my friends from Bongu and Gumbu, I considered this to be some kind of joke, adding that the attacks would harm not me, but the intruders. I then quickly changed the topic, asking would anybody like to accompany me to Englam-mana. The people told me that they were not on good terms with Englam-mana and if they went there, they were likely to be killed. However, the inhabitants of Gumbu were free to go there.

When the food was ready to be served, a Papuan ran through the village as if bringing some important news; soon after that a *barum* was heard. The people in the feasting area began to yell with all their strength and some of them sounded their instruments, but the noise they made was the sound of pleasure.

The influence of *keu* was quite obvious on some of the locals. They stood rather unsteadily on their legs and had little control over their tongues and limbs. Their faces had that expression the Germans would call *katzenjammer.* On the occasion of such a feast, the Papuans often painted their faces; some of the natives had their entire heads smeared with black, others used a red colour.

**6 May**

I went to Gorendu in the evening where my friend Ingo drew the figures of humans and animals for me in my notebook. I was quite surprised by the decisive movements of the pen, considering that he had never held such an instrument in his hand before.

Only today, the end of the eighth month of my arrival, I learned the Papuan words for 'father', 'mother' and 'son' — all in the Bongu dialect.

I used the arrival of four natives to help me pull my dinghy further up on the beach. We did so with the aid of a big log placed under the dinghy. With Olsson's help we carried the log about 20 yards before we reached an area of clear beach, and then rolled the log before us. Surprised at our strength, the four natives tried to carry the log on their own, but struggled to reach the dinghy. The natives seemed hesitant to apply much effort and made a considerable noise, encouraging each other to press on with the work. This seemed to help them achieve the strength they required.

**14 May**

Today I had many visitors from Englam-mana, Yambomba, Tuti, Bili Bili and other places. They brought me a rich meal from Gorendu consisting of boiled taro, baked breadfruit, sago and shredded coconut. I am still troubled with infected wounds on my legs, limiting my ability to move about.

The natives from Gorendu, very seriously, asked me today to stop the rain that had been so troublesome to all. When I informed them I was unable to do so, they nonetheless persisted that I could surely do it, but only if I wished to.

**23 May**

Tui arrived from Bogatim and I learned from him that many Papuans from neighbouring villages had gathered because one of the villagers had died. He went on to explain that this was the reason why, the previous day, we had heard the occasional sound of the beating *barum*. According to Tui, that was the practice when a man died; when a woman died, however, the *barum* is not sounded. Bua brought me a *mab* (possum) which I took in exchange for a knife. After I prepared the skeleton, I gave the extracted meat to Olsson who prepared it for the pot. He especially liked *mab* meat for its sweet taste and a strong flavour.

### 25 May

At sunrise I heard *barum* sounds from Gorendu, but not with its usual persistence. Tui explained to me that the *barum* was announcing the death of a villager from Gumbu; it was obvious that the natives were not sure whether or not I should have been informed. After some consultation, it had been decided that they would withhold any more news of the occasion.

We headed towards the coastal area where we caught up with a group of women, many of whom were carrying toddlers in bags or on their shoulders depending on the age of the child. We stopped at the approach to the village as I was told that the women must go ahead. We let them move on and soon heard their cries of lament, sounding much like the howling of the neighbourhood dogs.

Approaching the first hut, I was warned by the native next to me that I must be cautious, as an arrow or a spear could hit me. In a clearing surrounded by huts, a cry was heard, mixed with other human sounds. The group of natives near me, holding bows and arrows in their left hands and spears in their right, ran forward into the clearing to face a group of natives already there. I selected a spot that gave me both a vantage point from which to view the situation and some safety from stray spears and arrows.

Between the two groups of natives — defenders and attackers facing each other — there came a man from Gumbu, most likely a relative of the dead man. He made a very loud speech, accompanying his words with strong gestures and threatening the attacking group with his spear. Occasionally, from the opposing group appeared a man who was more virulent with his lungs than with his spear and arrows. Some of the villagers resorted to using their arrows and spears, but fortunately no one was hit. The situation seemed somewhat disorganised.

The natives did not act in groups but individually; each time a man emerged from one group, he would be faced by an opponent from the other. Observing this war game, I admired the physique of the Papuan — what grace and elegance as they moved! The warriors watched me with some mistrust as I was, after all, an uninvited guest. Finally, when the war games were over, they sat down in the clearing, the women and children behind them, and began to smoke and chat as on an ordinary occasion.

Some of the men were engaged in preparing what looked to be a 'Papuan coffin'. They brought an armful of palm fronds and joined these with vines into a large sheet. Then they used several pieces of the green sheeting folded together to form a box secured by more vines, making a coffin shape where the dead body might be placed. The natives did not hurry; while they worked they chatted and smoked. The crying from the hut where the dead man was kept became louder from time to time. Nearby, in a big cauldron, *baou* was being cooked. The hot food was then wrapped in broad leaves and tied among the branches of a tree near the hut, where there also hung a slaughtered dog. I was told that the food would be consumed later by guests.

A group of men went into the dead man's hut and moments later came out carrying the corpse, placed in a sitting position so that the dead man's cheeks were almost touching his knees. The head was bowed and the hands almost concealed between the body and the bent legs. The body was bound by the dead man's waistband so that his limbs were held in the appropriate position. The corpse was carried by three villagers, two of whom supported it from the sides and the third one actually carried the dead man.

A group of women, among whom were his mother and wife, joined the procession. Both females were smeared with black; they wore no ornaments and even their clothing seemed meagre, barely covering their bodies. This modest attire was to show that they had no time or inclination to decorate themselves, and both chanted a traditional lament. As the dead man was carried out, the crowd was silent for the remainder of the grieving rituals.

The dead man was placed in his coffin box in the middle of the clearing and his head covered with a *telrun* (plaited bag), similar to the one used by women to carry their babies. Then the flaps of the box were folded and tied with vines so that it formed a pyramid shape, and the vines holding the coffin together were tied to a large pole. While this preparation was taking place, a number of villagers came forward to place dried coconuts and a newly decorated girdle near the funeral box. Two men placed the ends of the pole on their shoulders and carried the dead man back into his hut. A third native collected the coconuts and girdle, and followed them. Thus, the ceremony came to an end. I went inside the hut, anxious to learn if the body would be buried or left to lie there. The box was actually raised up, tied to an overhead beam and left there.

On my way home I caught up with a group of natives who followed me to Garagassi, in the hope that they might get some broken glass from me to use for their shaving.

## 29 May

Even though burdened by headache and giddiness, I decided to go on with my visit to Gumbu, and journey from there the following morning to Englam-mana. Taking a dose of quinine, I set out on the trip accompanied by three lads from Gumbu who carried my baggage and equipment.

Following the shore line, I reached Gumbu at about dusk to find a group of young people awaiting me at the entrance to the village. They called: "*Maklai gena!*" (Maclay has arrived!) and "*E-*

*meme*". They took my baggage from the lads and led me to the village centre where I found a large group of natives enjoying their evening meal; *tamo* (adult men) sat on *barla* while *malassi* (young men) sat on the ground. The locals, as I knew, had their meal in honour of the dead villager; the men ate pork for the occasion while the *malassi* were served with *baou*. Being *tamo boro*, both an adult and a guest, I was provided with a large *tabir* of taro and a piece of pork. On a mat near the fire lay Kum who asked me for help, explaining that he had pain in the side of his body and stomach. I provided him with a few drops of opium (feeling better the following day, he complimented me and my medicine).

After dinner the entire village gathered around me. We sat in the dark, in the absence of a fire and moonlight. The locals asked me about Russia, anxious to know about houses, pigs and much else in my village. Later the conversation turned to the moon, now seen in the sky, which they had confused with Russia. They wanted to know whether there were any women on the moon and how many of them I had there; they asked about the stars, had I visited some of them, and so on. They listened carefully to each of my words. It was getting cold and damp and I wanted to rest, so I was led to a large *buambramra* belonging to Olum, the local villager who would accompany me the following day.

About half the *buambramra* was occupied by a wide plank bed; much of the remaining space was taken up by two large *barum*, leaving little room for humans. Feeling a slight chill from sitting outside, I was pleased to have everything necessary in my luggage to make a good cup of tea. A fire was already going in the hut and without waiting too long I obtained boiling water. After lighting a candle to see in the semi-darkness, I found a clean board and spread a cloth on which to place my teapot, biscuits, a glass and a spoon. The setting out of all that equipment surprised the natives so much that they were speechless for a while — gazing intently at each of my movements. By now I was quite accustomed to being courteously observed by the wide-open eyes of natives and took no notice of their presence, but hurried to finish my hot drink before retiring to bed. As I spread my blanket over the *barla*, the villagers expressed astonishment at the red colour and the softness of it. About six of them remained in the hut and chatted long after I went to bed. The village sank into the silence of the night and I fell asleep.

I was awoken by a rustling sound; as it was too dark in the hut to see anything I turned over and dozed off. In my sleep I felt a movement of my bed, as though someone else was on it. Surprised by the boldness of the intruder, I stretched out my hand to ascertain that someone was indeed lying beside me! Soon I touched a human hand, which then grasped mine. It was a woman, no doubt, and suspecting that her close relatives were involved in her coming to my bed, I immediately tried to see her out; she clung to my hand. I rose up, making it clear that I wanted only to sleep, but lacking sufficient Papuan words, I declared: "*Ni gle, Maklai nangeli avar aren!*" (Go away, Maclay needs no woman).

After my uninvited visitor had slipped out of the hut, I went back to the *barla*, but before falling asleep again I heard rustling accompanied by whispering voices outside. This convinced me that indeed the relatives of my unknown visitor had taken part in bringing her in. The following day I kept silent about the incident.

Although I got up at about 5.00 a.m. it was nearly two hours before we were ready to leave — by then the sun was already high. I divided my baggage between the two natives to carry; although not eight kilos for each of them, they complained about the heavy load.

We made our first stop near a small river. I had the scraps from yesterday's dinner with me and offered to share these with my companions. They declined, explaining that the pork was cooked with *taro*, eaten only by grown-up men, and if *malassi* touched the food they would become ill. The lads sounded serious, convincing me as it had on some earlier occasions, that *taboo* was practiced here as it is among Polynesians.

Ahead stretched the most difficult part of our journey — a constant climb up steep slopes covered with tall *unan* that pricked our faces with its thorny twigs. To protect their bare bodies, the natives walked ahead, each holding a branch in front of himself. The track was obscured by bushes, but we could feel the path under our feet and thus were able to follow it; as soon as we passed, the thorny *unan* branches would close behind us. As we climbed higher, the native huts of Englam-mana began to be revealed and soon the whole panorama opened up. Some distant islands off Cape Duperrey appeared also and the coast line at Gumbu stretched to the north-east. The course of the Gabenau and some other rivers were visible.

While I was occupied with sketching the view, my companions kept shouting to attract the attention of people working in the local native gardens, and some female voices answered. The native lads shielded me with their bodies, obscuring me from a woman who came forward to meet us. As the woman came close, my companions moved aside. The woman, who had never seen a white man before, halted stiffly in front of me as though rooted to the ground, unable to speak or cry out for a moment. She eventually recovered her senses, and then all the women began to run for their lives down the hill to the amusement of my companions. The youngest women dared to look back, but stumbled on the rough ground and fell. My companions shouted something which encouraged her to rise quickly; screaming, she followed the others.

Moving on uphill, we reached a small grove. After exchanging several words with the other natives, Obor broke off a branch and uttered some words over it. Then, walking behind our backs, he struck each of us with the branch. After this, he broke the branch into small pieces and buried them under dry leaves in the bush.

Unable to make fire, the Papuans go on a journey carrying their firebrands, especially when they travel long distances. On this occasion two of my companions had carried fire, but on learning that I could make fire any time it was needed, they disposed of this burden. I had demonstrated to them earlier, when we stopped for an occasional rest, how to obtain fire by lighting a match. I let them kindle a small fire to dry the tobacco they carried wrapped in green leaves, and it gave them the opportunity to inspect the match.

On hearing the calls of my companions, the inhabitants of Englam-mana came forward; on noticing me among the party, they timidly slowed down their approach. After the usual greetings, followed by chewing and smoking of *betel*, we proceeded. The pathway we moved on turned into a stairway made of roots and stones. Occasionally it traversed such steep terrain that the natives struck their spears into the ground between the stones, to give their feet purchase and save them from slipping. Here and there we walked over narrow bamboo footbridges spanning small ravines and crevasses; by destroying such passages, access to a village could be cut off.

I felt great relief on reaching the village after ten hours of strenuous journeying. On arrival, I immediately asked for a young coconut to quench my thirst. Unfortunately, only mature nuts were available, the milk in which is undrinkable, and so the natives offered *betel* instead and asked if I would like some *keu*.

After a short rest I took a walk through the village accompanied by a large procession. The native huts here looked relatively small, like the ones I saw earlier at Tengum and Koliku-mana. This village, like other mountain villages, seemed to be dirtier than those on the coastal area. Knowing that I was interested in *telum*, the locals led me into several huts and I was surprised to see much larger numbers of *telum* than the few seen on the coast; I sketched some of them. Whenever I stopped I was offered *areca* nuts, plentiful in Tengum and Englam-mana. On returning to my hut I noticed that the locals were preparing dinner for me. The sun was setting, so I chose a place near the fire and sat down to enjoy my meal. Around me gathered the entire male population of Englam-mana, and my companions sitting next to me told the locals about me. They even mentioned trivial details I could barely remember. Much of what was said was hearsay, passed on by word of mouth, one to another — stories about how I came from moon, could turn water into flames, could kill birds high up in the trees, and much else.

## 31 May

I woke before dawn trying to think of the best way to carry on my observations without disturbing the natives. As I got up I groaned and began to rub my legs. My companions asked if I were not feeling well, and I told them I had sore legs. They, too, began to groan, repeating the words "*sambo borle*" (leg hurts). I waited a while, then said: "Maklai has good water — rub the legs, pain go away," and they all got up to see what was going to happen. Taking out my hypsometer, I poured in some water from a flask, lit the lamp, and then adjusted the scale of the instrument. After making the appropriate measurement of the height and temperature of the local area, I wrote the figures in my notebook, discharged the used water into a glass and placed the instrument back in my bag. The natives observed my every movement. I took off one of my socks, rubbed my legs and then poured water on them from the glass, telling the Papuans that the pain should soon go away. They all sat around me, anxious to see the miracle of healing.

About ten minutes later, I carefully stood on my legs and then began to move slowly about while packing my belongings; afterwards I walked out from the hut to the great surprise of the natives, who saw that I was completely healed. They went through the village telling about the 'miracle' they had seen. The news of the 'miracle' attracted scores of sick people who called on me for help, expecting a speedy recovery with the magic of my water. I showed them my empty flask and told them they must come to Garagassi where I would provide them with medicine.

As the natives dispersed, I was left in peace to make a drawing of the hut where I had stayed overnight. Although the hut stood on a rise apart from the other village dwellings and was erected on a bald rock, it was structurally hardly different from the other huts. The eaves on both sides of the roof came down very low —

almost touching the ground. There was a low, narrow door (more like a window than a door) where on each side stood several *telum*, some the size of humans. Above the door hung cassowary bones, the skulls of pigs and dogs, skins of lizards, feathers of big birds, teeth of various animals, and beaks of *Buceros*. All these, together with the *telum* and the roof above overgrown with grass, gave the hut a unique character. There were four *telum*, but one especially attracted my attention. It was the biggest and was slightly different from the others as it held its hands in front of its chest, and carried a board engraved with irregular grooves resembling hieroglyphic symbols, old and much decayed.

Above the plank beds inside the hut was a ceiling made of split bamboo, from where hung various musical instruments to be used at the time of special ceremony *ai*. Talking in whispers to demonstrate secrecy, the natives showed me an old *ain* (wooden mask) with openings cut out for eyes and mouth, worn at the time of *ai*.

In the rear of the hut stood three large *barum*, large pots and a big *tabir*, together with three more *telum* stored on shelves. Lined up under the roof hung the bones of birds, turtles, fish and cuscus, all blackened from smoke and presumably the remains of some big feast that had taken place in the hut.

Unexpectedly, it began to rain heavily before I could finish my drawing or drink my tea. Unable to go home I had to shelter under the roof. While waiting for the rain to cease, I made a portrait of a Papuan with the most interesting features. The local inhabitants are of different height; their skin looks slightly lighter than the people from coastal areas and I saw ugly faces more frequently than I had in the coastal villages. The women had a rather sad appearance — after bearing their first child, they looked neglected.

I was informed that the inhabitants of the neighbouring village Sambul-mana, located north-east from here, were coming to meet me and they arrived soon after the rain had eased off. I came out into the village centre to greet them. I pressed their hands and indicated a place for each visitor to sit in a semi-circle around me. The moment I looked at any one of them, he would quickly turn away and look aside until I had moved my eyes to another person or object. Then he looked at me in turn, examining me in detail from head to foot. The inhabitants of Sambul-mana are similar to the villagers of Englam-mana and Tengum-mana, although they seemed to suffer more from elephantiasis and skin diseases, including smallpox. Englam dialect differs slightly from the dialects of Sambul and Tengum, so I wrote down some corresponding words from each of the dialects.

After a short rest I strolled through the neighbouring jungle and found that the tracks seemed even rougher than those of yesterday. I saw several birds I had not seen in the coastal area. After the rain a multitude of bird calls could be heard, but most were unknown to me. It seemed that the ornithological fauna was different here from that in the coastal area.

Driven by hunger I returned to the village. One of the first villagers I met on my return asked me if I ate chicken. I told him I did. They soon brought out two fowls, smashed their heads against the nearest tree, and then singed off their feathers instead of plucking them. They also brought out bundles of taro and started cleaning these. All the food was a present from individual villages as I was the guest of all the communities. One man cleaning taro asked me for a knife. Having no experience with it, the man used the knife clumsily and almost cut his hand instead of the vegetable, after which two natives began to make a bamboo knife. After selecting a piece of bamboo, they cut both ends with a stone axe and split it into thin strips. They then heated the strips on red coals and the dried bamboo became so hard that one could easily cut not just the soft taro, but meat or excess hair as well. I was witness to that when one villager accidentally stepped in a puddle, splashing some mud on the head of another native. The man who caused the incident took a bamboo knife and cut off a large lock of the muddied hair before the poor owner could object. Later I saw the natives using a similar knife as a bamboo razor while shaving the head of a young girl. It was done so skilfully it caused no pain.

A crowd of villagers followed me around; they smiled and were friendly whenever I glanced at them. I found such a following tiresome and was relieved when, due to the rain, the villagers retired to bed early, leaving me in peace to sit by the fire and write these notes.

## 1 June

Arising before dawn, I wandered through the village looking for a place with a wide view of the surrounding mountains. The high long ranges, one behind the other and covered with rich vegetation, attracted me immensely. If there were villages there I would head towards them, moving from one place to another, higher and higher. It seemed, however, that the ranges were unpopulated. I had not imagined that earlier, but learned today that Englam-mana was the last village; beyond it there was no trace of human habitation.

After breakfast about a dozen men offered to come with me, some to carry my belongings, others to carry a pig given to me, and yet others just for the sake of travelling. One, an old man of about sixty years, kept brushing his neck and the backs of his legs with a green branch, whispering all the while. I soon learned that because one needs to have good legs on a long journey, the old man was preparing himself for what lay ahead. He passed the green branch to the villager next to him so that he too, could prepare himself for the long trip.

The villagers brought out a pot of boiled taro, and the food was distributed in a *tabir* to each of my guides from Gumbu and my new companions from Englam-mana. Then one of the local natives took a smouldering brand and holding it under each dish, uttered some words, pleading that we all should successfully return home.

Due to the rain the track was slippery, but even so, going

down was easier than coming up. We stopped occasionally so that a group of women from Gumbu, who were returning with us from Englam-mana, could catch up with us. Despite babies, each had a large bag on her back with gifts of food from the people of Englam-mana, while their husbands carried only their weapons. We reached Garagassi at about 5.00 p.m. after a good eight hours of walking.

*6 June*

Old Bugai from Gorendu visited me with natives from Maragum-mana with whom Gorendu and some other neighbouring villages had established a peace. Bugai spoke enthusiastically to the visitors about the power of my terrible weapon called *taboo*, and how he and other Gorendu people had seen it in action. While we were talking, a large black cockatoo descended on the *kengara* tree above my hut to feast on nuts. I fired and the bird came down, but my visitors took off in fright. Bugai, even though frightened himself, succeeded in bringing them back, assuring everyone that Maclay was a good man who would do them no harm. The bird was a large one — the distance between the tips of its wings being 1027 millimetres. After my visitors had recovered from the effects of hearing the explosion from the gun, they begged me to hide the *taboo* inside the hut. I handed them tail feathers of cockatoos and a few large nails; although they were very pleased with the feathers, they seemed uncertain as to what one should do with the nails, but Bugai told them all the good uses they could be put to. After learning about the importance of the nails, the visitors from Maragum-mana wrapped them in an old loin cloth. I was unable to comprehend their words since their dialect was different from that of Sambul and Englam-mana.

I had invited natives from Gorendu to come and share the pig presented to me at Englam-mana. While we waited for them, Olsson went out to fetch some water, leaving pieces of meat unattended in the kitchen. In his absence I noticed a large lizard sneaking out of the kitchen with a big piece of meat, but on hearing a slight rustle the animal dropped its catch and disappeared. My guests arrived bringing *keu* with them and stayed until 5.00 p.m. They seemed to be as at home at Garagassi as in their own homes.

### 8 June

I caught the lizard seen yesterday. It was over a metre long and its skin prized by local natives, who use it to cover their *okam* (small drums).

### 13 June

The small cuscus I had obtained some weeks ago was growing and doing well. It ate rice, *ayan*, *baou* and liked bananas very much. During the day the young animal slept curled up, but at night it persistently chewed at the planks of the box in which it was kept.

### 14 June

A group of natives called on me with a request that I show them the place where they might find their lost *nenir* (basket for trapping fish) that had drifted away in the sea. They looked very disappointed on learning that I was unable to help locate it.

When visiting Gorendu, I found myself surrounded by local women asking that I give a name to a female child born only a few days earlier. I mentioned several European names including 'Maria', and this appealed to them. The villagers repeated the name and showed me the baby who would be so named. I was surprised at the infant's light coloured skin. The baby's hair was not yet curly.

## 17 June

The natives of Gorendu invited me to a big feast. The food consisted of eight big bundles of taro, a large pig, several dogs and a cuscus — cooked in forty huge pots. The feast differed from other feasts in that it took place in the village, accompanied by the sound of Papuan instruments: the *ai* and *barum*. This time the women also took part in the feast, although they sat separately.

## 18 June

When moving through a village and meeting the natives, I am often asked: "Where are you going?" or "What did you kill today?" They also like to know: "Where were you?", "What did you eat?", "With whom did you eat?" This is typical not just of Papuans, as village people in Europe ask similar questions.

Olsson constantly complains about ill health. His work often entails the boiling of beans and *baou*, and general meal preparation. He looked unwell today and told me that he felt the approach of another fever, so I had to do the cooking. I would be satisfied to eat raw beans and *baou* and not be bothered with making a fire.

## 20 June

The season of gathering the *kengara* had arrived. Several natives would simultaneously climb up a tree, break off the branches laden with nuts, and throw them to the ground. The ground under the trees had been cleared of scrub so that women and children could easily collect the harvested crop. At this time of the year black cockatoos feed mainly on *kengara* nuts, consuming a considerable quantity; one often heard the cries of natives who came daily under the trees to scare off the birds.

In spite of the headache that had been troubling me since morning, I went off to hunt. Feeling giddy and barely able to stand, I lay down in the jungle for several hours. I recovered slightly, but on returning home I was tormented by another violent headache, lasting long after midnight.

## 26 June

For some days now I had no need to go in search of game. The large *canarium* trees growing above my hut were covered with ripe nuts, attracting various kinds of pigeons which flew in early each morning to gather this food.

During the previous few days, a native called Kodi-boro had visited me. He is the brother of the Papuan who one of the officers from the *Vitiaz* described as 'savage like the devil'. Kodi-boro came with a persistent invitation for me to move to Bogatim. He assured me that everything was plentiful there and he even offered to build me a hut. He told me that the people from Bogatim would give me three wives and that there were far more women there than in Bongu. He seemed rather disappointed when his offer was declined.

## 30 June

After shooting a pigeon and a cockatoo in my tree, I let Digu climb for nuts. Digu scaled the tall smooth trunk the same way the Papuans climbed a coconut palm, using a rope slung between their feet. Once he reached the top of the tree, Digu began throwing down the nuts while Olsson, myself, and Bua's eight-year-old daughter gathered them from the ground. The young girl gathered more nuts than we two as she had such good eyes and was so agile; her bare body crawled everywhere among the prickly vines and bushes.

The Papuans have a practice of instructing others. If someone is seen doing something not in the most practical way, they will correct that person without hesitation. On many occasions I was shown, even by children perhaps only seven years old, the best way of doing certain work. This comes from the fact that the Papuans train their children very early in practical life. While they are still growing up, the children learn the skills and activities of adults. They hardly ever play, apart from the occasional throwing of a spear or using a bow and arrow. I have often seen small boys spend hours by the sea trying to hit fish with their arrows. The girls, on the other hand, help their mothers with domestic work at a very early age.

The weather is excellent and I swim several times daily — the temperature seldom exceeds 31°C.

## 1 July

Of all the various birdlife, the most impressive, after the black cockatoo, is definitely the *nareng* (*Buceros*) not only because of its large size and strong curved beak, but also because of the sound the bird makes during flight. It could often be heard from a considerable distance away. *Nareng* fly very high and usually in pairs, perch on tall trees, but fly off at the slightest sound. Even though I have tried hard, I have not yet shot a single one of them.

I wasted about three hours today on one *nareng*. I initially fired at the bird with fine buckshot but probably only slightly wounded it, so I followed the quarry further into the jungle. After firing another shot I most likely hit it again, since the *nareng* moved away but only to a neighbouring, higher tree. Taking note of the spot I returned to the hut for breakfast. On my way back through the jungle to find my quarry, I stumbled into a thicket of thorny vines that clung to my clothes and skin, holding me back for some ten minutes. Eventually I found the tree to see the *nareng* was still in the same spot, but it began to cry out loudly as I approached, objecting strongly to my intrusion, while climbing up still higher. The dense greenery concealed the bird but its loud cry gave away its presence. Another *nareng* flew in and circled above the tree with loud cries in support for its wounded friend.

Determined, I stayed near the tree. Pestered by ants and the hot sun and troubled by my tired legs, I subjected myself to voluntary torture. To follow the movements of the *nareng* so high up, it was necessary to constantly gaze in that direction; half an hour later, my neck felt very sore and my eyes so tired that I could scarcely see. But I persisted. The bird did not appear but responded to the cries of its friend who was a distance of some 100 feet away, flying around from tree to tree. Troubled by headache and giddiness I headed home for an hour's rest. On my return to the hunting spot I found the wounded *nareng* still there, but its companion flew off on my arrival.

## 4 July

The weather keeps fine. I carried out some microscopic research on the hair of Papuans and found great variation in its thickness and in the contours of the cross-sections. The hair samples were collected from various parts of the body of the same Papuan men. Among white people similar samples of hair would also vary in thickness and colour.

Passing the spot in the jungle where two days earlier I had left the wounded *nareng* perched in the tree and his companion nearby, I found both birds in the same situation as that of forty-eight hours before.

## 10 July

My friend Tui is building a new hut in his village with the help of people from Gorendu, Gumbu and Bongu, with whom he feasts every evening after work. To celebrate the building the natives sounded their *barum*.

## 11 July

A rain-storm swept the area at about 4.00 p.m. but it quickly cleared, so I went out on the verandah to do some sketching. Suddenly the big tree in front of my hut began to sway and for a moment I thought that I might be feeling dizzy. Before I could gather my thoughts as to what was happening, the huge tree began to lean — slowly at first, then more quickly until it crashed to the ground parallel to the front of the verandah, only two paces from the hut.

The tree appeared green and healthy but upon inspection I discovered that a few metres from the ground, its trunk almost eaten away by grubs and other insects. The fallen tree measured 29 metres in height and if it had collapsed on the hut, would have smashed through the roof, damaging much of my equipment and perhaps injuring us. That incident might have fulfilled the natives' prophecy made long ago, that the Garagassi tree could kill me. Strangely, there was hardly any wind blowing at the time the tree came down.

## 12 July

I have frequently been told by the natives: "Tomorrow we will burn the *unan* (tall grass); there will be many wild pigs and other animals. Maklai will bring his *taboo* to kill the pigs; we will bring our spears, bows and arrows." However, that "tomorrow" never seemed to eventuate. Today, again the villagers told me that they would definitely burn the *unan* and promised to come for me at about noon. We shall see.

## 13 July

At about 11.00 a.m. before I was due to go hunting, I heard the voices of approaching Bongu villagers who rushed in to see me, all equipped with spears, bows and arrows. Each man carried two spears; the spear heads were stained red as if with blood. As the men moved, colourful plumes swayed on the tops of their heads, decorated also with strikingly colourful hibiscus and other flowers. The warriors had called to tell me that the *unan* was already burning and I must leave with them immediately. I hurriedly dressed for the hunt, grabbed something to eat and followed the natives.

As we approached the end of the forest, we heard a sound similar to what one would hear from a massive waterfall. Coming out into the open I saw about 100 yards ahead the line of a grass fire moving in front of us, leaving only charred *unan* stalks and piles of ashes. A pall of smoke rose above Gorendu and other surrounding villages, stretching along the banks of the Gabenau River.

This was only the beginning of the fire and so we sat down in the shade of the jungle edge. This gave me time to complete my breakfast while my companions chewed their *betel*. Within an hour the fire had moved away from the edge of the forest about half a mile, driven by southerly winds that wafted the smoke away from us. We moved on across the scorched ground, now exposed and very uneven. Everywhere were small mounds, several feet in height and twice that size in diameter, and generally formed from soil mixed with pebbles. The origin of these was related to the *maleo* (species of megapod), a local bird; its strong claws dig up the ground to build a large nesting structure, relying on the heat of decomposing greenery to incubate its eggs. There were also similar mounds in the jungle but these were far more scattered.

We moved about ten yards within the line of the fire and each group occupied a site on one of the mounds, thus forming a hunting-line closely following the edge of the fire, at the ready to strike any quarry. The fire flared up and then abated from time to time. Sometimes a whole wall of smoke and flame rose high into the sky obliterating any view, while on other occasions the fire would die down, almost go out, and then rise again to engulf the whole area in flames.

The hunters stood ready to strike. Each held in his left hand a bow and arrow, and in his right hand he gripped a spear. They all carefully observed the movement of the fire line, waiting for their quarry to appear. A small group of young boys about ten years of age stood some distance from their fathers, learning in the field the hunting skills that were passed on from one generation to another. The burning *unan* crackled and burst periodically into a ball of flame, each time producing a cloud of smoke that now drifted towards us; the ash in the air penetrated our mouths and nostrils, almost choking us. From time to time the leaping fire was so intense that flames curled back towards us, forcing us to retreat. I was exhausted and drowsy, and would almost have dozed off had it not been for constant calls from the natives to move on as soon as the fire subsided. After two punishing hours we reached the other end of the hunting ground to meet another group of natives coming from the opposite direction. The eyes of the natives constantly searched the scorched ground, though it was early yet to see the appearance of any quarry. Then, after the last grass stalk disappeared from the ground and the air was cleared of ash fragments, I heard the hunters cry *"bul aren"* (no pigs) and we came down from the mounds.

Some villagers from Gumbu who formed the opposite line of the hunt, admitted that they had seen no quarry either. I stopped one of them who had an animal suspended from a spear across his back. The animal appeared similar to a big rat. It was a new animal for me and I wanted to inspect it more closely, as it had very interesting fur rather like flexible spikes. The animal was singed, especially on its claws and snout, and even its strong tongue was blackened, probably from suffocation by smoke.

As I examined its strong teeth I heard the hunting cry *"Bul, Bul"* about 100 yards away, and the sounds of many spears hitting the ground around a large boar. I retrieved my gun from the native carrying it, waited for the boar to come closer and then fired at it. The bullet struck the animal in the chest but below the heart. The boar stumbled but still moved on past me. I fired again, hitting its rear leg and the boar stopped for a moment, but again it stumbled on. I then pulled out my revolver and moved closer to the terrified beast, its lips curled to reveal a pair of deadly tusks. The boar made deep warning growls, indicating it was ready to fight to the death. I fired several more rounds as I moved closer and the boar fell, but struggled to fight on. The natives, moving closer, gave me no time to fire more rounds. One spear struck the beast, another missed but the three arrows that soon followed struck the boar in the back. Still the boar summoned enough strength to struggle forward, with the arrows stuck in its body. Wishing to end the beast's agony, I moved closer to the mortally wounded boar, ignoring the urgent warnings of the natives. Choosing the right moment I struck my long knife deep into the animal's side. A stream of warm blood shot up my arm and soon afterwards the boar collapsed for the last time. The natives who stood behind me unanimously declared that the catch was mine and began to praise my *taboo* and me.

We soon heard from another group of natives that they too were in pursuit of a catch, and I quickly loaded my gun. The hunters swiftly retreated in fear of my lethal weapon. I chose a vantage mound and waited. I could hear the cry "*Bul, Bul*". Then the natives informed me that two more boars in the hunting ground had got away because of the absence of me and my *taboo*. I was told by a group of natives from Bongu that they too had killed a pig. In the process, however, a man called Saul was knocked down and badly gored by the beast's deadly tusks, and had been taken back to Bongu. The natives who were with me then told them how effective my *taboo* had been and of the large boar which I had killed.

I approached the slain boar and the natives asked me where I wanted the catch to be taken. I answered that I only needed the pig's head and back legs, and that the rest would be a gift to the natives of Bongu. I also told them that I would call into the village to give treatment to Saul, but only after I returned home to leave my gun and hunting gear. The natives seemed content with this and we all moved on.

At Garagassi some forty natives sat down in the clearing to smoke and chat. I was able to count eight animals similar to the rats I had noticed earlier and which the natives called *gabenau*; there was also a large, silver-white *mab*. I purchased the *mab* and some other specimens for my collection and then hurried to Bongu to attend the wounded man.

I was met by a lamenting woman and Saul's son. Apart from a number of smaller gashes, I found two large wounds on Saul, one on the upper arm and one on the neck, but none of them appeared life-threatening. The dried blood mixed with ashes and mud gave the wounded man a very unfortunate appearance. Gesturing with one hand, he was able to explain how he struck the pig with his spear and how that pig had suddenly turned on him, broken his spear and knocked him to the ground. The animal had tried to run but collapsed. Saul's friends thought that he would have been able to handle the pig by himself and were so busy chasing other animals, they were too late to come to his aid. I asked for water, warmed it on the fire and washed the wounds; then I smeared on a carbolic ointment and finally bandaged the wounds.

The sun was already setting when I reached Gorendu and collected my share of the catch from the hunt. I cut off the boar's head and rear legs. Declining an invitation from the locals to spend the night with them, I put the catch across my shoulders and left for home. The load proved to be heavy and I had to rest twice on the way. Around 8.00 p.m. I finally sat down in my armchair to enjoy my dinner, feeling very hungry since much of the day had been spent on my feet with little to eat.

The sound of *barum* from Gorendu announced to neighbouring villages the beginning of an *ai* that was to continue throughout the night and the following day. The sounds of music from flutes and other instruments could be clearly heard in the quiet of the moonlit evening.

I was unable to fall asleep for hours and decided to return to Gorendu, anxious to acquaint myself with the *ai* and to learn more about the ceremony. I took Olsson who was also eager to witness the festivities. We carried a lantern as we could not rely fully on the moonlight, due to periodic clouding of the sky. We moved very slowly since Olsson was not familiar with the jungle pathways, and was often falling or stumbling. On nearing the village I covered the lantern's light and we approached quietly. In the village clearing, fires blazed under big pots cooking the pig meat. Sitting around or standing by, the natives were enjoying the music, each player competing to drown out the sound of the others with his instrument. Some of the audience had fallen asleep. Fat from the boiling pots spilled over into the flames, which flared, increasing visibility.

When I announced my arrival with a whistle, the music suddenly stopped and then cries were heard: "*O Maklai gena! Andi gena!*" and so on. I found a comfortable spot on the ground and the music continued, but I did not stay long as the sounds were becoming disturbingly loud.

## 16 July

The natives from neighbouring villages were busy again burning grass and hunting, but I stayed away. I had intended to paint a portrait of Nalai, only to be told by nearby natives that he would soon die if I did so. It is interesting that in some parts of Europe there is a similar belief.

## 17 July

I spent some time today tidying up my hut. Without doing so every now and again, it would be impossible to enter my seven square foot home.

I called at Bongu to see the wounded man Saul. The entire community gathered round, although everyone seemed occupied with doing something — a native was finishing his new *udya-sab* (a narrow spade) smoothing it with a shell; another villager, using a similar shell, tried to sharpen his *yur* (harpoon); the man next to him was shaving the end of his spear, broken during the last hunt, using a knife he had received from me. The women searched for lice in their husbands' head hair, and the half grown young engaged in similar activity amongst themselves. Two village women extended this grooming care to their dogs, busily catching fleas while the dogs relaxed on their laps.

I was about to leave when Bugai from Gorendu got up, wanting to go with me. When we reached the seashore, Bugai walked to a charred tree-trunk washed up on the beach long ago during a high tide. The man grabbed a handful of charcoal which he swallowed with some pleasure. Anxious to learn what type of tree this trunk might be, I also tasted the ashes and found them to be salty. The tree trunk had been carried by the waves for so long that it was now inhabited by sea creatures and had absorbed such a considerable quantity of salt, that the charcoal could be used as a substitute for ordinary salt. I learned from Bugai that the natives eat this ash with *ayan*, *baou* and other food. I considered this a most practical discovery, since my own supply of salt was fast diminishing and I was forced to eat everything except meat without salt.

I learned that the *dongan* (knife) stuck in Bugai's bracelet was made from a species of animal-bone that I had not yet seen. Called *tibol*, it lives in the jungle but may also be found in *unan*. According to Papuans the *tibol* has a long thick tail and can jump high.

### 30 July

Troubled by fever. I have lost several days. Olsson is also frequently ill.

On a small hill at Gorendu I noticed a little girl, about ten years old, throwing a coconut down the hill. Several boys of her age played nearby, throwing spear-like sticks to pierce the fibrous husk of the nut. I wished I had better artistic skill to capture the scene.

Sugarcane, absent for some time, now to be seen again, being chewed by the natives.

## 31 July

A group of natives arrived at Gorendu in their pirogue. Some of the visitors sat down by the steps leading to my hut, chatting about hunting and bird plumes. Suddenly one of them, as if bitten by a snake, leaped from the steps crying: "Maklai, *gene, gene*" (Maclay, come here). The other visitors did the same. I asked the natives what was happening, but there was no time for an answer. From the roof above my head, I heard a great crashing sound and saw a cloud of dust. Broken branches of various thicknesses fell to the ground near the verandah; some so sturdy that on falling from a height of 23 metres or so, could have seriously injured humans. It seemed that my visitor Bua, on hearing the tree-limb crack overhead, had jumped for safety, well knowing the danger. Papuans are very afraid of falling trees, often fatal to people below. Long ago I had been told by the natives that my hut at Garagassi was unsafe, and I was often advised to move to Gorendu or Bongu or build a new hut at another place. The natives were right, but the trouble of building and resettling at a new location was so inconvenient that I had kept putting it off, in the hope that disaster would not strike.

I went to Bongu every day to attend to Saul's wounds. Afterwards I joined a group of natives to smoke and chew *betel*, hoping to learn something new from their conversation. I asked about the names of various tribal groups and places, trying to find out if the people in the area shared a common name. My questions were well understood, but there was no common name. Instead, the natives gave me the individual names of people, adding to each of them the word *tamo* and the village name. I learned that the inhabitants of the mountain villages to the north-east, *tamo-deva*, made holes in their nostrils and placed plumes in them. Our conversation turned to the subject of my hut, the falling of dry branches, and so on, and the natives again suggested that I should build a new hut.

The feast at Bongu followed its usual course; it began with the drinking of *keu* followed by spitting and making of various grimaces resulting from the unpleasant taste of the drink. The meal consisted of shredded coconut, boiled *baou* and *kainda* (yams). The feast ended with the chewing of betel and smoking. This was the typical order of a native feast. I took no part in the first and last course of the meal, and so I left for home earlier than the others. On leaving the village I stopped by a hut to let a group of women pass, among them many guests from neighbouring villages. A group of men gathered around me and as the women came out of the jungle and caught sight of us, they became quiet, changed their gait, and dropped their eyes or looked aside. They moved on quickly with their skirts swaying.

My departure delayed and darkness closing in, I decided to spend the night at Gorendu. The bed turned out to be more comfortable than the one I slept on at home. I covered myself with a new mat and slept well, although I woke occasionally because of the hardness of the stout bamboo used as a pillow. When one lies on one's back the bamboo makes a reasonably comfortable pillow, but not so if you sleep on your side. One must learn to sleep on one's back and not to turn over.

## 4 August

Several pirogues drew up at the beach near Garagassi. The villagers from Bongu had come to chop a log some forty metres long into smaller pieces. The log had been brought up on the shore by a high tide in March — some five months ago — and the natives told me that tomorrow they intended visiting Tengum-mana. They would take log chips as a gift to the mountain people, who would burn them to ashes, later to be used as a salt substitute. The coastal people add a small portion of sea water to fresh water to provide themselves with a sufficient amount of salt, but the mountain-dwellers lack such a commodity and must use these salty ashes for their salt requirements. After loading up their pirogues and promising to return, the natives left.

## 7 August

The fever troubles me almost daily. It takes all my last efforts just to keep on my legs — there is not much quinine left.

All day yesterday the sounds of chopping axes could be heard in the forest, so I went to see what was happening. An area of forest had been cleared of bush and vines for a new garden, while the larger trees were trimmed of their lower branches; even some big trees had been felled and all in just a few days. I could not help but admire the workmanship, so effective and yet achieved with such a simple tool as a stone axe. Hordes of ants — black ones, yellow brown and white ones, big and small — much upset and deprived of their homes, all pestered me and I was forced to leave the clearing.

## 9 August

Villagers from Bongu, together with their guests from Bili Bili, visited me. One of the visitors pleaded to hear Olsson's mouth-organ. When Olsson went to fetch his instrument, the natives quickly placed a loin cloth over the head of a little boy to prevent him watching the *ai*. Only after Olsson finishing playing and returned to the hut, did they remove the boy's head cover.

## 13 August

I stayed at home to work on my anthropological notes about Papuan life to send to my academic colleague, Karl von Baer. Today, the natives who visited from neighbouring villages were a group consisting solely of *tamo boro* (elders). They presented me with a rather strange request — to come and live with them. I would be entitled to have one tree, two or three wives, and permission to stay with them forever. There would be no need for me ever to return to Russia, or indeed to go anywhere.

My visitors spoke to me very seriously, one after another, each repeating almost the same words; it was obvious that they had earlier discussed the idea at length. I advised them that even if I ever left (which I now doubted), I would come back; as for women, I had no need of such company since they talked too loudly and Maclay liked silence. Even though my answer did not please the visitors, they were glad to receive the tobacco I distributed to every one who was part of the deputation.

Every evening for the past six months, Olsson and I had left a big log on the fire to keep it going until morning, to save our dwindling supply of matches. From time to time we substituted the log with driftwood brought in from the sea and *à la papoua* would gather the white ashes for a salt substitute. It took some time for the seawater to evaporate from the wood, using up considerable wood-heat energy. The salt could easily have been obtained by evaporation of seawater through sun energy, but unfortunately we did not have a suitable trough for this latter practice. Fortunately I have become used to eating food without salt and as yet have not noticed any side effects.

## 15 August

During my morning hunt, as I walked along a footpath that passed by a native garden, I stopped on hearing the rustle of dried leaves. Upon investigation I saw at some twenty paces among the trees and next to a stump, a small reddish-grey kangaroo which the natives call *tibol*. I fired at it; the wounded animal was easy to catch and I returned home with my prize. It was only then that I realised I had not killed anything else for my dinner pot, but this was of little concern to me. It was now nearly a year since I arrived here and this was the first sample of *tibol* I had been able to catch.

## 20 August

I was sitting and chatting with the locals at Gorendu after a search for some young *ayan*, when I heard a sudden outburst of crying and lamentation. Though similar to those I had heard earlier at Gumbu after the death of Boto, this time the voices were female and soon a woman appeared looking very distressed. She was crying; both hands covered her eyes as she walked through the village followed by women and children — silent and with heads bowed and eyes downcast. I asked the natives why Kolol, the lamenting women, was so distressed. I was informed that during the night her large pig had been killed while trying to enter the village garden through a fence of deadly sharp stakes. Kolol went into her hut, crying as one would do for a lost child. The attachment of the women to their domestic animals in this part of the world can be explained by the fact that village women often wet-nurse young piglets. This proved to be very much the case here. I remarked, somewhat carelessly, that there were plenty more pigs about. This upset Kolol who showed her breast and told me that it was on that breast she had fed the now lifeless pig when it was just a baby. Two natives brought in the dead pig, which actually belonging to a man called Assel, and it was decided that the dead animal would be given as a gift to the villagers at Bongu. A *barum* announced the departure of the gift. Within an hour the answering sound of a *barum* from the village of Bongu acknowledged that the gift had arrived and that *ai* festivities would begin.

## 22 August

Last night I prepared to leave for Bili Bili Island and fastened my doors with rope. During the night the wind was weak but the sea was high. However, at dawn the sea quietened. After an hour of exhausting paddling due to the quietness of the sea, we approached Bili Bili.

A group of natives could be seen walking along the shore singing welcome songs, often mentioning my name. Several pirogues came out to meet us. The Bili Bili people frequently interrupted each other, all anxious to tell me how glad they were to see me. They tried to speak the Bongu dialect which I am more familiar with.

This very picturesque island with its thriving greenery, the natives decorated with leaves and flowers, their songs, the people's excitement — was all typical of a scene one would see on some isolated island in the Pacific, and often described in the diaries of seamen who had experienced such events. Choosing a spot on the beach for landing, I steered my dinghy towards it. As soon as I beached it on the sand, the front part of the dinghy was grabbed by a dozen native hands and dragged out of the water. It was about 9.00 a.m. and after a drink of coconut milk I would have liked a nap as I felt tired. However, this was not possible as my hosts were too excited by my arrival.

After a short rest I began to sketch the local scenes — everything that I could see — huts, pirogues, people's faces, the various native ornaments, wood carvings, and so on. As I walked through the village I stopped in front of many huts. Near one of the huts a group of natives worked on an oar. Here was a typical example of how iron would replace seashell and stone in time to come: a nail, sharpened carefully on a stone, had assumed the shape of a chisel and was used skilfully in the hands of the natives. Though the work was still tedious, the result was achieved faster with the nail than with traditional tools.

Near some of the huts hung many shields, newly decorated in black and white. Shields like this were not seen in neighbouring villages on the mainland, but were common to the islanders. They were round in shape and fashioned from a single piece of wood. On the front of the shield were two circles containing various figures. Anxious to show me their skills, some natives picked up their spears and, with a shield held in the left hand, began to make various movements to demonstrate their agility. The shields covered their heads and chests and thus protected them from possible arrows and spears.

## 24 August

The wind is unusually strong and the natives pleaded with me to
wait until it had died down. I do not mind staying longer, there is
always something interesting to take note of, or perhaps sketch as
the subjects here are endless. All the village youths boarded four
pirogues and headed to Bogatim to attend a special feast and some
kind of ceremony; the wind is very favourable in that direction.

Their faces, some I knew, were decorated with such various
colours that I often had to stare hard in order to recognise them,
as the decoration and colour considerably altered their
appearance. Various chest ornaments called *sari* and small drums to
be used during the ceremony were commonly seen among the
youths. In order to please me, before we loaded the pirogues the
natives performed the same dance there on the beach that they
were to perform at Bogatim. While they danced they held the *sari*
in their teeth and the small drums in their left hand while beating
with their right hand. The dance consisted of slow movements and
the natives sang, but as they had the *sari* in their mouths, their
singing was indeed a strange sound.

## 25 August

I woke during the night and noticed that the weather had
improved, so I dressed, lit my lantern, and went to wake Kain and
Gad with whom I was to travel to Tiara. After some objection,
Kain woke Gad and the two of them went to seek a sail and oars.
I packed my belongings together with the gifts into a small
pirogue. With their flaming torches swinging, the two natives
organised the sail, oars and other equipment. They also loaded
gifts; always carried with them when visiting neighbouring
people, and some goods for barter. The moon appeared from
behind a cloud to peep mysteriously between the palm fronds and
so light up the village. Now that the sea could be clearly seen, my
two native companions prepared to launch the vessel.

I took my place with all my belongings on one side of the mast. On the other side of the mast was a small fire contained in a pot. At the bow and stern, special places were allocated where one could stow bows and arrows. By 3.00 a.m. everything was ready and the pirogue was pushed into the water. My two companions jumped aboard and began to paddle energetically since there was no wind near the beach.

There was little else for me to do but sleep as I knew I would have the opportunity to view the surroundings on our return the following day. Besides, it was difficult to even make out the edge of the jungle near the beach. The bamboo platform on which I slept was reasonably comfortable and I had a good hour's rest before being wakened by Gad. He warned me that I might burn my shoes as my legs, stretched out in my sleep, had brought my feet close to the fire. The natives asked me for some tobacco and after lighting it, began to question me about Russia and the people who lived there; on the moon; and on the other stars. I learned from them that the natives call Venus *Boi*, Orion's constellation *Damang*, and the Pleiades *Baressi*.

As we passed the island of Yambomba, I got the impression of a complete bay forming part of the shore, but when daylight appeared it was obvious that the bay extended into a channel — towards which we headed. By now the sun had risen and the archipelago could be more clearly seen. In the background were the mountains and on both sides of us, rose coral reefs covered with dense vegetation. To the south lay the New Guinea mainland which the natives called *Beile*, while to the north lay Graged Island and the villages of Graged and Mitebog. There were two other islands further behind us, Bager and another, the name I have forgotten. Soon we found ourselves in quite a big bay surrounded by islands of various sizes, all part of a complete archipelago. The islands were formed from coral reefs and were covered with abundant vegetation. As we sailed further on I wrote down the names of the islands.

Appearing on the horizon, the sun lit up the archipelago

showing the calm surface of the bay with the mountains in the background. The strait between the mainland and Graged Island that led into the bay looked very safe. The bay was dotted with islands and protected from the open sea by a large reef, allowing several points of access — it provided the site for a perfect harbour. I named this area the Archipelago of Contented People. My companions began to tidy themselves, putting on clean loin cloths and arranging their hair using big combs; then they continued diligently paddling towards their destination. Not far away on the beach, we saw a group of Tiara people awaiting our arrival. Many of them called out my name. As soon as the pirogue reached the sandy beach, the locals pulled it further up the shore. Stepping down from the platform I distributed my gifts to the natives and then moved on to the village. On arrival we were shown to a big hut wherein I set up my portable table.

Among the locals who surrounded me I recognised three natives who had visited Garagassi some months earlier. I had written their names in my notebook, and after consulting this I read them out aloud. Surprised and pleased the men came forward, one after another, and took a seat near me. They kept close to me for the rest of the day, trying to please me as best they could. The whole village of Tiara constantly gazed at me and the things I had brought with me.

Here among the locals, as in some other villages, I noticed a few natives who had slightly different features. Mostly the differences were in their noses and some parts of their facial structure, but this was only in a few individual cases and the people in general were much the same as those in the mainland villages.

I distributed about half a pound of tobacco cut into small pieces, and shared this mainly among the elders. While the natives smoked I sketched the huts which, like those in Bili Bili, were either built on poles a metre above ground or were erected in an 'A' shape raised off the earth. Then I made a tour of the entire village. Although considerable in size, it was not as clean and tidy as the neighbouring mainland villages. On my return I found that dinner was being prepared for me. Pleased with their gifts of tobacco, each inhabitant of Tiara gave me one arrow, gratefully accepted since the objects were so skilfully crafted. I noticed that the locals possessed a very different breed of dog from that seen on the mainland of New Guinea. These dogs had a fat long body, short legs and thick muzzles — they originated from Karkar.

Our pirogue was ready to sail, and the entire village gathered on the shore to bid us farewell. The vessel was heavily loaded with the various gifts given by the island people to my companions. As we sailed out of the bay the pirogue began to rock on the turbulent water. Karkar was clearly visible and I was tempted to visit that island as it was so close; and also Bag-Bag where, so Kain tells me, the isolated natives do not bother to build pirogues.

## 26 August

In the morning as I was again preparing for departure, the pirogues or *robum* as the local villagers call them, returned from Bogatim to pick me up. The young natives on board looked very tired. On leaving I wanted to give some presents to the natives, but I had nothing better to hand than an empty bottle. I decided to smash the bottle, in which I had kept cold tea for the trip, and to distribute the pieces of broken glass among the natives. The bottle yielded a considerable number of pieces and the locals were delighted to receive them. Broken glass is used to shave wood, smooth tool-handles, and many other purposes when working with wood. The entire village, including women and children, gathered around the pirogue, each expecting to receive a piece of glass.

On returning home I found everything in order, even though I was sure there had been many visitors during my absence. However, no one was able to get inside since I had secured the entrance and the natives seemed to be suspicious of ropes such as those I used to fasten my door.

## 30 August

Today I went to Bogatim and arrived there after a six-hour journey. There was a small breeze at first but it became quite windy later on. Nearing that part of the beach that the officers of the *Vitiaz* and I had inspected some eleven months ago, I noticed a group of natives sitting down as my dinghy approached the shore. They stayed in that position until I asked them to help beach my vessel; they immediately did so.

On inspecting the village I got the impression that it was perhaps one of the biggest villages on Astrolabe Bay. The clearing in the middle of the village bore traces of a ceremony and feast in which the natives from Bili Bili had also participated. The high *barla* had been decorated with greenery for the occasion. Some of the natives were still eating scraps left over from the feast, even though this was the third day after the event had taken place, and I was given a part of it — a large piece of *ai-bul* (slaughtered pig).

The villager Kodi-boro again began talking about me moving to Bogatim and wishing to emphasise his desire, took me on a tour of the village. As we were going towards a hut, at his call there appeared a healthy, young and very attractive girl. He said something I did not comprehend and the girl looked at me, smiled, and then moved back into the hut. I was told by Kodi-boro that I could take the girl for my wife if I moved to Bogatim. We then proceeded with the village inspection. After we had walked for about five minutes, we reached a tall fence of stakes that guarded the gardens. We climbed over this and moved towards a group of women working on the land. Kodi called out to one woman, a beautiful young girl of about fourteen or fifteen years of age; as I already knew what was intended, I declined with a movement of my head. Kodi moved his head and pointed his tongue towards some of the other women, still with the hope that he could entice me. This showing of the tongue by natives is comparable to us pointing a finger at something. The inspection of young women was becoming tedious to me so I went back to the village. Since there was hardly any wind to travel back to Garagassi, I had to spend the night at Bogatim.

## 31 August

I spent a comfortable night covered with my Russian flag, though the night did not pass without an attempt from my friend Kodi to use darkness as a means of realising his match-making ambitions. I was on my own in the hut when I went to bed, but before I fell asleep I heard noises outside. I took no notice however and tried to rest.

At sunrise I made a sketch of the panorama of the south-west side with its background mountains. In return for a knife I was promised an *orlan-ai* (a musical rattle made of coconut shell). Somewhat furtively, Kodi took me to the back of one hut where I was led into a small *buambramra* and shown the *orlan-ai*. After I handed the knife to him, Kodi carefully wrapped the instrument in a mat so that no one would see what we were carrying from the hut. He then led me out across a bushy slope to my dinghy where he placed the *orlan-ai* in concealment under a pile of coconuts.

As the vessel was pushed into the sea I saw the natives sit down to watch Olsson busily hoist the sail. I sat down and called out my farewell "*E-aba, e-me-me*". Assisted by a fair wind we safely reached home in good time.

## 1 September

I had a strong attack of fever.

## 2 September

I accidentally cut my knee with my axe while mending the hut's roof. As the cut is rather deep I will have to stay at home for a few days.

## 3 September

Olsson, assisted by villagers from Gorendu, drew the dinghy higher up onto the beach as it had begun taking in water, about eighty buckets in twenty-four hours.

## 4 September

Troubled by my sore knee I was unable to hunt. Our provisions have dwindled almost to an end, so we must depend on food that the natives bring.

A cloudy day with fresh westerly winds; temperature about 26°C.

## 9 September

I am struck down by fever again, adding new troubles to those I already have with my injured knee. The last few days have been most unpleasant with fever attacks accompanied by violent headaches. To complete the misery I have to listen throughout the day to Olsson's routine complaints and lamentations. He predicts that we are both going to die from fever or hunger.

It has been cloudy during the last few days with occasional rain delivering large drops on my table and bed.

## 13 September

The *mab* died last night so today I spent some time mounting and drawing its brain. The animal had lived the last few months on the verandah.

I have recovered sufficiently from my illness to hunt while the weather is good.

Ernst Haeckel and Miklouho-Maclay at Arrecife in 1867.

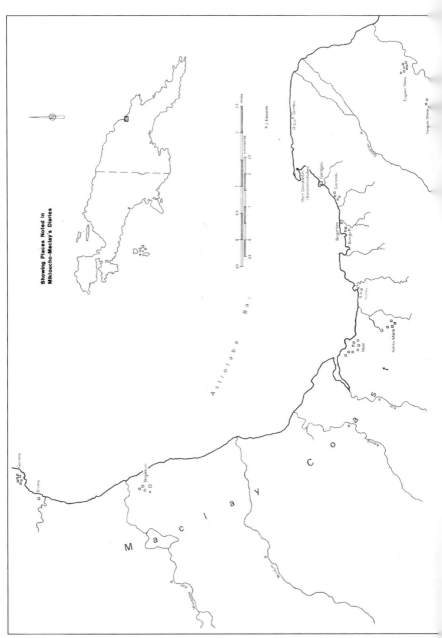

The coast of Papua New Guinea at Astrolabe Bay.

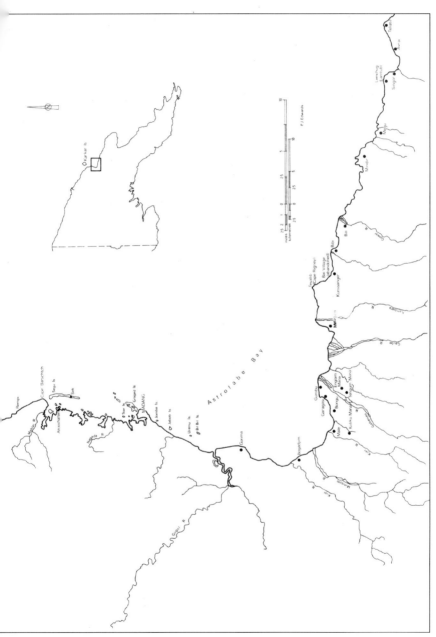

Astrolabe Bay and the adjoining coast of Papua New Guinea.

A participant in a ritual festivity.

A *buambramra* and huts on the Maclay Coast.

A *buambramra* in the village of Tengum Mana, 1872.

A Papuan playing the flute.

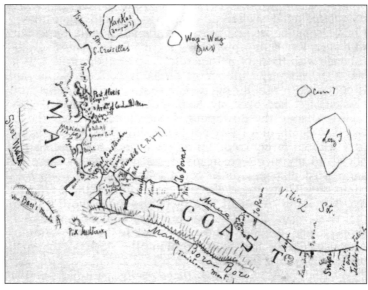

A chart of the Maclay Coast. Sketch by Maclay.

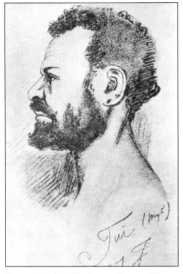

LEFT: Tui, a Papuan from Gorendu. Sketch by Maclay.
RIGHT: Asel, a Papuan from the village of Gorendu.

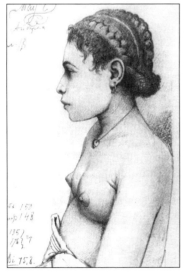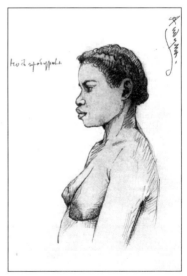

LEFT: A 17-year-old girl from Aiduma Island.
RIGHT: A woman from Aiduma Island.

LEFT TOP: A bride from the village of Bongu.
LEFT BOTTOM: Tui, at nine or ten. Bonem's son.
RIGHT: A Papuana participant in a ritual dance during *mun koromrom* festivities in the village of Bongu.

## 15 September

I have decided to keep the remaining provisions of rice and beans for the days when I may not be in fit condition to hunt, or when Olsson's illness prevents him walking to the village to bring back some food. Instead of beans and rice we live on yams, sweet potatoes and bananas. Occasionally we go hungry when there is no game about and several times I have dreamed of dining in luxury.

## 17 September

Olsson is struck by rheumatism and stays in bed the entire day.

On some days there are scarcely any birds to be seen. Even the black cockatoos, often seen in the branches of *kengara* trees, are absent. When strolling through the jungle I no longer hear even the pigeons. The appearance of various birds is connected with the ripening of fruit on local trees, which partially explains the birds' current absence; another cause is most likely the felling of trees in the area where I usually go to hunt. The natives of Bongu had cleared scrub and cut away branches to set up a new garden. When the cleared branches had dried, the natives set them alight and then erected a fence made from sugarcane and stakes split from logs felled during the clearing operations.

## 20 September

It is exactly one year today since I first set foot on the New Guinea coast. Throughout the year I have accumulated groundwork for my research for many years to come. I have established very cordial relations with the local people and can rely on their help and co-operation. I would like to stay in this area for several more years, but unfortunately my supply of quinine is fast diminishing. I am wearing my last pair of boots and I have only 200 percussion caps left.

During my hunt today I went so deep into the jungle that even with the help of a knife, I could scarcely move through the thicket of vines and thorny bushes. In that almost impenetrable growth I was surprised to come across a native garden surrounded by a fence. The natives are very good at finding remote and barely accessible spots deep in the jungle to establish their gardens. After climbing the fence I saw thriving plants of banana, sweet potato, sugarcane and yams. I found a gate in the fence from where a pathway led me through the jungle to the sea. Although I was near Gumbu I had no wish to call at the village and instead I rested on a fallen tree trunk on the shore. A group of women on their way to the garden and carrying empty bags passed by, chatting as they went. A group of men from Bogatim, fully armed, were heading in the opposite direction. I approached one of them and learned that they had left Bogatim at daybreak and had walked all the way following the line of the seashore.

24 September

Kodi-boro, accompanied by a group of villagers from Bogatim, brought me a piglet and I gave him in return a small mirror set in a wooden frame. The gift went from one hand to another so that everyone might gaze into it. The natives held the mirror before their faces; grimacing, showing their tongues, blowing their cheeks out, moving the mirror further away from their faces then bringing it close again, while uttering "a", "e", "o". Some of the natives held the mirror only very briefly and, as if frightened by something, would turn away hastily passing the object to another villager.

27 September

Two logs forming the foundation of my hut have partly rotted, or perhaps been eaten away by termites. The floor will soon collapse and I can see that it must be immediately repaired. Olsson lay groaning on his bunk claiming he was about to die, so I went out into the jungle to cut the new posts on my own. It was, however, beyond my strength to carry the posts back to the hut.

At 2.00 p.m. it started to rain, the sky covered with storm clouds. As I returned to my hut for shelter, I was aware that more heavy downpours could soon cause the hut's collapse. Instead of preparing dinner I decided to go to sleep — there was no sign that the storm would cease — "*Qui dort, dine ...* " (One who sleeps, eats less) I told myself, but I was aware the French proverb could apply for only one day, as sooner or later one must eat.

I was just falling off to sleep when a trickle of cold water fell on my face from a new crack in the roof. This had to be immediately dealt with to prevent my bed from being drenched, so using a piece of wood and a cord I fixed a sheet over my bed to keep it dry.

I have mentioned this episode in order to illustrate the problems I have to cope with every day in this uncomfortable environment — my extreme tiredness, regular headaches, moisture all around me, going hungry to bed, the possibility that the hut might collapse during the night, and so on.

## 10 October

I find it difficult to describe the conditions under which I work and live. The frequent fever attacks and perhaps my mainly vegetable diet have considerably weakened my muscular system, especially my legs; to walk up even a small rise becomes quite an effort, I can barely drag my legs along. Although there is a strong urge in me to work, I tire easily after any small effort. However, I feel no pain except for the occasional headaches associated with my fever; these pass as soon as the fever attack ceases. I tire so quickly that I can hardly go anywhere except to Gorendu or Bongu to obtain food, so I stay at home where there is still plenty to do. The solitude and camp life at Garagassi is pleasant to me, but the life we lead here has affected Olsson considerably. He has become sullen and very snappy. His frequent complaints and sighs disrupt my work, which irritates me.

I was visited some days ago by people from Biliya, one of the islands forming the Archipelago of Contented People. Among them were two or three natives with handsomely pleasant faces, perhaps as handsome and up-standing as Polynesians I have seen. The son of Kain, for example, even though not the most attractive man, reminds me of the young natives from Mangareva Island and Paumotu Archipelago.

There is rivalry among the Papuans where women are concerned, sometimes resulting in fights. When asking Kain about Kore, one of our acquaintances from Bili Bili, whom I considered to be a fairly intelligent man, I learned that Kore had been wounded in one of his legs. He had found his wife in the hut of another villager and as he tried to take her home, her lover resisted. Using his bow, Kore fired some arrows at his opponent thus wounding him; but the lover fired an arrow in return, penetrating Kore's thigh. A similar conflict happened some months ago at Bogatim when both participants were wounded; one of them nearly died after being stabbed in the shoulder with a spear. The rumbling of thunder is heard every day, very much like this time last year.

## 12 October

I have noticed lately that when there is not much to eat I become thirsty. I am anxious to find out what triggers my frequent bouts of fever. In the mornings, if I enter the water to about knee level or move about in wet boots, or if I spend time in the sun around 1.00 p.m. or 2.00 p.m., I will have an attack of fever almost without fail.

Today Olsson stood for about three hours in the water while washing his clothes. The water temperature was about two degrees lower than the air temperature. At about 3.00 p.m. he had another fever attack whereas yesterday he had been quite well.

## 21 October

Last night the *barum* sounded continuously from Bogatim, beating monotonously. I learned from Saul who was visiting me, that someone had died at Bogatim and a funeral was held this morning. I asked if a messenger had called to bring the news, but Saul explained that he had only heard the *barum* sound and had understood that there had been the death of a villager, though he was unable to learn the deceased's name. He knew from the *barum* sound, however, that the funeral had already taken place.

## 25 October

After spending the night at Bongu, I got up very early to visit Male. The sun was just rising and only a few villagers were up sitting by the fire to catch some warmth. One of them, Kale, on learning that I was to leave for Male, suggested that we go together and we took off.

We reached Male early. On arrival I was taken to a large *buambramra* and invited to stay overnight. Later, a native came by with a complaint about a *tamo russ*, referring to an officer or a sailor from the *Vitiaz*. The native explained that when the corvette was here, although his hut was closed and the entrance secured, the *tamo russ* had forced the door open, entered and taken away the native's *okam* (small drum). He had been without one ever since for the drums were made solely by *tamo Rai-mana* people, who used a material not found locally. My visitor pleaded for the return of his *okam* or at least to be reimbursed for his loss. A second villager complained that another *tamo russ* had taken his *nenir* (a basket for catching fish) and the entire catch that was in it. A third man claimed that my countrymen had made off with a very good spear from his hut.

Feeling that these complaints were genuine, I believed that the villagers should be properly compensated. Since *okam* are very highly valued by Papuans, I offered an axe in return; for the *nenir*

I suggested a knife, and the owner of the missing spear was promised three large nails. The natives were advised that they could collect the goods when next they called at Garagassi. My compensation offer came as rather a surprise and the natives called: "Maklai, very, very good man." It did not surprise me, however, that after fourteen months the natives still remembered what had happened when the *Vitiaz* was here.

The villagers brought two large *tabir* of boiled *ayan* for Kale and me. The food was placed in front of us and the crowd that had gathered around dispersed, leaving us to eat alone. As soon as we had completed our meal the villagers came back; some villagers offered to prepare *keu* for me but I declined. The people were most anxious to chat but I preferred to retire, explaining that I needed to sleep. I lay down on the *barla*, feeling no restraint at being in the presence of these villagers. The natives, noticing my eyes were closed, kept on chatting but in whispers.

After resting for about an hour, I went for a stroll into the jungle accompanied by a group of natives. While there I noticed many birds that I had not come across before. On my return to the village I explained that I wanted some *telum* and human skulls. I was soon shown several long wooden figures but all were broken and of no use to me. They also brought out two human skulls, each held on sticks. The skulls had no lower jaws and when I asked why, I was told only "*Marem aren*" (no lower jaw). After I declined to take the skulls the natives threw them away with the words "*Borle digor*" (bad rubbish). I was now convinced, based on this and on some earlier experience, that the natives do not appreciate the skulls and bones of their dead relatives, except for the jaws.

Some young villagers sitting opposite me were busy pulling out hairs from their chins, cheeks and eyebrows with the help of a thin, doubled thread. The thread was held very close to the skin and twisted so that a hair was caught in it, then pulled out by its roots with a single movement of the hand. Even though their pain was apparent, the natives continued with this practice of hair removal for some hours. Next to a smouldering log sat another group of natives placing their fingers into the salty ashes, and then licking them.

It was amusing to see a boy about three years old eating pieces of yam while sitting on his mother's knee, suddenly grabbing her big breast to suck. The woman was nursing another child but continued to eat yams herself, uninterrupted. The boy sucked for a while before returning to eat the yams.

That evening the natives prepared a meal of boiled *ayan* and bananas. The ripened fruit of pandanus was also cooked and served; although I found this latter dish not particularly flavoursome, it did have a most agreeable fragrance.

## 28 October

Loneliness is having a serious effect on Olsson. As I observe him I believe that his brain may be affected — he mumbles for hours, then after seeming to listen to something, begins mumbling again. It is pointless to try and advise him to occupy himself with some activity, for he is convinced that he will soon die. The only thing that seems to interest him is the cooking. He often rests for the whole day, pretending to be ill. I am disgusted with his behaviour and scarcely speak to him, not even to give him orders. It is enough for me to tolerate his antics and to feed him.

Occasionally I hear strange sounds like human voices coming from the distance. As one listens it seems that voices are coming closer and closer, but no one appears. Perhaps I am hearing the buzzing of some strange fly. Olsson tells me that he too hears the sounds; perhaps both of us are becoming deranged.

## 30 October

It rains and rains again. My roof leaks badly and water is falling on my bed and papers. My current situation is such: the food reserves have gone; the supply of quinine is coming to an end; only 100 percussion caps are left. Restricting my hunting to two caps each hunt, I often return home without any game. I had to dispose of some specimens collected earlier and there seems no point in acquiring new ones, since there is no spirit left. I am wearing my last pair of boots. The fever is wearing me out. My hut is in a sad state.

## 2 November

During the night a loud crash sounded outside — my verandah had collapsed. For a moment it seemed that the whole hut was about to collapse. It rained all day, preventing me from mending the verandah. No sounds of birds were heard from the jungle.

## 3 November

Tui called in this morning. It had been raining so I invited him to sit under the awning on the verandah near the door to the room where I was sitting. Tui had come to ask me to stop the rain. He told me that the people of Gorendu and Bongu had made as many spells as possible to try and stop the rain, but still it came. Maclay should make it stop. Tui stayed for some time seeking my help and I learned some important details about the natives from him. Even though I could speak the Bongu dialect reasonably well, I would need one more year to become familiar with the Papuan way of life. In the fifteen months that I have been here, I had never attended a wedding festivity or attended the *mulum* (circumcision ceremony) and there is so much more I have yet to see.

## 4 November

I left early this morning to look for yams, having eaten no breakfast since there was nothing to eat at my place. When I reached the village the natives gathered round me, pleading with me to stop the rain that was ruining their gardens. They brought food for me, asking for nothing in return except my 'medicine' against the rain. I wanted to learn how they charmed the rain away and suggested they perform the ritual for me, but Bugai told me that their traditional *onim* seemed to be of no help. He and the other locals were sure that I could have stopped the rain, but I did not wish to do so.

## 18 December

Accepting an invitation from the villagers, I went to Bongu to attend their ceremony *ai*. Preparation of food by the locals, drinking *keu*, and loud music — all proceeded as usual. It was too late to return home so I spent the night in Saul's *buambramra*.

## 19 December

Dawn penetrated the *buambramra* but I hesitated to get up as I had had an uneasy rest, often wakened during the night by the natives' music and shouting accompanying the *ai* festivity.

"*Bia, bia!*" (fire, fire) — I heard calls some distance away from the *buambramra* where I rested. Several extremely agitated villagers rushed in to inform me that fire and smoke could be seen near Karkar. "Well, why the concern? Karkar people must be burning *unan*," I told them without getting up. "No, it is not on Karkar; the smoke comes from the sea. Maklai, tell us, what is it?" I told them that I must first see the smoke before I could say what I thought it could be. At that moment several villagers rushed in crying: "*Maklai, O Maklai, ship russ gena — biaram boro*," (Russian vessel coming — big smoke).

I dressed and quickly went down to the shore without taking the news seriously, but as I looked towards the sea my scepticism soon disappeared. Smoke billowed from a large steamer, probably a naval vessel, some distance away and although the hull was yet out of sight, undoubtedly it was approaching. In any case I thought, I should hurry back to Garagassi and raise the flag outside my hut, then change into better clothes before going down to greet the ship. I reasoned that whatever nationality the vessel might be, the captain would surely not refuse to take on board my mail, give me some provisions, and take the sick Olsson to be left at the nearest port. I thought about all this while sitting on the platform of a native pirogue taking me from Bongu to Garagassi.

On arrival I found Olsson lying on his bunk groaning as usual, but when I told him that I needed the flag raised as a naval vessel was approaching, I was convinced that he had gone mad. The man called out incoherently, laughed and then wept, as if in a kind of fit. I hurriedly raised the Russian flag on the flagpole erected by the sailors from the *Vitiaz*. As soon as the flag was up and flapping in a light breeze, I saw the steamer now nearing Yambomba Island alter its course and head towards Garagassi. I immediately returned to my hut to change my clothes, but found this was futile as the clothes I had intended to change into were in the same sad state as the ones I was already wearing.

I walked to the shoreline and, after considerable effort, persuaded three natives to sail with me towards the approaching vessel. After we set off I was able to distinguish the Russian flag flying on the approaching vessel. My companions, Sagam and Digu, rowed very slowly, observing the ship's every movement and constantly pleading to be allowed to return to shore. Soon I noticed an officer on the bridge looking at me through binoculars. At last we were close to the ship which was moving at a very slow speed and I saw, with my naked eye, some familiar faces among the officers. They too, recognised me.

The emotional state of my companions, Sagam and Digu, attracted my attention. The sight of such a large number of people made them extremely restless. When on the captain's orders the sailors climbed the ship's rails and shouted a triple "Hurrah", my Papuan friends leaped from the pirogue into the water and swam back to the shore. Making a hasty departure, the natives had taken the oars or perhaps tossed them into the water. I had to paddle with my hands, slowly moving towards the Russian clipper before finally grabbing onto a rope thrown towards me.

On board the clipper *Izoumroud* [also spelt 'Izumrud'] I was met by Captain Mikhail Nikolayevich Kumani and his officers. I soon learned that the clipper had been sent by the Admiral of the Fleet. Chief Warrant Officer Rakovich had been transferred from the *Vitiaz* to the *Izoumroud* so that he could assist in discovering the spot where my papers were buried, since some European newspapers had spread rumours that I had been killed or had died. Several *Izoumroud* officers admitted that on seeing a man in European clothes coming out to greet them, they had thought this must be Olsson as they were positive that I would not be found alive. I asked the captain to let me return to shore and advised him that I would be back in a few hours to talk to him.

The unexpected arrival of the clipper had caught me without any planned course of action. However, I thought the most urgent needs would be the repair my hut with help from the clipper's sailors, restocking my provisions so that I could continue with my research, and to send the useless Olsson back to the nearest port. I also thought of mailing my diary and meteorological journal to the Geographical Society together with my anthropological writings on the Papuans, addressed to my academic colleague, Karl von Baer.

I returned to the *Izoumroud* around dinner time and was advised by Captain Kumani that on account of my poor health, I should immediately take up residence on board his clipper and leave the transfer of my things from Garagassi to one of his junior officers. Surprised by this suggestion I asked him: "Who told you, Mikhail Nikolayevich, that I am to go with you? That is far from decided. I would like you, if possible, to provide me with some provisions, take Olsson on board to be delivered to the nearest port, and take my letters with you. I have to remain here; there is considerable anthropological work about the local people here awaiting completion. I beg you to let me advise you tomorrow whether I shall leave with you or remain here." Captain Kumani agreed to my suggestion, but my words had obviously made a curious impression on him and his other officers. Some of them clearly thought that my brain must have been affected by the harsh environment and my various other deprivations.

I returned early to Garagassi and fell asleep like a log after such a long and exhausting day. I put off the decision to leave or not to leave Garagassi until the next morning.

## 20 December

Captain Kumani informed me of his intention to stay as short a time as possible, being aware that when the *Vitiaz* had last called here, several of the crew had became ill even though that visit was brief in duration. I knew that just a few days' stay would be too short a time for me to write a detailed dispatch for the Geographical Society and to thoroughly check my diary before I sent it away.

I learned from Captain Kumani that the Dutch government was about to dispatch a naval vessel to explore New Guinea for scientific purposes. The news was of special interest to me. I thought that if I left, I could return again to the Maclay Coast on the Dutch ship with my health restored, and with new strength and supplies. I definitely must come back.

My knowledge of the native languages and the trust I have established with the local people have paved the way for my future anthropological research for years to come, and should flow on with considerable ease. With this in mind, I decided to leave Maclay Coast temporarily and return at the first opportunity.

When I informed the captain of my decision, he asked me how much time I would require to prepare myself for departure. I told him that I would need only two more days to pack my things. Captain Kumani kindly let me have one of his cabins and I started ferrying some of my things from Garagassi to the clipper.

That evening natives from Bongu, Gorendu and Gumbu came to see me, carrying torches. Among them were villagers from Male and Koliku-mana. My friends Tui, Bugai, Saul, Lako, Sagam and others whom I had often seen at Garagassi, felt very sad at the news of my departure. They pleaded with me to stay with them for always. They promised that if I stayed, the natives would build a house for me in each of the local villages, that I would be at liberty to choose the best girl in every village to be my wife, and I could have as many wives as I wished. I politely declined their offers but assured them that I would be back and that we would see each other again. The villagers from Gumbu begged me to visit them; they said that natives from Tengum, Englam and Sambul-mana would also be there — all wishing to see me again before I left. I felt that it would be unwise to decline and accepted the invitation.

At Gumbu the villagers begged me not to leave and as their pleadings continued throughout the night, I barely had any sleep. My legs were hurting badly and were now very swollen as the last few days had been very hectic for me. It had become too difficult for me to walk back to Garagassi. In fact, the pain was so strong that the villagers decided to make an improvised stretcher from some light saplings and they carried me on this to Cape Gabina. From there I was ferried to the clipper where I finally received some treatment for my sore legs and exhausted state.

On the captain's orders a mahogany board was to be erected near my hut at Garagassi, with a copper plate affixed to it which would read:

***Vitiaz* Sept. 1871**

**Miklouho-Maclay**

***Izoumroud* Dec. 1872**

In spite of my sore legs I went looking for a suitable tree to mount the copper plate. I chose a large *Canarium commune*, the tallest and most impressive tree at Garagassi. I spent the rest of the day in the hut packing my belongings knowing that I had only one more day left to do so.

## 21 December

Before I went to sleep in my hut for the last time, I realised that in all the fifteen months I had spent here, I had never found time to make myself a comfortable bed. When I stretched on top of the two baskets my body flopped over the edge; as one of the baskets was slightly higher than the other, my legs were not level with the rest of me. It would have been far more comfortable if I had put boards over the baskets and made a base to stretch out on. However, I never thought of that since there were other things of more importance occupying my mind.

Yesterday I persuaded the natives to accompany me and inspect the clipper. Many natives turned up at Garagassi but only a few were willing to be ferried to the vessel; when we arrived, even fewer still were prepared to venture on deck. On board they became confused and frightened at the sight of the seamen and strange looking equipment around them. Indeed, the natives followed me so closely, they even held on to me in their fear. I asked one of the seamen to give me a length of rope and after winding it round my waist, I handed both ends of the rope to the natives to hold on to — thus as I moved, they followed me on the tour of inspection. The Papuans looked at the big guns with horror and then turned away from them, pretending to look at some other equipment. They were especially interested in two young oxen and they asked if they could have one of the animals. As soon as I told them the Russian name *bik* they all repeated the name "*Bik, bik, bik*".

On our way to the officers' mess we passed the vessel's steam engines; these fascinated the natives, even though they did not know the purpose of the machines. The Papuans were delighted with the large mirrors in the mess room which could reflect several people, full length, at the same time. They were very impressed with the piano and its sound; I told them this was *ai-boro-russ* but when they asked if they could take the piano back with them, I hurriedly took them back up on deck.

One of the natives asked again for a *bik*, even though he had difficulty remembering the Russian name and referred to it as "that big pig". He said that he would very much like to have a big Russian pig with two large teeth on top of its head. Suddenly one of the natives remembered the name *bik* and again they all started to repeat "*Bik, bik, bik*". By this time I felt that my Papuan friends were becoming more relaxed so I let them to move around on their own. The last of my belongings were now on board. Olsson had also been ferried across and as he was not well, he was accommodated in the sickbay. Before we parted Tui wanted to know how many moons would pass before we met again. Even after fifteen months I was still uncertain of the Papuan word for 'many' so I had to use the word *navalobe* loosely meaning 'in due course'.

## 22 December

All morning a group of pirogues had been encircling the ship and it was periodically reported to me that the Papuans wanted to see me. When I went on deck the natives began to cry out to me. However, the ship was about to depart and the noise of the anchor being hauled aboard together with the churning propellers frightened them. As the pirogues moved away the Papuans cried out to me "*E-meme, E-aba*" (O father, O brother) and I could hear their cries for some time after the clipper began moving away. Passing Cape Gabina, we heard *barum* from Gorendu and Bongu sounding simultaneously; as we sailed further along the cape, *barum* could also be heard coming from Gumbu.

The drums still sounded in the background even as we neared Bili Bili where I could clearly see through my binoculars, a group of natives moving along the rocky shoreline slopes, waving me signs of farewell. We sailed past the Archipelago of Contented People and Port Grand Prince Alexei, and rounded Cape Croiselles to enter the strait between New Guinea and Karkar Island. I made a note on my map, naming it Izoumroud Strait.[4]

# Expeditions to West New Guinea and the Malay Peninsula

Passing through the Malay Archipelago, the *Izoumroud* stopped at the Moluccas where Miklouho-Maclay called on the Sultan of Tidore to enquire about the local slave trade and find out what danger the Papuans might be exposed to. The sultan must have sensed what was on his visitor's mind and presented Miklouho-Maclay with a gift — a Papuan slave-boy who had been taken away from his people and given the Muslim name, Achmat. For the slave traders, Achmat could just as well have been a native from Arnhem Land of Australia, for that too fell in their slave catchment area. The boy learned Russian in a matter of months and remained faithful to Miklouho-Maclay for years.

While the *Izoumroud* was anchored in Manila, Miklouho-Maclay made an expedition to the Limai Mountain in search of the Negrito indigenous tribe, and acquainted himself with the anthropological characteristics and way of life of the original inhabitants on the island. He somehow sensed that the Philippine islands may be another Easter Island disaster in the making — the colonial masters of the islands and missionary religious interference were fast edging out the indigenous population, altering the ethnic structure and bringing ecological and cultural change.

When the *Izoumroud* reached Hong Kong, news was sent off to Europe and the rest of the world that Miklouho-Maclay was still alive after an absence of many years. He sent to Karl von Baer in Russia his anthropological findings, which proved that the indigenous people were not subhuman as the British and Americans claimed (to support their colonial expansionism) and, indeed, had a culture of substantial merit. However, instead of going to Russia and a heroic welcome, Miklouho-Maclay left the *Izoumroud* at Hong Kong and journeyed to Batavia (Jakarta), only to learn that the expected voyage of the Dutch naval vessel to New Guinea had been put off due to an insurrection by the Achins natives in Sumatra. Undaunted, Miklouho-Maclay asked the Dutch colonial authority for permission to visit West New Guinea as half the island was under their colonial administration at that time (in 1828 the Dutch annexed the western half of New Guinea). After meeting considerable resistance from the Papuans, the Dutch retreated to the Moluccas from where they nominally administered control over West New Guinea. The Moluccas islands at that time were the centre of the slave trade industry in South East Asia.

A few years before Miklouho-Maclay landed in West New Guinea, the naturalist Alfred Russell Wallace had visited the north coast. Wallace, whose work has been associated with that of Darwin's, was a brilliant naturalist and field researcher, mainly with plants and animals. However, he lacked an understanding of the mind of indigenous people. At the time it was a common scientific belief in the west that the best way to handle the natives was to keep them at a distance, in range of firearms. They were seen as sub-human and inherently violent — a mere link between apes and humans. It was Miklouho-Maclay who broke with that perception, showing that the natives are just as human as Europeans and, if approached cordially, there should be nothing to fear from them.

Wallace reported initially that the north coast of West New Guinea was inhabited by the most treacherous and bloodthirsty Papuan tribes: "Many crewmen from earlier discovery ships have been murdered in the south-west part of New Guinea, known to the natives as Papuan-Koviai, and scarcely a year now passes without some lives being lost." Miklouho-Maclay went there and stayed in the area of Triton Bay at Papua-Koviai coast for some months. He even ventured into the mountainous inland, discovering Lake Kamaka-Ballar. On this visit he found that

Papuans, either living at Astrolabe Bay on the north-east part of New Guinea or on the south-west part of the island, were the same people — the colonial powers set the borders dividing the island regardless of the people who lived there.

On his return from the West New Guinea expedition, Miklouho-Maclay handed to the Dutch colonial authority a report about the lethal impact on local tribes of West New Guinea by slave raids carried out by the sultans of Ternate and Tidore. At that time bands of Macassans from Celebes roamed through the Arafura Sea, seizing non-Muslim indigenous people from Papua and Australia to trade as slaves. In that report Miklouho-Maclay stressed that slave traders had forced the coastal Papuan tribes to abandon their traditional land and move further inland, into rugged and inhospitable ranges which drastically affected their cultural and traditional way of life.

This pattern of destruction was continued even a century later — when Indonesia took over the rule of West New Guinea from the Dutch in the 1960s, with the blessing of the United Nations, it began colonising the area with Muslims from Java, thus the indigenous Papuans were passed from one colonial master to another. The slave raids on the Arnhem Land coastline (carried out by Macassans on the pretext of collecting sea-slugs) were outlawed by the Australian government at the beginning of the twentieth century

After spending some time recuperating as a guest of the Dutch Governor at Bogor and his fragile health partly restored, Miklouho-Maclay left for the Malay Peninsula in search of the original inhabitants, an aboriginal tribe reported to be living in the remote mountainous interior. Little was known about those tribal people even to the local ruler, the Maharajah of Johore. Miklouho-Maclay hoped that on this expedition he might be able to find out about the racial characteristics of the original inhabitants of the Malay Peninsula before outside cultural and religious changes came to dominate the area; he also wanted to learn if the tribes he was looking for could be related to the

Papuans, the Australian Aborigines, and to other people of the region.

The Malay expedition took Miklouho-Maclay 170 days. He penetrated deep into the remote area of Johore and travelled further into the Kingdom of Siam, where on the upper reaches of the Pahand River he came across pure-blood non-Malay natives, the Oran-Sakai, small Negroid people similar to the Negritos he had found earlier in the Philippines. This finding was of immense importance when determining the origin of the Papuans as well as the origin of the Australian Aborigines.

On his return from this expedition, Miklouho-Maclay wrote from Singapore to the Russian Geographical Society about his Malay discovery, proud of his ethnic and racial mapping of an area that had existed prior to the religious changes and the impact of colonisation. With that mapping Miklouho-Maclay hoped to demonstrate the link between Papuans, Australian Aborigines and other tribes of South-East Asia. Knowing how lethal the consequences of colonisation were, Miklouho-Maclay wrote to the Czar of Russia asking that he use his influence to declare the east part of New Guinea a protectorate.

Troubled with financial difficulties as he received no funding from Russia, Miklouho-Maclay offered his anthropological collection as security to a Singaporean merchant for a loan. He then made arrangements with the skipper of the *Seabird*, a small schooner trading in the Pacific, to drop him off at the Maclay Coast of New Guinea. The skipper, an American called O'Keefe, deceived Miklouho-Maclay, as once aboard, Miklouho-Maclay found the vessel heading for the Pelau and Caroline Islands; it would then proceed to the Admiralties Island and after four months at sea Miklouho-Maclay was finally dropped off at the New Guinea coast. With him Miklouho-Maclay had his servants, a Malay man called Sale and two young islanders from Pelau (Mebli and his young wife Meri), and supplies for six months. As agreed, the *Seabird* was to call back in six months to pick them up.

# The Second Visit to the Maclay Coast

*June 1876 – November 1877*

## June 1876

I arrived back on the 27 June on a small schooner, the *Seabird*. I noticed that some changes had occurred in the appearance of the surrounding mountain peaks.

The natives were very pleased to see me, although some were not at all surprised as they had always held the belief that I would return. Soon after I embarked at Gorendu a large crowd of men from neighbouring villages gathered to welcome me, but the women and children were absent. Many natives were crying, becoming quite emotional about seeing me again. Some of my older friends were not present — they had died during my absence — but a number of lads had reached manhood and some of the young girls had become mothers.

As before, people from all the villages pleaded with me to settle with them but, as I had explained to them during my earlier visit in 1871, I preferred to establish myself outside a village. After inspecting the areas around Gorendu and Bongu, I chose a promontory near Bongu village as a convenient spot to settle. The following day many natives, under my direction and with help supplied from the ship's carpenters, cleared a site for my hut and made a wide road connecting my new home to *Uleu*, the nearest beach.

This time I had brought with me from Singapore a small hut made from timber panels, to be erected on stilts and roofed on location. Not wanting to unduly delay the schooner's departure but in need of the carpenters, I did not pay sufficient attention to the quality of timber required for the roof and stilts during construction. This was to cost me dearly later on when I found out that the timber selected was prone to termites, a menace in this part of the world. Here on the Maclay Coast there are trees naturally resistant to termites, but I failed to make the proper selection during construction, just to save time.

## July

My hut was completed in six days. The construction party comprised myself, two Europeans, my four servants, and several dozen Papuans who helped carry and cut timber for the roof. Help also came from the local women who contributed to the clearing of bush around the hut. The stilts on which the hut rested were about two metres in height, giving me considerable space underneath for storage. I had brought some seventy boxes with me, some large baskets and much baggage of various sizes. At last I was able to advise the schooner's captain that he could now depart.

Helped by my four servants (one a Malay who would be my cook and tailor, the other three Micronesians from the Pelau Islands) and the local Bongu natives, I soon brought my local residence into a liveable state.

I learned some very useful information from the local natives about an earthquake that had occurred during my absence, responsible for the changes in the mountain peaks of Mana-boro-boro (Finisterre Mountains). When I left in 1872 the peaks were covered with greenery, but now the peaks and the slopes below were barren. The natives told me that during my absence, earthquakes had occurred on a number of occasions, violently shaking the coastal area and ranges. The tremors caused human tragedies; in particular, people were killed by falling coconut trees smashing down on their huts.

Villages along the shoreline suffered much tidal wave destruction. As the huge waves rushed inland, trees and huts were swept away. I also learned that even before my first arrival here, there had been one such tidal wave, the aftermath of an earthquake which had struck during the night. It had completely swept away the village of Aralu, lying between the Gabenau and Koli rivers, and its entire population. Only a few men, who had been absent visiting another village, survived. After the tragedy the survivors had settled at Gumbu as this village was further inland and had escaped destruction. The fate of Aralu was well remembered even by the younger men, so I concluded that those events must have happened between 1855 and 1865. After the catastrophe various unexplained illnesses spread to the neighbouring villages causing even more fatalities, probably as a result of contamination by the rotting corpses left behind after the sea retreated.

## August

On 12 August I decided to climb Constantine Peak. Rising at 9.00 a.m. I set off by dinghy from Bongu where I could see the entire mountain range very clearly; there was not a single cloud in sight. Assisted by a good wind I reached Bogatim after about one and a half hours' journey. The villagers awaited me, to help ferry my belongings from the dinghy to the hut of Kodi-boro. They advised me that it was too late to climb the mountain and that it would be best to leave this for the following day.

I arose about 3.00 a.m. and woke my men. After coffee and distribution of the loads among my carriers, we set out on the track still lit up by moonlight. Following the dried bed-line of the River Yor, we made good progress.

As I carried no food rations I had to call in at the village of Yaru for supplies. My native companions did not wish to continue accompanying me up the mountain range, but this did not concern me as I had enough men in my team, perhaps even more than was necessary. Some villagers from Yaru joined us and we continued along the dry river bed. In some places we had to climb over rocks smoothed by the rushing water of rapids, making our travel more difficult than before.

About 3.00 p.m. it began to rain and the entire mountain range was veiled in cloud; there seemed no point in hurrying ahead so I instructed the natives to erect the tent. I settled down for the night after measuring the height of our location using my Renault instruments, which proved their accuracy as the figures were identical to those provided by my aneroid equipment. The height measured 262 metres.

Because of heavy rainfall during the night, it became very chilly. My canvas roof overhead held well so I stayed dry, although the air around me was very damp and I suspected another fever would occur the next day. Rising at 6.00 a.m. I observed that my men were not ready to leave, so I set off by myself, telling them that *tamo bilen* (good people) should follow me up and that *tamo borle* (bad men) remain. This seemed to have an immediate effect on my companions as all were willing to join me.

The rain during the night had made the river flow again making the rocks very wet and slippery, so we had to move very cautiously. We walked for a while before climbing up over some difficult banks to follow a sketchy track. My companions tried to convince me that since there was no definite track, we should not proceed any further. To my regret, I began to realise that my exposure to yesterday's rain and the dampness during the night would soon cause me to suffer a fever attack. Already I was feeling somewhat faint, giddy and consumed with weakness. Fortunately the slopes were well covered with forest so one could hold onto branches and vines or roots as we struggled upwards. In one steep place as I stretched my hand to reach a vine, I suddenly lost my concentration and my senses followed ... as I regained consciousness I heard human voices but on opening my eyes to see jungle all around me, I could not think where I might have been. Exhausted, I fell back into a dizzy state, feeling pain in various parts of my body and muscles. Finally I was able to ascertain that I was in a rather awkward position — lying with my head positioned far lower than my legs, but I was still not fully conscious of what was happening. Later, I again opened my eyes and heard a voice say: "I told you that Maklai is not dead. He has only fallen asleep." Some of the natives were peeping at me from behind trees. As I looked at them, my consciousness returned and I began to remember that while I was holding onto that vine, it had snapped under my weight and I tumbled down towards a ravine. Fortunately, no bones were broken and although my back was very sore, I felt my condition improving. I looked at my watch to see the time but realised that it had stopped after the shock of my fall. The sun was already high in the sky, so I guessed that I must have been unconscious for some hours.

I told myself not to waste any more time since I could expect rain again around 3.00 p.m. Fortunately, one of my aneroids was undamaged and I was able to find out that we were at a height of 400 metres. I moved downhill to find a safer gully before proceeding with the journey. We were heading towards Gumugua at heights reaching up to 573 metres. Beyond that a narrow gully led towards another mountain of 730 metres in height.

At last we reached the dome-shaped summit of the Tayo Mountains, 817 metres in height and only visible from the seaward approach. At the top, despite the altitude many tall trees flourished. My native companions lit a big fire in order to signal the surrounding villages that we had reached the summit. I gave a piece of white linen attached to a rod to two Papuans and suggested that they tie this to the top of the tallest tree. Branches had to be removed so that the flag could be seen from a distance. After that we began to descend. I was somewhat disappointed with my excursion because the heavy vegetation obstructed the view from the top, and I had not brought sharp axes with me to make a small clearing at the summit. Without any difficulty we descended to the place where we had camped the previous night; after our lunch there we headed back to Bogatim.

Natives from neighbouring village joined us, so my company became two hundred men. Even though I was exhausted I did not stop for a rest and as darkness fell, we used torches for the last leg of our journey. We reached Bogatim at about 10.00 p.m.

## 21 August

I headed for Bili Bili Island where the natives had built a hut for me at Airu. Although rather dark inside, it was cool in the tropical weather. I intended to visit Airu from time to time.

On my way to Bongu I visited the villages Englam-mana, Seguana-mana and Sambul-mana.

## 20 September

I visited Garagassi today and found that the undergrowth had taken over the area. Of the coconut palms I had planted earlier, only five survived. The copper plate erected by the *Izoumroud* crew on the big Kengara tree was still firmly attached to its trunk, though the red wood seemed to be partly eaten by termites. I reinforced the plate by driving in a few more nails. The stilts on my old hut had been so affected by termites that a light puff of wind might bring the whole structure down. In the area round about I noticed far more birds than in my new place at Bongu; the sound of the birds revived memories of my stay in 1871–1872. I instructed my servant Mebli and a few villagers from Gorendu to clear the bushes surrounding my old hut and around the coconut palms growing there.

## October

My new situation afforded me much more convenience to concentrate on my comparative anatomical studies. The comfortable hut and three servants had a stabilising effect on my health. Towards the end of September and the beginning of October, I harvested the patch of Indian corn I had planted in July. After harvest, I planted in the same patch some other seeds brought with me. In the area adjacent to the hut I planted twenty-two coconut palms and these seemed to do well. Some sores and blisters on my legs seemed to be larger, due perhaps to the effects of seawater that I frequently came into contact with. If neglected, wounds heal very slowly here, often restricting my movements.

As well as my writing, I now found time to do the anthropological research not possible at Garagassi. The natives feel relaxed with me and do not object to my anthropological measurements, but I do not feel at liberty to take measurements of the village women. The men here are rather possessive of their women and I do not wish any misunderstanding to occur.

The opportunity arose for me to learn about *u-ravar* or *mulum* (a circumcision ceremony). All *uleu tamo* (coastal natives) follow this custom apart from some people on the Archipelago, but it is not practised in the mountain villages.

### November

I still suffer from frequent attacks of fever and the sores on my legs have not yet healed well. Whenever possible I am busy with my research or reading. During the night the pain in my legs becomes so strong that I must take chloral in order to sleep. I feel most chilly in the mornings when the temperature drops to perhaps 21°C; I shiver, like the natives, with my whole body.

### 5 December

After several days' preparation, the villagers in Bongu began their *mun* festivities. It was, perhaps, the most impressive ceremony I have yet seen here. I shall try to describe it.

### Mun festivities in Bongu, 5–6 December 1876

The festivities begin after a long preparation lasting several days. In the time leading up to *mun* the natives from neighbouring villages practise every night their dancing and singing, and the *barum* sounds day and night.

The programme was to begin on the evening of 5th December in Gorendu, and then on the following nights festivities would take place in Bogatim and Gumbu. Prior to the commencement of *mun* a procession left Bongu carrying brushwood to be thrown in the sea. These people then went back to the jungle to dress themselves for the festivities. Their *sanguin-ole* (three-tier head-dress) is constructed on a bamboo ring set on top of the head. From the ring projects a bamboo pole some five metres tall; the bottom part is split and fanned out so that it will hold firm in the coarse Papuan hair. The lower part of the pole is decorated with cassowary plumage, the middle section with cockatoo feathers, and the top part with birds of paradise plumage; constructed so that the feathered pole sways with every movement of the dancer. Tucked in the dancer's waist are green branches which sway with his movements. The dancers also wear *sagyu* (bands of greenery) around their arms and legs.

Apart from *diu* (plaited hair bands), some natives also decorate their heads with dog teeth. Around the dancers' necks hang *yambi* (a small bag) and *bul-ra* (boar tusks). The European-made cloth that I had given the natives during my earlier visit is also used for decoration.

## Mun-Koromrom

Accompanied by the sound of *okam* (ceremonial drum), the dancers swung two by two in rhythm as they moved onto the ceremonial ground to make an arc formation; they then slowly began to move around, sometimes in pairs, sometimes solo, forming a long line. In front of them moved a villager from Bongu but he was not decorated like the others. He had several red hibiscus flowers in his hair and carried a spear with its head pointing backwards, with a piece of coconut shell jammed on the point so as not to injure any of the dancers by accident. The singing and dancing was rather monotonous. The dancing consisted mainly of slow movements and small steps with occasional bending of the knees. The dancers often bent their entire bodies; letting their head decorations swing forwards. Gradually women wearing newly made *mab* (loin cover) joined the dancers. The women were also decorated with several necklaces and some had *sagyu* (arm bands) made of greenery. Some of the women were obviously pregnant while others nursed babies in their arms. The women's dance was even simpler than that of the men and mainly consisted of a swaying of the buttocks.

The ceremony of *mun* continued till dawn; young people from Gorendu and Bongu also participated.

### Mun

From Bogatim I went to Bongu while there was still daylight. It was about 5.00 p.m. The ceremony *mun* engaged many more participants than *mun-koromrom* and the dancers' movements were somewhat different. The male dancers, dressed in *sanguin-ole* and *gubo-gubo*, were encircled by a group of women who held the men's bows and arrows; the women also carried large bags on their backs. Also present were a large number of armed natives who took part in the singing while clapping sticks against bundles of arrows.

The movements of the dancing procession were quicker than the previous ceremony. Two principal dancers, their eyes closed, performed complicated movements with their legs, kicking them outward. Ceremonial drums hung at the back of their necks. I was most impressed with the mimic dancing which depicted the hunting of wild pigs and how parents lulled their infants to sleep. In that scene, one native man was dressed in women's finery and his ceremonial drum placed in a bag to represent a child. This scene came after one in which a young woman was hiding behind a man to avoid the attentions of an admirer who was persistently pestering her.

A comic scene followed, showing a local medicine man administering *onim* (traditional remedy). A native sat on the ground portraying a sick man; he was visited by a healer who began dancing around him, kicking him in the sides. The healer then moved in a circle over the ground, chanting some words to a branch held in his hand. He then returned to the patient and

repeated the earlier treatment of kicking him. Finally, worn out
and puffing and sweating, he threw the branch on the ground and
began stamping on it.

In the morning the ceremonial procession moved to encircle
a palm tree; then came to rest. One of the participants in the *mun*,
a native from Bongu, climbed up the palm tree and shook the
trunk, bringing down most of the nuts for the participants to eat.


## 22 December

A funny thing happened today at Bongu. As I mentioned earlier,
during the day the villages are almost deserted by the men who
are out hunting or fishing, or visiting neighbouring villages, or
tending gardens. They usually return at sunset so I was surprised
to hear the sound of the *barum* calling the men to return to the
village. In response I hurried to the village where I found Bua. In
a nearby hut I could hear the cries of Lako's wife. I was told by
Bua that earlier in the day, when Lako came unexpectedly home,
he found his wife in his hut with another man called Kaleu, an
unmarried villager of about twenty-two years. The people here
usually walk very quietly so the lovers were taken by surprise.
Kaleu was able to escape, although unscathed or not was as yet
unknown, but Lako took out his anger on his wife by beating her,
stopping only long enough to beat his *barum* and thus summon his
friends.

When I arrived I saw Kaleu at his hut looking downcast. Lako
was busily punishing his wife, but then he suddenly rushed from
his hut, armed with bow and arrows, and stared at the crowd now
gathered. When he saw his rival Kaleu, Lako immediately began to
select an arrow — at the same time a villager handed Kaleu a bow
and arrows. Observing Lako's fury, I doubted that he was in a fit
state to hit his rival and I was right. A moment later the shot
missed Kaleu widely. The second shot also missed as Kaleu dodged
it in time. I failed to see if Kaleu fired back at Lako but I was later
told that he had fired, missed, and then fled. His rival now gone,

Lako focussed his anger on Kaleu's hut, breaking the walls and tearing down the roof. The villagers now found it necessary to intervene and to restrain Lako.

The following day I found the two rivals sitting together on the shore, engaged in friendly conversation while sharing a smoke. Noticing that I was approaching they started to laugh. "Did you see what happened yesterday?" asked Lako. I told him that I had and asked: "What's happening today — is Kaleu a good or bad man?" Lako told me: "He is good, good." Kaleu also indicated his approval of Lako.

On my way to Bongu, I met Undel and mentioned how Lako and Kaleu were sitting together. Undel told me that Lako had turned his wife out and that she was now living with Kaleu. Cases like this, however, happen infrequently.

*January 1877*

I am progressing with my anthropological work. So far I have measured the heads of 102 men, 31 women and 14 children. I have also inspected their arms, legs and nails. The hair of newborn children is not curly.

### The fear among Bongu natives when hearing bulu-ribut

For some reason I have not been sleeping well lately, and concluded that listening to music might help relieve me from troublesome thoughts at night. I recalled that during my travels through the Malay Peninsula, I went to sleep on several occasions charmed by the plaintive sound of *bulu-ribut*, the traditional Malay instrument. Speaking to my servant Sale about it, I found out he knew how to make *bulu-ribut* so I suggested that he make several of them in various sizes.

This instrument is known among the Malays of Johore and Java and consists mainly of a bamboo cane, sometimes 18 metres in length. The internal pith of the bamboo is removed and at various distances on the pole, vertical openings differing in size are made on the tube. The bamboo tubes are then hung from the roof of a hut or a tree in the village, and are even sometimes found hanging in the jungle. As the wind travels through the slits in the tubes, it creates curious sounds; since the slits are positioned on various sides of the tube, the sound can be heard regardless of from which direction the wind blows. The sound quality of a *bulu-ribut* depends on the length of the pole, the thickness of the bamboo, and how dry the bamboo is; it also varies with the height the instrument is hung at.

After three days of hard work Sale made five sets of *bulu-ribut*, some over twelve metres long. With help from my other servants, we hung them from the tree tops around my hut and even placed one on my verandah. According to Sale's instructions, *bulu-ribut* have to be hung straight up and down, so we put considerable effort into making sure they stayed that way, and that they were securely tied to the trees and could not be blown away by the wind.

We had to wait until nightfall to hear how the newly-made instruments would sound. Throughout the day the wind here is usually very strong, so the rustle of leaves from the jungle and the sound of waves crashing on the reef around the cape drowned the melodic sound of *bulu-ribut*.

Busy with my daily work I completely forgot about our new musical instruments. Only after I had retired to my bed and was about to fall asleep did I hear the drawn-out, melancholy sounds around the hut, followed by a shrill whistle. Moments later I could hear Sale and Mebli chatting about our Malaysian 'harp'. During the night I was occasionally wakened by a whistling from the verandah; similar sounds could be heard from the adjacent jungle. The whole area seemed alive with our *bulu-ribut* calling to each other from their scattered positions in the darkness.

No natives called to see me the next day and they stayed away the following day as well. I thought that something must have happened at Bongu to cause their absence as it was very unusual for a day to go by without local villagers calling in to chat with me or my servants. I went to Bongu to find out if my friends had been offended by something.

I reached the village at about sunset, when the natives are usually back from their daily work, and found them occupied with preparing dinner. A group of them hurriedly cleared a place for me on a *barla*.

"Why have you not called at *tal* Maklai in the last few days?" I asked.

They looked down at the ground: "We were afraid."

"Afraid of what?" I felt surprised.

"Of the *tamo* Russ."

"What *tamo* Russ? Where did you see them?" I persisted.

"We only hear them."

"Where then?" I felt puzzled.

"Near *tal* Maklai, for the last two nights; a crowd of them … they spoke loudly."

Now it became clear to me — the *bulu-ribut* near my hut were the cause of the natives staying away. I smiled. The natives, who watched me carefully, must have thought that I agreed with them and asked: "When did the *tamo* Russ come? How? No ship was seen hereabouts. Would they stay for long? May we come to see them?"

Unable to withhold my laughter I explained that there were no *tamo* Russ visiting me. I invited the natives to come and see for themselves when I returned home and they followed me rather shyly. They seemed confused at finding no visitors at my place and concluded that the *tamo* Russ must come only during the night to chat with me. From then on the natives always left my place at sunset.

In the beginning the penetrating sound of *bulu-ribut* would waken me during the night, but as time went by I became accustomed to the sound. Even if wakened I soon fell asleep again and the soft plaintive sound accompanied by rustling trees and murmuring waves, often lulled me to sleep.

February

I decided to journey to the Archipelago of Contented People and visit Erempi. Since my friend Kain, with whom I stayed at Airu, did not know the way to Erempi, we visited Segu Island first and collected two natives to be our guides. We sailed with our pirogue to the rim of the bay then, after following the course of a river, we found ourselves in a small lake encircled by jungle. There we left our pirogue and journeyed inland along a narrow path almost over-grown by *ratang*, a kind of native vine. An impressively tall, wild *banaba* caught my attention. It had small greenish fruit full of seeds, however the fruit was not edible; the vine leaves were very narrow. We travelled westward and after about another hour's walk, reached Erempi. The villagers seemed very frightened by our sudden arrival and at my appearance — I was told by Kain that they had never seen a white man before.

The sounds of the local *barum* summoned the people to return from their jungle gardens to the village. The inhabitants of Erempi live in small huts scattered throughout the jungle and only from time to time do they visit the main area of the village. Their huts are mainly built on stilts. The people did not differ in their appearance from the Papuans on the Maclay Coast. I measured the heads of several villagers and wrote down some words of their village dialect.

Although it was said to me earlier that the people from Erempi are cannibals, I did not see a single human tooth or bone used by the locals as ornaments, nor did they use human bones for making their weapons. My friend Kain though, claimed that the Erempi people dispose of human bones by throwing them into the sea. The local people here make oblong shields of different sizes, while the shields made by the Papuans from neighbouring islands are circular.

On our way back the following morning, I was surprised by a sound coming from the jungle and far louder than that emitted by any animal known locally to me. So loud was the noise that I thought it must come from a creature of considerable size. My companion Kain assured me, however, that the sound belonged to an adult cassowary and was often heard in the jungle.

*March*

## The marriage of Mukau

A group of youths from Gorendu arrived to tell me that they were bringing a bride from Gumbu. They led me to the sandy bank of a stream where I found several natives from Gumbu accompanying the bride. Most of them sat down and smoked while two young men were occupied with the bride's toiletry. She was called Lo and had a shapely figure, looked healthy although not very pretty, and was about sixteen years of age. Also accompanying Lo were three girls aged between eight and twelve years, whose presence seemed customary. It was the young men who carefully groomed the bride from the top of her head to her toes. They smeared her skin with *suru* (red ochre) excluding no part except the skin covered by her traditional loin cloth. While the bride was being smeared, a few men sitting some distance away came closer and spat a chewed-up pulp containing *onim-atar* (magic spell) on her. The last man to approach turned up the front of her loin cloth and began spitting chewed pulp over the lower part of the bride's abdomen. The spitting completed, he uttered some words that brought the *onim-atar* ritual to an end.

Three horizontal lines of white ochre were painted across the bride's face and a long line along the ridge of her nose. The men hung many necklaces made from dog teeth around her neck and placed bracelets on her arms packed with palm leaves, tipped with red colouring. While being decorated, the bride patiently offered each part of her body to be smeared. Over her maidenly waistband a new loin cloth called *mal* was placed made of yellow and red bands and reaching down to her knees; it was open on both sides to expose her legs and thighs. Finally, red ochre was smeared on the three girls accompanying the bride.

Lo had her hands placed on the girls' shoulders and they held onto each other in the same manner as they walked along the path towards the village. They moved slowly, heads lowered, eyes upon the ground. All wore the *goon* (woman's large bag) on their heads and a group of Gumbu natives followed them walking in single file. Apart from the bride and her three companions, there were no other females in the procession. I walked among the first group of natives behind the bride in order to see everything.

Entering the village we found local men and women waiting at the doors of their huts. As we came to the village clearing near the bridegroom's hut, the girls suddenly stopped and abandoned their walking positions. Bongu women sat in the village clearing preparing *ingi* (food); the men also sat clustered in small groups.

A brief silence settled upon the crowd, interrupted by a short speech from Mote who approached the girls and placed new *mal* (loin cloth) on their heads. After him Namui appeared from his hut, uttering some words as he placed a new *tabir* on Lo's head. A Gumbu woman came forward from the crowd and took off the *tabir*, the *mal* and the *goon* and placed these on the ground beside her. Then the Bongu villagers brought out their gifts — *tabir*, scores of male and female *mal* and *goon*, and other objects. Two men each brought a *hadga-nangor* (a new spear). On delivering their gifts some natives gave a short speech; others approached quietly and stepped aside as soon as they had left their offerings near the bride.

After the last gift had been delivered, friends of the bride began sorting the objects into appropriate groups and the crowd fell quiet again. An old native approached the bride and while leaning on his spear, wound a tuft of her hair around one of his fingers. He addressed Lo with a short speech while she sat at his feet.

As he spoke the old man occasionally tugged the bride's hair to focus her attention on what was being said. He was soon replaced by another old villager who, before speaking, also wound a lock of the bride's hair around his finger and pulled it so hard that Lo jumped up, trembling and crying. All seemed to go according to a customary programme, which each participant was familiar with and well knew the role to be played.

The crowd remained silent throughout the ceremony so the speeches, not particularly loud, could be heard. The bride and bridegroom appeared in such a secondary role that the main protagonist, old man Guna, even forgot that Muku was the name of the bridegroom and asked for help. The crowd laughed. The bride's parents barely took part in the ceremony.

After the old men had delivered their speeches of wisdom, reinforcing their words by pulling Lo's hair, hence causing her to sob louder and yet louder, the ceremony came to an end. The villagers who had come with the bride began to prepare for the journey home. The women packed the gifts into bags and piled them near Lo, whom they farewelled by pressing her arms above the elbow and stroking her gently on her back. Still weeping, the bride awaited the arrival of her future husband.

I learned that the entire Bongu village community had contributed gifts, not just the relatives of Muku, and that the gifts did not all go to the bride's family but were distributed among the wider Gumbu village community. The bride's relatives would play an important role in the distribution of the gifts, particularly as there were obviously not enough *tabir* for everyone.

Later when I visited Muku's hut, I found the young bride already occupied with preparing food for the guests. Muku is about fourteen years old and Lo a year older. He had not been through the *mulum* (circumcision ceremony) yet and this concerned some Bongu villagers who voiced their disapproval. But other villagers mentioned the case of Asol, married some years ago, now with two children and still uncircumcised. So I concluded that the *mulum* custom was not strictly practised on the Maclay Coast.

The following day I found a group of young Bongu men taking Muku to the sea to bathe him; they spoke loudly and laughed. The bathing was related to the marriage ritual but I do not know if the girls took Lo to the water also. The bathing was the last part of the wedding festivity.

On 20 June 1877, I witnessed another wedding where the bride was abducted by force. It was actually a purported 'abduction' for appearances sake, as the marriage had already been arranged. It all went as follows: at about 3.00 p.m. the *barum* sounded from Bongu as though calling men to arms. A boy ran into the village bringing news that a group of armed men from Koliku-mana had raided a garden where Bongu women worked and had taken off with a young girl. Several young Bongu men ran after the raiders and a fight took place, but even that was pre-arranged. The men then made for Koliku-mana where a feast awaited everyone. Among the group engaged in the chasing the raiders, was the father and uncle of the 'abducted' girl. They all returned with gifts from Koliku-mana and the girl supposedly 'abducted' stayed as wife of one of her abductors.

*29 May*

## The illness and death of Mote's wife

I was told this morning that Mote's wife was very ill and was asked to go and see her. Around 1.00 p.m. a messenger brought the news that the woman was dying and that her husband had begged that I take some medicine to her. I left for the village and on arrival heard women lamenting and wailing from various parts of the site, so I thought that the sick woman had already died. However, I was directed to Mote's hut by some local women sitting nearby breast-feeding their children. It was very dark inside the hut and for a moment I was unable to see very much. Several women rushed up to me from the semi-darkness, begging for medicine.

When my eyes adjusted to the darkness I saw the sick woman lying and tossing about on the bare ground. Around her was a group of women trying to hold and comfort her. Beside them stood more women; some children were also in the hut. The dying woman kept clenching her teeth and occasionally tried to get up.

Outside the hut as well as inside, the people spoke of death and the sick woman herself cried out from time to time: "I am dying … dying."

As I returned to my place, Mote came after me pleading for medicine and I told him that I would bring it soon. I hurriedly weighed out a small dose of morphine and left for Bongu. On my way I met a group of natives who accompanied me to the village, convinced that I carried a safe remedy for the illness. The people inside the sick woman's hut felt the same, but the dying woman refused to take the medicine despite all efforts to convince her to do so. One of the natives then tried to force her clenched teeth apart with a *dongan* (traditional knife) and pour the medicine into her mouth. She kept repeating: "I am dying … "

### 30 May

At sunrise the short beat of *barum* could be heard from various parts of the village announcing the death of Mote's wife. As I hurried towards Bongu I could hear the wailing women from some distance away. The village men carried their bows and arrows as they moved about. I saw Mote near his hut pacing about; then he began to run as if chasing someone. He held an axe which he swung round as if cutting the roofs of nearby huts or coconut palms. I went inside the hut where the dead woman lay, but because of the darkness I could only see that she lay on a platform surrounded by lamenting women.

Lako and other relatives of the deceased made a kind of high chair from paddles and poles and placed it in the fore-part of the hut. One of the natives carried the dead woman, whose body had become considerably emaciated during her last days, and handed her to another native who placed her in the high chair. The dead woman's legs were bent and tied at the knees and then she was wrapped in the female *mal*. Around her head and along her body were placed branches of *coleus* and other colourful leaves.

In the clearing in front of the hut, visiting natives from

Gorendu and Gumbu made warlike cries and gestures. Speeches were made but they were all spoken so quickly it was impossible for me to understand the words. Meanwhile, Mote demonstrated his grief and despair — he was dressed in a new *mal* and on his head wore the *katazan* (a huge crest-like fan made from plumes) worn only by *tamo boro* (the head of the family). He carried a large *goon* (bag) hanging from his armpit and an axe on his shoulder. Mote alternately paced up and down, then squatted — a kind of ritual dance performed by the husband of the deceased wife — while the village women wailed in accompaniment.

Driven by despair, Mote began to furiously chop at a coconut palm with his axe. One of the wailing women, presumably his sister, quickly approached Mote, telling him that it was pointless to ruin a perfectly good tree. After she had spoken, he made a few light strokes of his axe against the tree trunk and then moved off to vent his grief by smashing an old and useless fence.

A group of Mote's friends from Gumbu, in expression of their sympathy, brought *tabir* and placed them at the entrance of the deceased's hut; the gifts were soon taken away by family members.

Mote wailed in grief all day; throughout the evening he repeated the mourning song, *alamo-amo*: "The sun is setting already but she is still sleeping; the dark is already falling but she does not come: I call her — she does not appear." The natives moved the dead woman deeper into the hut where a group of women again surrounded the bed on which she lay. Still wailing, the women made a fire and talked.

When visiting Bongu that evening I found little had changed — the women kept vigil in the hut; the men gathered around a fire in the village clearing. Several times during the night the *barum* sounded and was answered by another one somewhere far up in the mountains. It was from the village of Buram-mana, but I was only to find this out later.

31 *May*

At Bongu this morning I found an entirely different atmosphere. People were chatting among themselves in an amicable way as they prepared *ingi* (food). Judging by the number of pots near the fire and the piles of yam and taro peelings (being busily consumed by grunting local pigs), it was to be a large gathering. Most of the preparation for the feast had been made during the night and I was told that the deceased's relatives from Buram-mana, where she had grown up, were expected to come to *gambor-rosar* (to tie the baskets).

Entering the deceased's hut, I found that the corpse had already been placed in a *gambor* (a basket coffin made from *goob*, woven palm leaves) but the dead woman's head was still visible. Coming closer to the box I noticed that the necklaces and other ornaments I had seen during yesterday's showing of the body had been removed. Even the *mal* was gone and only the *coleus* branches still remained.

On hearing terrible cries outside, I left the hut to see a group of warriors from the mountain village of Buram-mana emitting war cries in the village clearing, much as the Gorendu people had done yesterday but with even greater noise. They were followed by a file of women heading directly to the deceased's hut and all began to wail loudly.

As the Buram-mana villagers had to return home the same day, the Bongu inhabitants had prepared the banquet in such a way that it could be taken home in baskets and eaten there by their visitors. To make that possible, each *tabir* was lined with banana leaves in which to wrap the boiled *ingi* and pieces of pork for the guests. Apart from the packed food, the guests also received *tabir*, *goon*, *mal* and other objects.

Two Buram-mana men carried the *gambor* containing the deceased from the hut; behind them walked a group of wailing women. The basket that held the body was then tied up with vines and attached to a bamboo pole. Two more natives held the pole-ends on their shoulders while other men wrapped more vines around the basket. The wailing women formed a circle around the basket and began to dance, swaying with the middle parts of their bodies. Some of them rubbed the *gambor* containing the dead body with their hands, as if trying to comfort it, continuously lamenting. The basket was then taken back into the hut and hung from a crossbeam in the corner.

At the funeral's end the Buram-mana natives loaded their gifts onto their women and left for home with far less noise than when they had arrived.

## 2 June

This morning I found all the natives, even the younger ones, with blackened faces. Some of them had even smeared black colouring on their chests, limbs and backs. Mote, the deceased's husband, had decorated his entire body with *kumu* (a black earthen colour). I was informed that the body smearing activity had been carried out during the night, and that today the Bongu villagers would remain in their huts and no soul would venture out to work. The men drank *keu* and helped themselves to food from *tabir*, while the women busied themselves within the huts. The women wore no ornaments but their skin was heavily smeared with *kumu*.

I approached Mote and asked for some *kumu*, with which I was immediately provided. The villagers watched approvingly as I scooped some *kumu* onto my index finger and marked a black spot on my forehead. Mote, squeezing my arm, kept repeating: "*E-aba, e-aba.*" The other natives echoed his approval.

Upon entering Mote's hut I noticed a large cylinder made from coconut leaves. It was about two metres long and placed in the same corner where the *gambor* was seen yesterday. On parting the leaves I saw that the *gambor* still hung from the beam, but the cylinder of palm leaves had been arranged around it. Two fires were burning inside the hut to cover the decomposing body's noticeably strong smell.

225

*June*

## Visit to Gorima

While eating my meal on the *barla* near the hut of Kodi-boro at Bogatim, I overhead a conversation between my host and his son Ur, who had just returned from another village. They were chatting while chewing betel and although I scarcely understood most of their words, I recognised my name mentioned several times. After finishing my meal I left the *barla* intending to stroll through the village, but Kodi-Boro held on to my sleeve as I was passing by him.

"Maklai, do not go to Gorima [a coastal village about six kilometres from Bogatim]."

"I do not intend to go there — I will be returning to *tal* Maklai tomorrow."

"That is good," said Kodi.

"Why should I not go to Gorima," I was puzzled.

"People there are bad," he explained.

I let the matter rest since I had other work to do — namely trying to determine the position of some peaks on the Mana-boro-boro ranges, now exposed to the evening light. When darkness fell I stayed awhile, chatting with some old village friends by their fires before returning to my *buambramra* where I was to spend the night. Nearby Kodi-boro busily attended to his fire. I stretched my blanket on the *barla* and began taking off some of my apparel — boots, gaiters, and so on. Before lying down, however, I called to Kodi-boro: "Why are the people of Gorima *borle* (bad)?" Kodi hesitated. I pressed some pieces of tobacco into his hand.

"If you don't tell me I shall return home for my dinghy and head for Gorima."

"O Maklai, stay away from Gorima — the people there are very nasty."

"Why? What did Ur tell you today?"

Seeing that I was determined to find out, Kodi told me that

when visiting in-laws at Gorima, Ur had met two local villagers who spoke about me and how I had many goods in my home. They discussed how Bongu people should kill me and take all my belongings. The two villagers wanted to go to *tal* Maklai and ransack my place after killing me — and this was why Kodi called the Gorima men *borle*. He begged me not to go there.

"What are the names of those men?"

"Abui and Malu,' Kodi told me."

After handing Kodi another piece of tobacco I told him I would now like to sleep — but in my mind I had already worked out a plan to handle the matter. I was surprised that after knowing the natives for so long, there were still those among them who plotted to kill me. As to Gorima, I had visited that village only once during my earlier stay here and was therefore less acquainted with the people there than in other places. However, I did not believe that they seriously intended to carry out what they had said; even in the most extreme circumstances they would surely hesitate to openly attack me. They might, however, throw a spear from behind my back or ambush me with their arrows — that was more probable. I was more concerned with the fact that the natives were talking about an idea that might incite someone from my closer neighbours to do the same. A villager could think: "Why wait for the Gorima people to kill Maklai and take all his goods. I should do it myself." Before falling asleep I decided that I would go to Gorima, perhaps tomorrow, should all go well.

Wakened early by roosters, I got up after a good night's rest. Some cold tea and pieces of taro left from yesterday's meal served as my breakfast. I left part of my baggage in the *buambramra* placed in a knapsack and tied up with white cord, and took with me only a blanket and some pieces of taro. No one saw me set off for the trip; leaving the *buambramra* I made straight for the sea to avoid going through the village. I did not know the road to Gorima but expected that one could get there by following the shore line.

The day warmed up fast and by 11.00 a.m. it felt burningly hot. I had to cross the Kior River in water waist deep. Travelling on, I reached another river that looked shallower. I hesitated to take off my boots, as I was uncertain as to whether I would be able to put them on again if they became wet. The ground along the river bank was covered here and there with sharp stones, slowing me down. Moving on I took a wrong path that led me into the jungle, away from the shore; but I soon realised this, took another track and then changed course again to avoid going deeper into the forest. At last the sea was in sight, but it was already 3.00 p.m. so I stopped to rest and eat my taro pieces. Gorima was not far away and I wanted to arrive there after 5.00 p.m.

Only now I remembered perhaps the most important thing, for which I had come unprepared — the Gorima dialect was unknown to me and the locals were probably unfamiliar with the Bongu dialect. But it was too late to do anything about this now and I must just hope for the best.

Gorima lies on a promontory; heading that way I came across a stretch of mangrove forest, slowing me down considerably, thus I doubted if I would reach the village during daylight. Fortunately, I noticed a pirogue drawn up on the beach and heard human voices from the nearby jungle, so I went to the pirogue and awaited the natives' return. Soon three of them appeared, shocked to come back and find me by their pirogue. They were about to run back into the jungle, so I hurriedly approached the eldest: "Are you from Gorima?" I asked in Bongu dialect. The native raised his head slightly and I understood this to be a positive answer. I told him my name and explained that I would like to go with them to Gorima. The natives looked confused as to what to do, but they had to return to the village and seem pleased at the prospect of being rid of my presence once they got there. I gave each some tobacco and we all set off.

The village lay further along the shore than I had thought and the sun was already setting when we got there. Because of my white jacket and hat I had been noticed by the villagers from some distance away, and now a large crowd waited for me on the shore. No local native spoke Bongu dialect so I had to rely solely on my gestures and signs, placing one of my hands on my empty stomach and pointing a finger to my mouth. The villagers understood that I was hungry; one old man said something and the people began to prepare a meal. By placing one of my hands under my cheek and laying my head down, I demonstrated to the locals that I would like to stay overnight in the village. The message was understood and I was soon shown to a *buambramra*.

Although I was unable to express my apology for my unexpected arrival, I was most gratified that I would not go to bed on an empty stomach or spend the night in the open and thus attract fever. Feeling hungry and in expectation of a *tabir* with food, I barely acknowledged the arrival of a man familiar with the Bongu dialect. When the food was served, the *tabir* contained the biggest meal I had ever eaten in New Guinea.

With dinner over, I thought it would be a proper time to have a talk with the locals, since there was now a man present to help as an interpreter. I asked this interpreter to summon the headmen of Gorima for me to talk to. He left and returned shortly to tell me that all the *tamo boro*, the chief men of Gorima, were coming to see me. I asked that some dry branches be thrown on the fire to better illuminate the interior of *buambramra*. I sat on *barla* near the fire and looked at the now well-lit faces of the natives: "Abui and Malu, are they among you here?" Before saying the names of the men I had to look in my notebook where I had written down the names the previous evening in semi-darkness. The natives were quiet and after a while I was told that only Abui was present. "Call Malu," I requested and someone immediately left to seek him.

When Malu appeared I stood up and indicated to him and Abui two places near the fire opposite me — they hesitantly sat down. I then addressed the whole gathering through my interpreter: "I heard yesterday from some people at Bogatim that two Gorima men — Abui and Malu — want to kill me, so I have come here to have a close look at each of them. I think it is very unfair because I have caused no harm to either men or to anybody in Gorima. Now, since I have come here from Bogatim on foot, I feel very, very tired and want to rest. If Abui and Malu want to kill me, let them do it while I am asleep, since I intend to leave Gorima tomorrow." After speaking these words I walked to the *barla*, climbed up on it and wrapped myself in my blanket. Before falling asleep I heard much talking with my name often being mentioned; I woke several times during the night, not because of fear but because of my heavy evening meal.

The following morning, before I departed from Gorima, Abui brought me a big pig as a gift. He and Malu insisted on accompanying me back to Bogatim and even to 'tal Maklai'. The news of this spread throughout all the villages in the area, to be told and retold and has left a strong impression on the natives.

## 11 July

I was away for six days journeying with Kain and other Bili Bili natives in their *wang,* visiting Tiara and some other islands in the Archipelago of Contented People. On my return I was met on the beach at Bongu by Meli and other local natives who told me of the death of Vangum during my absence. Vangum from Gorendu, about twenty-five years old and healthy and strong, had unexpectedly fallen ill and died two or three days later.

Melbi informed me that natives from Bongu and Gorendu were in a state of shock and alarm about the death. The father, uncle and other relatives of the deceased, of whom there were many in both villages, were persuading other natives to set out against the mountain villagers in revenge. The situation sounded serious and on hearing the news, I decided to try to prevent an attack on the mountain people. I restrained myself, however, from immediately voicing my objection, in order to give myself time to consider the matter more calmly.

Conflict between Papuans is often triggered by the belief that the death of a villager, even an accidental one, could have been caused in some way by *onim*, magic brought about by their enemies. Relatives and friends of the deceased gather after the death ceremony and speculate from which village the *onim* may have emanated, who had initiated it and why. It often leads to exhaustive debate. After determining who the culprit is, a plan is prepared on how to attack him and his village and to forge alliances with other villages sympathetic to the cause.

*15 July*

Yesterday I learned some details which should be very advantageous to my plan — the natives of Bongu and Gorendu could not agree on the exact village where the alleged enemy of Vangum lived, or the father of the culprit who supposedly prepared the *onim* that had caused the death. However, the natives overcame their differences by a decision to attack one of the suspected villages first, and then proceed to attack the other.

A delegation from Bongu called on me today to canvas my support, but received only my refusal. The men kept trying to persuade me to ally myself with them, so I raised my voice: "Maklai *ballal kere*" (Maclay has said enough), upon which the delegation left.

I left for Gorendu to discover what the people there thought and found that the locals spoke of nothing but the forthcoming war on the mountain villagers. I walked into Vangum's hut. In one corner near the *barla* hung a *gambor* and by the fire burning on the ground sat the young widow, naked but for a covering of soot. There was no one else in the hut and she smiled, plainly weary of her new status as the distressed widow. I learned that she would have to go to her deceased husband's brother.

Without having achieved what I had intended during my visit, I left. On my way out of the village I saw Vangum's father busily making a fire on the beach under the pirogue of his dead son, completed only some days before the young man died. The craft was already cut in several places and was now about to be totally destroyed by fire. Knowing that I would object to a possible war over his son's death, the old man barely glanced at me.

Several days passed without an attack on the mountain villages, though this was not due to my influence, but to some disagreement between the two villages — Bongu and Gorendu — about the warring strategy.

## 23 July

At about 3.00 p.m. today, while I sat on my verandah, Sale suddenly appeared. Trying to catch his breath, he told me that he had heard from some Bongu people of the sudden death of Vangum's younger brother. Alarmed at the consequences that could result from the death of two brothers in such a short time, I sent Mebli off to Bongu to find out if the news was indeed true. On his return I was informed that earlier in the day, a young man called Tui — about ten years younger than his brother Vangum — had accompanied his father and other Gorendu villagers to the Ganbenau River to fish. He was bitten on one of his fingers by a small snake, its venom known to be so powerful that the frightened father gathered the boy in his arms and ran back to the village. On their arrival Tui was already dying. I hurriedly collected a lancet, liquid ammonia, Condy's crystals and some bandages and ran to Gorendu. On my way there I became exhausted but was fortunate enough to be able to catch a pirogue heading for Port Constantine, and thus take me on to Gorendu.

Before reaching the village we were met by two messengers, Ion and Namui, sent from Gorendu to tell me that the poor boy Tui had died and that the huts of the *yambau-tamo* (uncircumcised mountain people) were to be burnt. The beating of the *barum* could be heard from Gorendu telling of the boy's death. This second death, happening in the same village and to the same family hardly two weeks after the earlier tragedy, had brought not only grief to the inhabitants of both villages but the urge for revenge — and fear as well.

War now seemed imminent; even old people and children were talking about it. Some locals looked at me with considerable reservation and others with a certain degree of hostility, since they knew well that I was against war and were suspicious that in some way I may even have contributed to the Tui misfortune. Only my old friend Tui — as usual friendly towards me — kept shaking his head. There was nothing more for me to do in Gorendu — the people were too agitated to listen to me. I went along the shortest path to Bongu, helped by bright moonlight.

On my return to my hut, Saul tried to convince me of the need to raid *mana-tamo* (mountain people) as he felt strongly that both deaths had been caused by *onim* and unless they fought back, the Bongu and Gorendu people could be wiped out. So even here, at home, the word *onim* haunted me. My servant Saul told me that in Java *onim* is called *doa* and he believed in it. According to my other servant Mebli, the word for it on Pelau Island is *plai* and belief in sorcery is just as powerful.

### 24 July

I went to Gorendu in the morning; the natives appeared calmer than yesterday but remained sullen — even my old friend Tui seemed gloomy: "Gorendu *bassa*," (the end of Gorendu) Tui said, offering me his hand. I asked Tui to explain to me exactly how the *onim* worked. He believed that the *mana-tamo* had got hold of some taro or meat left uneaten by the Gorendu people, cut the food into small pieces, uttered some magic words and then burnt it.

We went to the hut where the dead boy Tui lay. Groups of people were gathered around the hut. A sharp whistle, *ai*, sounded and the women and children broke from the groups and dashed into the jungle. I expected to see some kind of procession arriving but instead a solitary man appeared, constantly blowing a *monki-ai* (musical instrument made of coconut shell). When he passed near the hut where Tui lay, the man glanced inside and then moved on.

Only when the whistling *ai* had ceased did the women return to carry the dead boy from the hut. The old man Bugai smeared

Tui's forehead with white ochre, then drew one line downwards along the nose. The rest of the body was already smeared with *kumu* (charcoal). Earrings had been inserted into Tui's ears and earlobes while from his neck hung *gubo-gubo* (chest ornaments). Bugai added to the existing decorations with a new comb of white cockatoo plumes which he stuck in Tui's hair. The boy's body was then wrapped in *gub* (palm fronds) but this would be only a temporary arrangement as a proper *gambor rosar* (coffin basket) was being made in Bongu. Sangam, the dead boy's uncle, placed the body over his shoulders, cushioned on some palm leaves, and set off along the track to Bongu followed by a long procession of mourning natives.

Accompanied by several village men, I took another track and reached Bongu at about the same time as the procession. In the main village clearing Tui's body was placed in the new *gambor*, also made from palm fronds. No ornaments were removed from the boy's body, but his head was covered with a bag.

While the male relatives of the deceased were busy with tying the body into the *gambor*, several women daubed with charcoal were wailing and dancing around it, stroking the coffin with their hands. Most active among them was Kallol, Tui's mother, who dragged her feet along the ground as she wailed and clung to the coffin.

Finally the *gambor* was taken to Sangam's hut. There we were offered some *onim* to keep evil away from us and I was most curious to know what this magic potion consisted of. One of the natives called Ion, spat the *onim* from his mouth, so did all of us, and then we all walked to the beach to wash our hands in the sea. My old friend Tui asked me if I could prepare a special 'Maklai *onim*' to keep a powerful earthquake away from the coastal people, but let it destroy just the mountain villagers.

That evening the *barum* was heard sounding from Gorendu. Later on I was wakened by Mebli who had just returned from there. He secretly told me that the villagers had decided war on *mana-tamo* and probably Tengum-mana as well, but that he had been instructed not to say anything about this to me. The wars here result in a relatively small number of human casualties, but they are very prolonged and personal vendettas which drag on for years. The warring villages stay cut off from each other and the people live either in constant fear of being killed, or in an agitated mood to kill.

I felt compelled to help the native community at Bongu, only five minutes walk from me, and influence them not to wage war. My thoughts and opposition to any warfare had been made quite clear to them earlier on, so to remain silent on the matter now could be misunderstood, as though I had given up my objections. Besides, if I were silent now I would have to remain silent later on should the conflict spread. Even though I hate meddling in the affairs of other people, I decided to intervene. My determination to prevent war would have to match the natives' strong desire to seek revenge, so I had to think of a way to stall them until passions had cooled off.

*25 July*

I lay awake long into the night. Even after falling asleep I frequently awoke, pondering what to do. It was already dawn when I eventually managed some proper sleep. On waking I was able to formulate a plan of action but, feeling that I must not rush things or appear over-anxious, I restrained myself and waited for sunset before setting off to Bongu.

As expected, the villagers were preoccupied with current events, yet were anxious to know my view. I told them that although Vangum and Tui were both young and healthy and that their father was now left alone, I must still hold to my earlier view: "There shall be no war." My words spread fast throughout the village community. A large crowd had now gathered, but only old men entered the *buambramra* into which I withdrew. Each tried to convince me that war was inevitable. It would have been pointless to debate the groundless theory of *onim* since my knowledge of their language was still very limited. Besides, even with the best oratory, it would have been impossible to convince them of what I had to say. I let each native state his view. Then, when the last had finished talking, I rose in readiness to leave, repeating: "Maklai says there shall be no war; if you attack the mountain people, grave disaster will strike the people of Gorendu and Bongu." Silence fell in. Then the natives asked: "What will happen? ... What will Maklai do? ... ," and so on. I thought it best to leave them to think about the consequences and only said: "You will find out if you go to war."

As I left for home and was passing a group of natives gathered in the village, I felt convinced that my words were already making an impact on the locals — everyone seemed anxious to know what my predictions were. As I reached the doorstep of my hut, an old native caught up with me and with laboured breath from such a long run, asked: "Maklai, if *tamo-Bongu* go to the mountain, will a *tangrin* (earthquake) strike us?" These words from an old man struggling to regain his breath, were proof that what I had said earlier had made a strong impact on the Bongu villagers: "Maklai did not say there will be an earthquake," I told the old man. He answered: "No, but you did say that if we raided the mountain people, a great evil will strike us — *tangrin* is a great evil; the people of Bongu, Gumbu, Gorendu and Bogatim – we all fear the *tangrin*. Will the *tangrin* strike? Please tell me!" I replied: "Maybe."

The old man was going back towards the village, but was met by two more natives running from the opposite direction. They were not far off and I clearly heard the old man saying: "Did I not tell you – there will be a *tangrin* if we go against the mountain people." Then the three of them ran towards the village.

I kept away from Bongu for some days, leaving it to the natives to solve the riddle, and depending on the Russian proverb: "Fear has great eyes." I felt certain that the village men would think seriously of what I had said and as they did so, their emotions would gradually begin to cool off. I restrained myself from enquiring as to whether any definite decision had been reached, but it became obvious their preparations for war had ceased.

About two weeks later I was visited by my old friend Tui who confirmed rumours that the Gorendu people intended to resettle their village. "Why?" I felt most curious. "We fear that if we stay in Gorendu, we will die one after another. Two men have already gone because of *onim* from *mana-tamo*. It is not just the people who are dying but the coconut palms look sick — their fronds are becoming red and they will soon die. Our enemy has buried *onim* in Gorendu so that everything in the village dies. We intended to wipe out *mana-tamo*, but we are afraid to do so now. Maklai objects to it and warns that disaster may strike us. The Bongu people fear *tangrin*. Should *tangrin* strike, the neighbouring villages would blame Bongu for causing it and they would all turn against us. That is what we are afraid of. The village of Gorendu has such a small number of men that they will be no match against *mana-tamo* if they go to war alone. That is why we have to leave our village." Tui explained that some of the people would settle in Gorima, others in Yambombi and Mitebog; only a few villagers intended to remain at Bongu.

(I came across customs like this some years ago during my visit to the tribal people on Luson Island, off the Malay Peninsula and to the tribal people of West New Guinea. There is a practice common among them and the people of Maclay Coast, to abandon any village in which one or more villagers have been thought to die accursed.)

## August

I have made it a custom to visit my neighbours at Bongu at 6.00 p.m. daily. Today I went there in anticipation of meeting inhabitants from other villages who were also expected to call into Bongu.

On reaching Bongu I went towards to a *buambramra*, attracted by the loud voices of a conversation going on inside, but the discussion ceased as soon as I appeared. The locals were most likely talking about me, or of something secret. The setting sun's red light penetrated into the hut, revealing the faces of people from Bongu, Gorendu, Bili Bili and Bogatim. It was a large gathering and obviously rather an important one. The natives kept silent and I sensed that my presence had interrupted an important discussion. My old fried Saul approached me. I have a special affinity with him and we often sit together on my verandah chatting about various transcendental topics. Now, putting his hand on my shoulder and looking into my eyes, he asked, pleadingly: "Maklai, tell me — can you die — can you be dead like the people of Bongu, Bogatim and Bili Bili?"

The question, coming so unexpectedly and with such a pleading tone of voice, surprised me. I looked around to find from the expressions on the faces of the other natives that it was not only Saul who was expecting an answer. It was most likely that the natives had been speaking about this and that my arrival had interrupted their discussion. To a simple question one should respond with a simple answer, and the natives knew that Maclay would give them an honest reply. Their proverb '*Balal Maklai hudi*' (You can take Maclay at his word) is a belief that must be upheld. I did not like to say "No' since tomorrow or some day afterwards, an accident could happen which would show the natives that I did not speak the truth. On the other hand "Yes" could tarnish my authority, especially important now, a few days after I had not sanctioned the war.

I stood up and paced about the *buambramra*, looking upwards while searching for an appropriate answer. The soft rays of the setting sun illuminated the objects hanging from the roof — skulls of fish and jaws of pigs. My eyes moved over the weapons above the *barla*; bows, arrows and spears of various shapes — I found what I was looking for. Taking down from the wall a solid, sharp spear that with a single thrust could have caused death, I approached Saul who watched my movements from the middle of the *buambramra*. I handed him the spear and then made a few steps backward. Facing Saul, I took off my hat to expose my face to the light, so that the natives could see that I was very serious and would not blink whatever might happen: "Let us see if Maklai can die," I told him. Astonished, Saul made no attempt to raise the spear but begged: "*Aren, aren*" (No, no)." Some natives rushed and stood between me and Saul to protect me with their bodies if necessary. After this scene, I was never again asked if I could die.

## September

The ceremony of *mun* in Bogatim.

The seeds I had given the natives to plant in their gardens are growing well.

Crocodiles are frequently seen swimming in the bay.

## October

The burial of Tanoka at Gumbu.

The natives of Gorendu are thinking seriously of resettling in a new location.

## 6 November

The arrival of the schooner *Flower of Yarrow*.

## 9 November

The death and burial of seaman Abu.

## 10 November

At 6.00 p.m. we raised anchor. I left most of my belongings in my hut, locked away and in the care of Bongu natives.

# Revising Darwin

It should be noted that, even with the best intentions, Miklouho-Maclay occasionally intruded on the traditional Papuan way of life. One example was his well-intentioned interference to prevent war between different villages. Disputes like this had often taken place and helped isolate one community from another for a long period of time, thus preventing the spread of disease and interbreeding. Miklouho-Maclay himself admitted that such disputes resulted in minimal loss of life, in contrast to disease fatalities. Also, Miklouho-Maclay's introduction of a variety of seeds foreign to New Guinea and his bringing of cattle from the outside world would be seen as unwise by today's ecologist. His monumental achievement came, however, by placing the accumulated wealth of his field work into practise, thus revising Darwin.

When after two months the *Flower of Yarrow* reached Singapore in January 1878, Miklouho-Maclay looked in a sad state. While on the ship, he contracted beriberi from which several crewmen had died. He was very ill and was confined to bed for three months. The doctor advised him to leave the tropics if he wished to survive. He thought of returning home but there was no Russian ship to take him on board. With some money that he had received from the Russian Geographical Society, Miklouho-Maclay was able to leave on the SS *Somerset* which was sailing for Sydney, calling on the way at Cooktown, Townsville and Brisbane. In Australia he hoped to make anthropological studies of the Australian aborigines. Awaiting him was the most crucial part of his scientific work — to revise Darwin's theory on the origin of the species and natural selection, and to find out how the Papuans and Australian Aborigines (with their dingoes) happened to be in their particular part of the world.

Miklouho-Maclay blended into the small scientific community in Sydney without difficulty, and did not challenge the old colonial concept that the Australian natives are subhuman; he pretended to be chiefly concerned with the Papuans. At the time of his stay in Sydney, many colonial expeditions perished in the harsh Australian interior, for reasons that the whites opted to die rather than ask local Aborigines for food and water that would have seen them survive the desert country. The British colonial concept of *terra nullius*, meaning that the continent was not inhabited with people but only sub-human natives, was much on the white men's minds.

The Russian explorer was already well known in Sydney. On arriving there in July 1878, he was befriended by Sir William Macleay, a wealthy grazier interested in anthropology and exploration, who invited Miklouho-Maclay to stay at his home. Miklouho-Maclay badly needed comfort in order to recuperate from years of exhausting work and deprivation. Writing to his sister Olga in Russia, he talked of how well he had been received by the Sydney scientific community. He even became a member of the local Linnean Society, writing various papers on anthropological subjects for their periodical *Proceedings* as well as campaigning for the rights of indigenous people.

When in New Guinea, Miklouho-Maclay had noticed that the Papuans lived in small but well-functioning communities, very conscious of their dependence on local natural resources. They moved their cultivated garden plots from one area to another, giving opportunity for that part of cleared jungle to rejuvenate the ground. They would even resettle a whole village if the latter were affected by sickness or some other disaster. Most importantly, however, was the finding that Papuan women had a modest number of children, thus eliminating or averting the danger of rapid population increase, which would inadvertently put a strain on local resources and lead to ecological disaster. The Papuans were much in control of their destiny, provided that ills were not brought in from the outside world. Arriving in Australia, Miklouho-Maclay was anxious to find out if the Australian Aborigines also had some kind of population control, similar to that practised by the Papuans.

Miklouho-Maclay's stay in Sydney was interrupted by another trip, when in March 1879 he sailed to New Guinea and neighbouring islands; New Caledonia, New Hebrides, Banks Island, Santa Cruz, and the Admiralty Islands, endeavouring to discover the ethnic and racial relationship between people living in those places and the Papuans. This time he travelled on a three mast schooner, the *Sadie F. Caller*. The vessel's skipper, an American captain called Webber, who was purportedly involved in trepang (sea slug) trade, called at various remote islands and the northern coast of Australia for his 'catch'. The 'catch' was not trepang however, but captured natives to be traded as slaves. Miklouho-Maclay insisted on a written agreement with Captain Webber that should he (Miklouho-Maclay) be killed by the natives on one of the islands, Webber should not take punitive action against them. The schooner was to call at the Maclay Coast for two weeks and then proceed to Karkar and Bagabag Islands, but Miklouho-Maclay called off the visit so as not to expose his Papuan friends to this unscrupulous slave trader. The schooner sailed instead to the Trobriand Islands, the Solomons, and the Louisiades.

Feeling most uncomfortable on board the *Sadie F. Caller*, Miklouho-Maclay left the schooner and caught the steamer, *Ellangowan,* belonging to the London Missionary Society, which took him back to Australia. Captain Webber, who had on board cases of scientific material collected by Miklouho-Maclay during his twelve month expedition, died unexpectedly and the cases went to San Francisco where they disappeared forever.

On the *Ellangowan* Miklouho-Maclay met the Reverend Chalmers who had pioneered a mission station in New Guinea at Port Moresby.[5] The missionary made it possible for Miklouho-Maclay to visit some native villages in that area. The missionary steamer then called at Thursday Island in the Torres Strait before reaching Brisbane. This last trip provided Miklouho-Maclay with the racial and ethnic characteristics of people living in the regions of the east coast of New Guinea. The regions lying south and north of New Guinea had been covered by his earlier expeditions. Now, only the southern part — Australia — was left to be explored in order to complete his ethnic map.

In May 1880 Miklouho-Maclay reached Brisbane where he soon established good contact with the local authorities. He was provided with laboratory facilities and was given human bodies of prisoners executed in Brisbane gaols, for dissection and research. Many of the bodies belonged to Aborigines and *kanaks*, native islanders brought to Australia by slave traders. Miklouho-Maclay obtained a similar offer of bodies from local hospitals.

From Brisbane, Miklouho-Maclay made several expeditions to the Australian outback to study tribal Aborigines. He noticed that the tribal people were skilled in fire making (a skill still not known to the Papuans). On the other hand, the Aborigines did not know about the bow and arrow, although they had a highly developed use of boomerangs, spear throwers, and some other unique tools. And there was always the question of where the Aborigines and their companion dog, the dingo, came from — if indeed, they had come from some other place at all. The official scientific view at the time was that Aborigines were sub-human and that they had crossed to Australia from Asia some thousand or so years prior to the arrival of Europeans. The extensive research that Miklouho-Maclay had earlier carried out in the Malayan archipelago and New Guinea, gave him an advantage over other scientists of the time when it came to the origin of the natives. Even a century after his death, he remained ahead of other scientists with his findings.

Miklouho-Maclay soon noticed an immense richness and diversity among the culture of the tribal Aborigines. There was also a strong linguistic diversity which he was able to detect. This convinced him that the Aborigines must have been in Australia ever since the Ice Age, and even earlier. They survived the climatic changes and successfully adapted their way of life to the new and dry environment. He saw them as part of Australia, and with a culture of considerable substance that could be the envy of many other peoples in the world — a radical view in the 19th century. He found that those same people had long been practising a highly effective system of population control, similar to the Papuans, which was of such importance to their survival that the system was embodied in tribal belief.

The tribal Aborigines were conscious that even a small increase in human population in the dry, often semi-desert, environment would lead to their extinction. Miklouho-Maclay remained quiet about his findings. On his expedition into the Australian interior, he discovered at Glen Innes the remains of a prehistoric pouched animal *Diprotodon Australia*, a giant kangaroo *Macropis titan*, and a giant wombat *Plascotomas gigas*. The findings showed that life in human or animal form had been in Australia since time immemorial.

Miklouho-Maclay took a special interest in carrying out research on dingoes, which he thought may hold the clue as to how long humans may have been inhabiting the Australian continent — did the dingo follow the hunter or the did the hunter follow the dingo? Miklouho-Maclay may have also sensed that the dingo could reveal secrets on the theory of evolution. (Even a century after his death he remained the sole scientist who conducted positive research on this Australian animal.) The dingo was the only animal domesticated by the Aborigines and was totemically related to many tribal groups, often portrayed in their art and oral literature. Miklouho-Maclay was puzzled about the dingo's presence in Australia. The animal was outlawed by the white settlers in Australia and was being driven towards extinction — sharing the same fate as the tribal Aborigines. No consideration was given to the fact that the dingo was especially intelligent and, being the only carnivorous animal on the Australian mainland, had checked the spread of various marsupial species, and even some insects that could have devastated the fragile Australian environment.

In Australia the dingo has evolved into several sub-species — the desert dingo, the rainforest dingo and the Alpine dingo — characteristic of the area and the environment where they lived. They all shared a common breeding pattern — to produce a litter in accordance with the amount of food available, or to severely curtail offspring production in times of severe food shortages.

The Australian Aborigines depended on the dingo for their hunting, just as the Papuans depended on their native dog. Did the hunter lead the canine or the canine lead the hunter? Miklouho-Maclay carried our comparative research on the dingo and the Papuan dog looking for this answer. He thought that the dingo might provide him with just the perfect specimen to work on, and perhaps revise Darwin's work on the selection of the species. Darwin held that humans are only a link in the long chain of evolution, meaning that their predominant role on the planet is only temporary. In his research among the Papuans and Australian Aborigines, Miklouho-Maclay had found, however, that those people had developed a culture and the way of life which co-existed with nature. The Papuans, without even discovering the skill to make fire, had stabilised a way of life that, if it had remained free from outside interference, could have lived on to eternity. The Australian Aborigines have gone even further in surviving drastic climatic changes; faced with the drying out of the Australian continent, they cocooned their culture in order to ensure their survival. They lived in that state for thousands of generations and may have continued living that way for eons of time, if they had been spared from European interference. Miklouho-Maclay thought that if Europeans could learn from Papuans and Australian Aborigines how to live harmoniously with nature, it might be possible for man, as a species, to avert self-destruction.

At the beginning of the 1880s when Miklouho-Maclay was still in Australia, another Russian scientist, Prince Peter Kropotkin, published his Mutual Aid theory, showing that many species are grouped and socially organised in order to secure their existence and survival, like flocks of birds, packs of wild dogs, and herds of other animals. Kropotkin also wrote about the grouping of humans in the struggle for survival, thus elaborating on the undivided family or extended family, which was practiced among Southern Slavs — Serbs and Bulgarians under the organisational term *Zadruga*. These social phenomena came about because most Southern Slavs had lived for several centuries under the tyrannical Ottoman occupation. The impoverished families had to resort to self-sufficiency, caring for their sick and elderly and bringing up their children within a system of oral tradition. Kropotkin believed that humans could organise themselves far better and live safer lives, by being stateless i.e. without rulers and bureaucrats — a belief for which he was unjustly labelled an 'anarchist'.

In his work, Kropotkin actually refers to Miklouho-Maclay using references from Miklouho-Malcay's notebook about the life of the Papuans, and heralds those notes as a finding of immense importance. The details from the notebook appeared in *Izvestia*, the journal of the Russian Geographical Society, in 1880, sent by Miklouho-Maclay from Australia. Kropotkin died in exile without seeing most of Miklouho-Maclay's work published. The work proves that Papuans and Australian Aborigines lived in a social system of extended families, without tribal chiefs, rulers, or any bureaucratic structure above the family as a basic unit. The people harvested their crops from the land, built seafaring vessels, made spears and successfully educated their youngsters to do so as well. Dingoes had families of their own or shared one with humans.

When Miklouho-Maclay finally returned to Sydney in January 1881, he received a welcome warmer than he ever expected — Sir Henry Parks, Premier of New South Wales, had a small cottage put at Miklouho-Maclay's disposal for his scientific pursuit. On the recommendation of Sir John Robertson, former premier of that colony, a marine research station was built at Watson's Bay on the outskirts of Sydney — one of the first stations of that kind to be built in the world.[6] It was expected that the research at the new station would revitalise Miklouho-Maclay's interest in comparative anatomy and lead his mind away from Papuans, Aborigines and dingoes. It happened, but only temporarily.

Miklouho-Maclay began his work at Watson's Bay Station in November 1881 where he eventually developed his Maclay Coast Scheme for the protection of the Papuans, their culture and habitat. He urged the colonial authorities to help implement his scheme. At that time it was widely held that due to European expansionism and 'development', the Australian Aborigines would soon become an extinct race; so would their companion animal the dingo and a host of other Australian species. Even Darwin himself expected it to happen, and had stated that wherever the white man treads, death pursues the aborigines. Campaigning from his Watson's Bay station, Miklouho-Maclay hoped to reverse the trend of destruction, thus revising Darwin's theory of the 'survival of the fittest'. The white man had achieved the upper hand by his successful development of superior tools. If given time, the Australian Aborigines would survive, just as they had survived the harsh climatic changes of the Ice Age and adapted to the dry environment that followed. Miklouho-Maclay expected that the strength of their earlier experience would see them through. From his base at Watson's Bay, he put his entire energy into halting the tide of human and environmental destruction.

The Russian scientist seldom mentioned Darwin, but Darwin must have often been on his mind when he was carrying out his research. He may have felt more comfortable with the findings of the naturalist Alfred Wallace, whose field research had actually accelerated Darwin into fame. In his student days Miklouho-Maclay followed Darwin's theory but now, after such extensive field work, he had strong evidence that Darwin's work was flawed and could be easily manipulated. Australian Aborigines and dingoes survived mutually in Australia through eons of time — with the large influx of whites into the country with their lethal tools, the two species could be wiped out in a single generation, as happened in Tasmania. At his new Watson's Bay station, instead of researching marine life, Miklouho-Maclay was more interested in studying the brain of the dingo, as he felt its extinction was probable.

Miklouho-Maclay kept quiet about his findings on the Australian Aborigines and the dingo, in order to preserve cordial relations with his Australian colleagues, as he hoped to realise his dream of making New Guinea an international protectorate, to help save the Papuans and their culture from colonisation. With that idea in mind Miklouho-Maclay left Sydney in February 1882 for Europe; he was back in Russia after twelve years' absence.

At that time much of the world was colonised and divided by European imperial powers. The eastern half of New Guinea was still free but was being contested by Europeans, all anxious to seize it. While in Russia, Miklouho-Maclay negotiated with the imperial Russian authorities to have East New Guinea proclaimed a protectorate, democratically run by the Papuans themselves in accordance with their traditional culture, and to be protected from colonial exploitation and the slave trade. The Russian fleet was to be given access to Port Constantine at Maclay Coast, a port badly needed for re-supply of the Russian fleet travelling to the Far East from their European ports. It was a highly secret deal and Miklouho-Maclay returned to the Pacific with his trip paid for by the Russian Czar.

While he was in Europe, Miklouho-Maclay joined Dr Otto Finsch in a lecture at the Berlin Anthropological Society on the poetry of the Pacific. As a scientist, Finsch was very much interested in the culture of people from the Pacific islands and befriended Miklouho-Maclay. It was unknown to Miklouho-Maclay, however, that his colleague was working for a German financial institution planning to set up the *Neu Guinea Kompanie* on the Maclay Coast, which would lead to colonisation of the whole area.

Before leaving Europe, Miklouho-Maclay met in London with Sir Arthur Gordon, the British Commissioner for the West

Pacific and friend of Prime Minister Gladstone, who assured him that the British had no interest in annexing New Guinea. Considering his European trip successful, Miklouho-Maclay returned to the Pacific.

# The Third Visit to Maclay Coast

*March 1883*

## March

I was travelling on the English steamer *Chyebassa* from Port Said to Brisbane in Australia, when at Port Batavia (Jakarta) I met Admiral N.V. Kopitov who was in charge of the Russian corvette *Skobeliev*. The admiral informed me that on their way to the Far East, the corvette would call at some islands in the Melanesian group and perhaps even New Guinea. This provided me with the unique opportunity to visit the Maclay Coast and see, once again, my Papuan friends. I hastily organised that my baggage be sent to Australia on the *Chyebassa* before transferring to the corvette *Skobeliev*, and the following morning we sailed off.

On our way we called at Macassar in Ambon where I asked the admiral if he could obtain for me a young bull, a heifer and two goats. The animals were already acclimatised to the Malay Archipelago environment and I intended to give them as a gift to my native friends on Maclay Coast. The admiral obliged and the animals were purchased at the expense of the Imperial Navy as well as other gifts — Malay *parangs* (knives), red cotton fabric, beads and mirrors – to be given to the natives. I myself bought a variety of seeds: durian, mango, breadfruit, oranges, lemons, coffee; also several pineapple seedlings and some other plants that my Papuan friends would find useful to grow in their gardens.

After passing the straits of Buru and Saiguyen between the islands of Salavati and Batanta, we reached the northern coast of New Guinea on 12th March. The admiral decided not to call at Dore so we headed straight to Maclay Coast. Some days later, as we passed Humboldt Bay on the New Guinea Coast, Volcano Island could be seen with its still active volcano, as it had been during my earlier visit in 1877. We eventually passed Izoumroud Strait between the mainland and the Archipelago of the Contented People on 17th March and about 5.00 p.m. that day, dropped anchor at Port Constantine.

As I walked onto the shore at Cape Observation, I was greeted by a group of old friends from Gumbu. I told them that I would be at Bongu the following morning and that my countrymen on the corvette would need some pigs, taro, bananas and other supplies. Fearing that I might attract a fever attack I restrained myself from visiting the other villages and spent the night on the corvette.

On 18 March, accompanied by Admiral Kopitov and some other officers, we embarked on the shore near Bongu. The natives soon approached me with questions; where would I settle and where would my hut be built this time? The village of Bongu looked somewhat smaller and more neglected than during my 1876–77 visit and I soon discovered that part of the village, including a number of deserted huts, had been reclaimed by the bush. I was told by locals that some of the people who had once lived in them had since died and others had resettled elsewhere.

At the end of my earlier visit, I had instructed the natives to move all the girls and young women further in from the coast and hide them in the jungle. The natives had done this, leaving only old women in the village; they had also taken notice of my other advice on how to appear on the beach in front of strangers, without weapons and wearing no ornaments. The natives meeting me today looked rather sad without their usual finery and reminded me of humble Europeans wearing tattered clothes. This meeting was especially poignant for me as the welcoming crowd consisted mainly of elderly people. Some of villagers were absent, taking part in big *ai* and *mun* ceremonies at Bogatim, but others were probably in the jungle guarding the women.

I learned from my old friend Saul that during my absence a *tamo inglis* had called at Garagassi presenting himself as '*abadam Maklai*' (Maclay's brother). The visitor had probably been the

British Deputy Commissioner for the Western Pacific, a man called Romilly, who visited the area in 1878 on the schooner *Dove* with a group of gold prospectors. The visitors found my old hut in the same condition as I had left it, with the main door securely locked and the garden around it well cared for. As the visitors reached for the lock, scores of Papuans appeared from the bush and held them back, explaining with their gestures that the place belonged to Maclay and to keep off. I suddenly became aware of the absence of my old friend Tui and was soon told: "*Tui muen sen*." (Tui is dead). As Saul repeated the words I felt saddened by the loss of good old friends.

The Bongu natives were excited by the news that I had brought them an ox, a heifer, and male and female goats. The villagers kept repeating the names for the animals and wanted to see them immediately. I told them that they needed to fence off a pen area so that the animals did not wander off into the jungle. The people talked about this at some length, but no one did anything about the actual work. I had learned during my earlier visit that to give something to the native community instead of to an individual often meant that the gift would be neglected. I was uneasy, however, about giving the animals to a single villager or to just a few of them.

Informing the villagers that the animals would be brought in towards the end of the day, I left for my hut built during the 1876–77 visit. On reaching the site I could hardly recognise the area as it was already reclaimed by bush and jungle trees amongst which appeared, here and there, the coconut palms and banana bushes I had planted earlier. Towering above them were the large trunks of *Carica papaya* that I had brought in and which had adapted perfectly to the local conditions. The old tracks around the hut site had disappeared and it was now difficult to move about. Among the bushes I located several old stumps, about all that still remained of my old hut. I remembered how hard I had worked to build that hut and to cultivate the garden around it, and now it was all reclaimed by the jungle during just six years of absence. The fertile soil had much to do with the thick re-growth.

I instructed the natives on how to clear the area around the spot where I once grew sweet-corn as the jungle looked less dense there. With so many hard-working hands the area was soon cleared and bushes pulled out — a group of sailors from the corvette arrived with spades to dig up the ground. With the help of my servant Jan and two sailors, I began to plant the seeds I had brought with me but decided not to plant the coffee. Instead I handed the seeds to Saul and some other natives with a request to pass them on to the mountain villagers where the climate would be far more suitable for growing coffee than on the coastal area.

The natives were quite interested in seeing me set up my garden but I was uncertain whether anything planted would grow, or whether it would perhaps be devastated by wild pigs since there was insufficient fencing around the plot. The natives who could have helped with fencing were too excited by the arrival of visitors from the corvette and with making a yard for the cattle.

I made for Gorendu to see my old friends there but had so much difficulty in following the track, now partly reclaimed by the jungle, that I could scarcely find my way. Eventually I reached the village but was shocked by the changes that had occurred. The village was now overgrown by bush, almost beyond recognition. It so saddened me to see Gorendu derelict and deserted that I hurried back to the sea shore where I returned to the corvette.

After lunch and a brief siesta I left for the shore again, feeling that Bongu was my home. No other part of the world where I had lived during my wanderings had left such a deep impression on me as this coast of New Guinea — even the local trees seemed to be old friends. As soon I arrived at Bongu a crowd gathered around me. So many faces seemed unfamiliar, most likely belonging to those who were just children when I was last here, and only among the aged people did I recognise old friends.

Two things became very apparent; any jubilant mood of the people at seeing me was somehow lacking and it seemed as if it were only yesterday, not six years ago, that I was last at Bongu. The feelings were understandable though, as I did not like demonstrations myself, particularly emotional ones, about my return. Some of the local natives leaned on my shoulders, shed tears, and through their sobbing told me the names of those who had died during my absence. They all asked me to settle among them, as they had asked in the old days. They wanted to know when I would be going back and what they should do if the *tamo inglis* called in again.

A group of native lads ran into the village bringing news that *tamo russ* with *boro russ* (big Russian pig) was heading for the village shore in a *kabum ani boro* (very large boat). The natives rushed to the beach and I followed them to find that a large launch was already close to the shore but was unable to find an appropriate spot for landing. The officer in charge of the vessel ordered his sailors to roll up their trousers and jump into the water. A large crowd of natives from Bongu, Gorendu and Gumbu silently watched from the shore every movement of the approaching seamen. The sailors, now in the water, held the end of a rope tied to the horns of the bull. The boat tilted and the animal jumped out to make his own way across the water to the shore with the sailors still trying to hold on to him. The natives, about one hundred of them, panicked at the sight of such a large animal and ran away. They had never before seen anything bigger than a wild boar and in their desperation some climbed up trees while others dashed into the sea.

After the bull, the heifer was landed but she was somewhat easier to handle. She was followed by the pair of goats. Leading the animals by ropes the sailors made for the village. I hurried on ahead to organise the villagers with the help the visitors would need. The natives had made a pen 15 metres by 15 metres for the bull and heifer but the sailors had a hard time getting the animals to enter the enclosure. As soon as the animals were inside, the gateway was immediately fenced in while the animals settled down. The sailors cut down some leafy branches from nearby trees and threw the foliage inside the pen. The heifer was attracted to the greenery and began eating but the bull kept pacing and looking for a way out of the enclosure. The presence of the sailors who had looked after the animals during the voyage eventually calmed the bull, so the ropes were removed from his horns and it seemed that he had settled down in his new home.

In the absence of a pen for the goats, I suggested that they be placed in one of the huts and the following morning the women should bring the animals some young *unan*. One of the sailors reminded me that the natives should be shown how to milk the goat. The sailor was handed a *tabir* and he soon began to milk the animal with the whole village gathered around him to see the miracle. However, no villager in the crowd was brave enough to taste the milk when offered, so it was drunk by the sailors.

Sunset was close so I told the sailors it was time to return to the corvette. Two sailors were in the pen and had to climb out over the fence since there was now no gateway. I was busy advising the natives what to do in case of future unexpected arrivals of white men when I heard urgent calls from villagers and I turned my attention to the penned animals. Since the sailors' departure the bull had again become agitated and was pacing up and down while trying to break out through the fence.

I hurried to the pen to find that the bull had damaged the fence. Further agitated by the frightened natives now running about in panic, the bull charged at the fence again, knocking out several more supporting stakes. There was no time to send a villager after the sailors so I helplessly watched as the bull backed away from the fence, charge forward and, with a mighty effort, leapt right over it. Now free of all restraint the agitated animal ran through the village as natives fled in panic; soon afterwards the heifer also jumped the fence to follow the bull. I hastened to the beach and caught up with the sailors who thought that they should be able to catch the bull since they considered the animal to be very tame. On our return to the village we found that both bull and heifer had fled into the jungle. I asked the natives to stay away from the animals while the sailors tried to drive them back into the village. The attempt to retrieve the animals failed — as soon as they saw people approaching, the cattle fled further into the jungle.[7]

It was already getting dark so we returned to the corvette. I felt so exhausted by the events of the day that I was unable to keep my promise to return to Bongu and spend the night with the natives.

At dawn on 19th March the *Skobeliev* weighed anchor and we sailed for the island of Bili Bili. As planned earlier we were to survey the site of the envisaged Port of Prince Alexei. It was essential for us to have interpreters on board since there were many dialects throughout the Archipelago of Contented People unknown to me. I hoped to find someone at Bili Bili on whom I could rely to come with us. The depth of the water allowed us to come reasonably close to the shore and a boat was lowered for me. A large crowd of locals waited on the shore, greeting me with calls: "*O Maklai; e-meme, e-aba gena.*" As we neared the shore several pirogues approached; aboard one was Kain while in the other I noticed Maramai, Hassan and some other familiar faces. Wasting no time on welcoming formalities I suggested that they all follow me to the corvette where I would give them tobacco and nails. Kain, followed by the others, immediately came onto my boat so that we could chat.

Once finding themselves on the deck of the corvette, the natives became confused by the engine noises and the presence of such a large number of sailors. They begged me to let them leave. I told Kain and Hassan that we were going to Segu Island and that I needed their help in order to talk to the locals there. I immediately gave all of them the tobacco and nails I had promised, allowing most of the natives to return home while Kain, Hassan and Maramai stayed with me on board. However, once the corvette began to move I had to hold Kain by force while Hassan, seizing the right moment, clambered to the upper deck and jumped into the sea!

As we sailed past the island of Uremu where in 1877 I had

planted coconut palm seedlings, I noticed with pleasure that the seedlings were growing into tall trees. Actually it was Kain and Maramai who pointed them out to me, repeating the words: "*Nui Maklai, monki Maklai*" (Maclay's island, Maclay's coconuts) and "*Navalobe Maklai uremu i na tal atar*" (Maclay shall come to Uremu and build his home).

Passing through the narrow strait between Graged Island and Cape Beile of the New Guinea mainland, the corvette proceeded to sail along the side of Segu Island to determine that the passage was completely safe. With the strait behind us we eventually reached the western coast of Segu Island. There was still enough time left that same day to carry out a survey of the site.

I set off with several officers in the steam launch to look at the extensive bay of the future Port Alexei. On my return I was informed that Kain and Maramai, taking advantage of a passing pirogue, had jumped into the sea and been safely picked up by their fellow natives. Although I understood their fear of being on the corvette, I felt very angry at their abrupt departure.

## 21 March

I reached the village of Segu before sunrise in a dinghy I left on the shore. Although there was not a soul to be seen I felt confident that the natives would soon appear. They did so indeed and, not only the men, the women as well. My friend Kain also appeared. Joyfully he shook my hand and explained that his reason for running away from the corvette was fear at being left with so many *tamo russ* without me being around. He convinced me that he would follow me wherever I went so I asked him to accompany me to Bomassia, a village I had heard of when I was here in 1876 but had never visited.

As well as Kain, I also took my Ambonese servant Jan with me and we sailed up the Ayu River in a small pirogue. Then we followed the river's tributary, the Maus that led us to a small lake, Ayu-Tengai, surrounded by jungle. After drawing our pirogue up on the shore we set off on foot. It took us about half an hour to reach the village which looked very similar to Erempi village I had visited earlier. The natives were ready to flee at the sight of us but words from Kain calmed them down. I began distributing gifts to all the villagers including the women and children who flocked around me. I gave tobacco and nails to the men while the women received beads and strips of cloth.

Here, as in Erempi, the natives are cannibals. I enquired if I could obtain some skulls but Kain explained that the local people boil the skull, brain and much else and, after everything is eaten, all the bones are thrown into the sea. I was offered the opportunity to buy a long shield made not from wood but plaited from *rotang*. These shields were originally traded into here from Karkar. The owner of the shield wanted an axe for it but I did not have one with me. I suggested that I would send the axe later by Kain but the owner declined the offer and kept his shield. I had more luck in obtaining a very well-made spear and a bow with arrows, thus enlarging my collection of Papuan weapons. The arrowheads were carved with considerable skill, with various notches and strokes.

When the locals offered us boiled taro for lunch, I tried to find out if the same *tabir* were used when human flesh was prepared for meals. I was told that human flesh is cooked in ordinary pots and served in ordinary *tabir*. Since there was no meat being prepared for our lunch, I felt easier knowing that I would not be served human flesh.

We returned to the corvette just before a stormy downpour. On my return I learned from the admiral that he intended to weigh anchor the following day. The news rather disappointed me since only half of our work on marking out the Prince Alexei harbour was completed. Much of the southern part of the harbour, including the islands Riwo, Tiara, Graged and many of the anchorages nearby, had yet to be included on the maps being drawn up by the officers on *Skobeliev*.

Several times I tried to explain to the admiral the importance of surveying the entire harbour and that maps completed by

Russian officers on a Russian vessel would be invaluable. Nonetheless he was determined to leave, explaining that the most necessary work had been done and that time was rather limited. I was most disappointed that the Russian navy missed a rare opportunity to map this excellent harbour.[8]

## 22 March

I was up before dawn hoping to sketch from the corvette's bridge the view of Mana-boro-boro (Finisterre Ranges) and the Archipelago of Contented People. A strong wind blowing against us postponed the departure and this gave me time to visit the small island Malaspena which, although covered with dense vegetation, offered several very suitable spots for mooring. From there I was able to cross to Segu Island where I found Kain. I asked him to enquire of the local natives whether they would allow me to build my new home on Malaspena and settle there when I returned. The natives agreed and seemed very pleased at the news that I intended to be their neighbour.

## 23 March

At about 6.00 a.m. we weighed anchor and two hours later passed through the Izoumroud Strait between New Guinea and Karkar Island. Far to the south-west I noticed several pirogues on the sea sailing between Karkar Island and the mainland.

# *Disillusionment and Death*

On reaching Hong Kong on his return from New Guinea, Miklouho-Maclay learned from a newspaper article that Queensland had annexed the entire free part of New Guinea. It was purported that the annexation was necessary to prevent a foreign power moving into the region. Technically this meant that Queensland, being a British colony, had obtained a colony for itself. The white settlers in Queensland at that time relied heavily on *kanaks*, slaves brought in from the Pacific islands, including New Guinea, for the development of vast areas of land taken over from the Australian Aboriginal tribes. In spite of the British Abolition of Slavery Act of 1833, slave trade was still a flourishing business in the Pacific. Though publicly quiet about the brutal treatment of the Australian Aborigines, Miklouho-Maclay feared that once Europeans were in New Guinea, the Papuans would be subject to a similar fate.

Miklouho-Maclay felt that he may have precipitated the annexation by canvassing Russian support for a possible protectorate for New Guinea. Consequently a strong wave of anti-Russian hysteria swept Australia and on his arrival back in Australia, Miklouho-Maclay saw a gun crew at Cooktown, guarding the port from possible Russian invasion. At Cooktown he met with Reverend Chalmers who, with other missionaries from New Guinea, strongly objected to the annexation, especially as the Queensland colonial government had a dismal record of dispossessing its own indigenous population.

After settling in Sydney, Miklouho-Maclay wrote to the British Prime Minister Gladstone, Lord Derby, Queen Victoria, and anyone he could think of, asking them to use their influence to see that the New Guinea people were properly protected. He received no positive answer but learned from a newspaper article that a manipulative British land developer had issued a prospectus offering one-thousand acre parcels of land on the recently colonised land at Maclay Coast of New Guinea. Desperate, Miklouho-Maclay turned to Bismarck of Germany for help, urging him to see that the New Guinea natives were protected. Bismarck already had contact with the British, opening the dialogue about colonies in the South Pacific including New Guinea, but not in the interests of the Papuans.

Hoping that the New Guinea natives could be saved from the dreadful fate of colonisation, Miklouho-Maclay settled at Watson's Bay with Margaret, daughter of Sir John Robertson, whom he had married in February 1884. His colleague, Dr Finsch from Germany, unexpectedly turned up in Sydney to see him. Dr. Finsch explained that he was leading a scientific expedition to the Pacific. Miklouho-Maclay welcomed him and spoke in detail about his last visit to the Maclay Coast. In all his innocence he even acquainted his German colleague with words and signs for Finsch to use if he wished to be welcomed by Miklouho-Maclay's Papuan friends on the Maclay Coast.

Miklouho-Maclay was unaware that Finsch had read every article and paper he had so far published on the Papuans, including *The Dictionary of Bongu Language*. Finsch was actually working for the German *New Guinea Kompanie* which was making preparations to set up trading stations in New Guinea, already claimed by the British. The Germans had hired Dr Finsch to select suitable areas where they could expect cooperation from the natives. Their ship *Samoa* was manned exclusively by a German crew and, with Dr Finsch on board as leader, the expedition left Sydney in September 1884 and arrived at Port Constantine on 11 October. As Finsch walked out on the New Guinea shore, he called "*Aba* Maklai." The Papuans came forward and welcomed him with open arms.

For a while the Papuans had two colonial masters: British and German. However, a deal was negotiated later to split the colonial

loot; the southern part of New Guinea went to the British and the
northern part to the Germans.

Broken hearted and disillusioned, Miklouho-Maclay sailed to
Europe and from Crimea went to see Czar Alexander III at his
summer residence in Livadia, in the vain hope of reversing the
wheel of colonisation and save the Papuans. Russia, however, was
at that time in no position to challenge the European colonial
powers for the rights of natives in the Pacific. Miklouho-Maclay
then turned to the Russian author Tolstoy for help. Tolstoy told
him:

"You were the first to demonstrate beyond question by your
experience that man is man everywhere, that is, a kind, sociable
being with whom communication can and should be established
through kindness and truth, not gun and spirits."

Tolstoy advised Miklouho-Maclay to edit his New Guinea
Diary in a style accessible to the ordinary reader and felt confident
that such a book could become so popular that it would save the
Papuans from colonisation. Czar Alexander III offered to publish
Miklouho-Maclay's entire work at Imperial expense. Miklouho-
Maclay began preparing his work for publication, but he was a
broken man, ill and disillusioned. His health, after living so many
years in the tropics in deprivation, had deteriorated beyond
recovery. Miklouho-Maclay made a brief trip to Sydney to bring
Margaret and their two children to Saint Petersburg, knowing that
his days were numbered and hoping that after he died, his family
would be better looked after by his relatives in Russia than in
colonial Sydney.

Nikolai Nikolaevich Miklouho-Maclay died at the age of 42
years and was buried alongside his father and sister Olga in Saint
Petersburg's Volkhov Cemetery on 16th April 1888. He left
behind his widow Margaret and two sons, one aged two and
another three years old. He also left a will asking that all his papers
and diaries should be destroyed, a request Margaret fulfilled. Soon
after his death, distressed and disillusioned, she burned most of her
husband's papers. Margaret was later invited by the Czarina to visit

her and was offered 5000 roubles for her needs and expenses to return to Australia, and a pension for life. She received this pension until the abolition of the Russian monarchy in 1917. Before Margaret died in 1934 she left bundles of Miklouho-Maclay's papers and bundles of his drawings of the Papuans to the Mitchell Library in Sydney, to gather dust for almost a century.

The sole lost copy of Miklouho-Maclay's *The New Guinea Diaries* and discovered in 1949, could well have been the same copy he gave to Tolstoy who advised him to make the work appealing to a mass readership. Tolstoy was right — after *The New Guinea Diaries* eventually appeared in print in the 1950s, millions of copies of the book were sold in Eastern Europe and Miklouho-Maclay became a scientific hero. By then, however, the Papuans of New Guinea were long colonised.

# *Afterword*

I have often wondered just how close Miklouho-Maclay must have come to making a very important scientific discovery in his work on comparative anatomy of species. Some years ago, almost by accident, I found some answers. For that I am indebted to my pack of dingoes.

While living in Arnhem Land and the tribal bush up north, I observed the relationship between the tribal Aborigines and the dingo. The animal was extensively portrayed in tribal art and oral literature and was totemically associated with various tribal groups and individuals.

Many years later at my property, 'Dingoes Den', south of Melbourne, where I settled after retreating from the sub-tropical north, I kept a pack of dingoes — sharing with them my house, my food, and even my bed.

At that time it was illegal to keep dingoes, considered vermin, even on 200 acres of bush property and the animals could have been shot at the whim of state authorities. I split up my pack, giving some of the animals to my Aboriginal friend, Professor Eve Fesl, and a dingoess, Kashovanka, to my friend, Lynda Bilcich. We were joined by a dingo breeder, Bruce Jacobs, in forming the National Dingo Association.

Some years ago, a young dingoess, Sarah, was expecting her first litter, even though she was barely a year old. She was very timid and came from a father who was a full-blooded Alpine dingo born in the wild of the Bogong High Plains, Victoria, Australia. Her mother, Kashovanka, once gave a record litter of fourteen pups although she had only ten nipples. She was well looked after and sensed that there was plenty of food about;

therefore she produced a very large litter. All our dingo pups were born black but as they grew up the black fur gradually turned into golden brown. The dingo has its litters about July when the Alpine hills are well covered in snow. The black colour of the fur keeps the pups warm and helps them to survive. The animal must have lived in that region for eons of time, since the Ice Age, for such pigmentation to develop. Similar principles of pigmentation occurred in seals in the north of the British Isles. During the Ice Age they developed white fur disguising them from predators.

We had often observed the way Kashovanka rotated her suckling pups — picking up a pup from the end of the queue and placing it in front of nipples where the best supply of milk flowed. All her pups survived, even a little runt we called Annie. Annie stayed close to her mother and, as a grown-up dog, she was the only one of the siblings allowed to eat from Kashovanka's food bowl. She would often come to her mother to be groomed, or licked dry after being in the rain.

It was Sarah who helped us unravel the mystery of Annie's attachment to her mother. Sarah, young and inexperienced, had a little runt in her litter of twelve, half the size of the other pups, whom we feared would not survive — at least according to Darwin's theory of natural selection. The pups were nested in the back room of our house. Twice I observed Sarah taking the little runt out into the backyard, looking for a secluded spot, but the other adult dingoes of the pack kept interfering.

Some days later I found the little runt on my bed. The bed was almost a metre high from the floor and it would have been impossible for the little runt, barely weeks old, to climb up on. Anxious Sarah had followed me into the room to observe my reaction. Sarah then jumped up on the bed to allow Runt to suck her. As this feeding pattern was repeated during the following days, it became obvious that Sarah was taking Runt away from the puppy nest to give him the extra feeding he would need to survive. "Good old Miklouho-Maclay would have been very pleased with you," I patted Sarah.

I named the little runt George, after my New York publisher George Braziller who was visiting us at that time. The pup has grown up into a normal-sized dingo, thus contradicting the theory that only the fittest will survive.

Miklouho-Maclay must have known about such dingo behaviour even a century ago, as did the tribal Aborigines for thousands of generations before him, during the Ice Age and long after.

# *Notes*

1. Astrolabe Bay discovered in 1827 by the French explorer Dumont d'Urville and named after his ship *Astrolabe*. He did not disembark but observed the coast from the ship.
2. Miklouho-Maclay collected Olsson and Boy on the island of Samoa where the *Vitiaz* made a stop in transit to New Guinea. Olsson was a Swedish ex-seaman and Boy a young Polynesian from New Ireland.
3. In the biography of Miklouho-Maclay by F.S. Greenop (*Who Travels Alone*), the author claims that the natives thought the explorer's shoes were a part of his body.
4. The *Izoumroud* was actually the *Vitiaz*, refitted and renamed, and is perhaps the only ship to have two straits named after it.
5. In 1873 Captain Moresby of the Royal Navy sailing on a reconnaissance voyage along the southern coast of New Guinea, found a suitable harbour site which he named after his father, Admiral F. Moresby. The missionaries soon followed. Miklouho-Maclay arrived in New Guinea about two years earlier in 1871.
6. Miklouho-Maclay, in association with Anton Dohrn whom he met at Messina University when in Europe, was the first to develop the idea of the marine biological station; Dohrn opened the first in Naples in 1871 and Miklouho-Maclay the second at Watson's Bay in Sydney.
7. Some years after Germans colonised New Guinea, it was found that the bull had been killed by the natives for breaking into their gardens and destroying the crops. By that time the bull had mated with the heifer. The offspring of the cattle were sighted and reported toward the end of 1886.
8. Admiral Kopitov had sensed the imminent fate of the Maclay Coast. A year later the Germans invaded New Guinea and soon after, Port of Prince Alexei was renamed Alexihefen.

# Glossary

| | |
|---|---|
| *aba* | friend, brother |
| *abadam* | brother |
| *ai* | festivities forbidden to women and uninitiated youth |
| *ai kobray* | musical instrument made from bamboo pipe |
| *ain* | wooden mask |
| *aka* | bad |
| *alama-amo* | cry, distress |
| *amb* | hut (term from Bili Bili) |
| *aous* | cane-like plant with edible flower (*Saccarum edule*) |
| *aren* | no, negative |
| *arur* | sea-shell |
| *aue* | good |
| *ayan* | yams (*Dioscorea*) |
| *ballal* | word, to speak |
| *baou* | taro |
| *barata* | to burn |
| *Baressi* | Pleiades |
| *barla* | bench, platform |
| *barum* | drum |
| *bassa* | end |
| *bia* | fire |
| *biaram* | smoke |
| *bilen* | good |
| *Boi* | Venus (star) |
| *borle* | bad |
| *borle digor* | bad rubbish |
| *boro* | large, great |
| *buam* | sago palm dish |
| *buambramra* | hut |
| *bul* | pig |

268

| | |
|---|---|
| *bul-ra* | ornament made from boar tusks |
| *bum* | day |
| *Damang* | Orion's belt (constellation) |
| *darem* | hut (term used at Bili Bili, Yambomba and Yelyata) |
| *degargol* | sweet potato |
| *diglan* | thorn |
| *digor* | rubbish, litter |
| *dim* | bark of tree (Yambomba term) |
| *diu* | plaited braid for tying up and supporting hair |
| *dongan* | knife made from bone |
| *dum* | small, fowl-like jungle bird (*Cemtropus*) |
| *dyuga* | cassowary |
| | |
| *e-aba* | o brother (greeting) |
| *e-meme* | o father (greeting) |
| | |
| *gabenau* | animal, similar to a large rat |
| *gamba* | shell of coconut used as a cup. |
| *gambor* | large container for holding a corpse made from palm fronds |
| *gare* | skin, bark |
| *gate* | skull |
| *gatessi* | locks of hair at the back of the head |
| *gena* | to come, come here |
| *gitan* | stone |
| *gle* | be off |
| *goob* | woven palm leaves |
| *goon* or *gun* | bag |
| *gub* or *goob* | palm frond |
| *gubo-gubo* | chest ornament |
| | |
| *hadga nangor* | a new spear |
| *hudi* or *gudi* | one |
| | |
| *ingi* | food |
| | |
| *kaaram* | moon |
| *kabum ani boro* | very large boat |
| *kainda* | species of yam |
| *kale* | Papuan dish |
| *kanum* or *ganum* | mirror |
| *kanya* | ancestral figure carved from wood (Tengum-mana term) |

269

| | |
|---|---|
| *katazan* | comb decorated with fan of plumes and worn as a head dress |
| *kaz* | tobacco |
| *kengara* | nut-bearing tree (*Canarium commune*) |
| *kere* | enough, finished |
| *keu* | intoxicating drink made from the root of *Piper methysticum* plant |
| *kiringa* | girl |
| *kobray* | cockatoo |
| *kobum* | pirogue (Bili Bili term) |
| *kobum* | spider |
| *kobum barla* | platform on a pirogue |
| *koko* | native bird (*Chlamidodera*) |
| *korog* | north-west wind |
| *kumu* | black earth used for body decoration |
| *mab* | cuscus |
| *mal* | loin cloth |
| *malassi* | youth of both gender |
| *mana* | prefix meaning 'mountain' |
| *marem* | lower jaw |
| *meme* | father |
| *moem* | to die |
| *mogar* | species of bean |
| *mondon* | afterwards, later on. |
| *monki* | coconut |
| *monki-ai* | musical instrument made from coconut shell |
| *monki-lya* | Papuan dish made from coconut |
| *muen sen* | died |
| *muliki* | pigeon (Bili Bili term) |
| *mulum* | circumcision ceremony |
| *mun* | festivity |
| *nangeli* | women |
| *nare* | one |
| *nareng* | bird (*Buceros*) |
| *navalobe* | in due time |
| *negrengva* | to draw or write |
| *nerin* | fish trap, basket |
| *ni* | you |
| *niri* | star |

| | |
|---|---|
| *nui* | island |
| *nyavar* | to sleep |
| *okam* | ceremonial drum |
| *onim* | sorcery, magic, traditional remedy |
| *onim-atar* | magic spell |
| *orlan* | species of tree (*Pangium edule*) |
| *orlan-ai* | rattle made from shell of *orlan* fruit and used as a musical instrument |
| *palam* | arrow with a broad bamboo head |
| *pat* | stone (Bili Bili term) |
| *rak-rak* | floating log used as a canoe |
| *robum* | no need |
| *robum* | pirogue (Tiara dialect) |
| *rosar* | to bind or tie up |
| *rotei* | ancestral spirit (Bogatim term) |
| *sagyu* | bracelet worn around the upper arm or the lower part of the leg |
| *sambo* | leg |
| *sanguin-ole* | large ceremonial head decoration up to 5 metres in height |
| *sari* | chest ornament |
| *shelupa* | spoon shaped knife |
| *sing* or *sing niri* | sun |
| *subari* | tree (*Calophyllum inophyllum*) |
| *surle* | bones |
| *suru* red | ochre |
| *tabir* | wooden bowl or dish |
| *tal* | hut, home |
| *tamo* | man |
| *tamo deva* | man from mountain village |
| *tamo-gate* | human skull |
| *tangrin* | earthquake |
| *taun* | dish prepared from nut |
| *telrun* or *telgun* | woven string bag worn by women |
| *telum* | carved wooden figures |
| *tibol* | species of kangaroo |
| *tyumbin* | bamboo flute |

| | |
|---|---|
| *ubu* | stone (Gorendu and Gumbu term) |
| *udya* | digging stake used for cultivation |
| *udya-sab* | narrow wooden spade used to break up soil |
| *uleu* | sandy beach |
| *uleu-tamo* | coastal villager |
| *unan* | species of tall grass (*Imperata*) |
| *uramar* | vine (Bili Bili term) |
| *u-ravar* | circumcision |
| *u-tibol* | species of kangaroo |
| *uyar* | to eat |
| *vab* | clay pot |
| *val-tibol* | species of kangaroo |
| *vang* (Bili Bili) | a large vessel with sails |
| *wang* | sea vessel with sails (Bili Bili term) |
| *yambau tamo* | uncircumcised mountain man |
| *yambi* | small bag carried around the neck |
| *yarur* | shell used for scrapping coconut flesh |
| *yavar* | north-west wind |
| *yur* | spear for catching fish |

# Bibliography

Gammage, B, 1976, 'Maclay comes to Gorendu', *Oral History*, 4(1):64–72

Greenop, F., 1944, *Who Travels Alone*, K.G. Murray, Sydney

Miklouho-Maclay, N.N–Notebook, containing photographs, newspaper cuttings and drawings, 1886. Available for reference. National Library of Australia MS 3375

Miklouho-Maclay, N.N. *Sobraniye sochineniy (Collected Works)*, 1950–54, Akademiya Nauk SSSR, Moscow-Leningrad. With much additional material, biographical essay and discussion of Miklouho-Maclay's work, and extensive annotation.

Vols I, II Journals and reports of travels
Vol. III pt 1, Articles on anthropology and ethnology
Vol. III pt 2, Articles on zoology, geography, meteorology and organizational questions
Vol. IV Correspondence
Vol. V Illustrations (drawings by M.M. and potographs of objects in his ethnological collection)

Miklouho-Maclay, N.N. 'Second sojourn on the Maclay Coast in New Guinea (from June 1876 to November 1877)', *Izv. IRGO*, 16(2):149–70; *SS*, II:386 (Russian)

Miklouho-Maclay, N.N. 'Sojourn in Sydney (from August 1878 to March 1879)', *Izv. IRGO*, 16(2):41624; *SS*, II:435 (Russian)

Miklouho-Maclay, N.N. 'The proposed zoological station at Sydney', *Proc. LSNSW*, 4:103–6

Miklouho-Maclay, N.N. 'Travels in the islands of Melanesia and fourth visit to New Guinea', *Izv. IRGO*, 17(1):131–42; *SS*, II:559 (Russian)

Miklouho-Maclay, N.N. 'On the practice of ovariotomy by the natives of the Herbert River, Queensland', *Proc. LSNSW*, 6:622–4

Miklouho-Maclay, N.N. 'Remarks about the circumlocutions of the cerebrum of *Canis dingo*', *Proc. LSNSW*, 6:624–6

Miklouho-Maclay, N.N. 'Cranial deformation of new-born children at the Island Mabiak, and other islands of Torres Straits, and of women of the S.E. peninsula of New Guinea', *Proc. LSNSW*, 6:627–9

Miklouho-Maclay, N.N. *New Guinea Diaries, 1871–1883*, 1975, translated, with biographical comments and notes, by C.L.Sentinella, Kristen Press, Madang

Miklouho-Maclay, N.N. *Travels to New Guinea*, 1982, Progress Publishers, Moscow. With introduction and notes by D.D.Tumarkin

Miklouho-Maclay, R.W. de, 1974, 'Nikolai Nikolaevich Mikluho-Maklai', Australian *Dictionary of Biography*, vol. 5, Melb. Univ. Press, Melbourne

Miklouho-Maclay, R.W. de, 1974, 'Nikolai N. Mikluho-Maklai (1846–1888), pioneer educator in New Guinea and Melanesia', *Educational Perspectives in Papua New Guinea*, Australian College of Education

Mikluho-Maklai, Margaret–Diary 1888. Fisher Library, University of Sydney. Microfilm XT79

Putilov, B., 1978, 'Lev Tolstoy and Miklukha-Maklai', *Soviet Literature*, no. 8:95–102

Stanbury, P., 1975, 'Baron Nikolai Nikolaivitch Miklouho-Maklai, or the complete nineteenth century international explorer and scientist', in *100 Years of Australian Scientific Explorations*, ed. P. Stanbury, Sydney

Thomassen, E.S., 1882, *A Biographical Sketch of Nicholas de Miklouho Maclay the Explorer*, privately printed, Brisbane

Tumarkin, D. D., 1963, 'A great Russian scientific-humanist', *Sovyetskaya etnografiya*, no. 6 (Russian)

Tumarkin, D. D., 1997, 'The Papuan Union (from the history of the struggle of N.N. Miklouho-Maclay for the rights of the Papuans of New Guinea)', *Rasy i narody*, 7 Nauka, Moscow (Russian)

Valskaya, B.A., 1972, 'Unpublished materials on the preparation of N.N.Miklouho-Maclay's expedition to New Guinea in 1871 and on the voyage of the corvette *Skobelev* to that island in 1883', *Strani i narody vostoka*, 13(2), Nauka, Moscow (Russian)

Webster, E.M., The Moon Man, Melbourne University Press, 1984

Wongar, B,. 'Miklouho-Maclay and his dingo', in Striking Chords (ed. Sneja Gunew and Kateryna Longley), Allen & Unwin, Sydney, 1992

Worsley, P.M., 1952, 'N.N.Miklouho-Maclay, Pioneer of Pacific Anthropology', *Oceania*, 22:307–14

# Index